Intermediate Programming for the TRS-80®(Model I)

David L. Heiserman has been a freelance writer since 1968. He is the author of more than 100 magazine articles and 15 technical and scientific books. He studied applied mathematics at Ohio State University and is now Associate Professor of Electronics at the Ohio Institute of Technology. A member of Mensa, he is especially interested in the history and philosophy of science.

Intermediate Programming for the TRS-80®(Model I)

By

David L. Heiserman

Associate Professor ot Electronics
Ohio Institute of Technology

Howard W. Sams & Co., Inc.
4300 WEST 62ND ST. INDIANAPOLIS, INDIANA 46268 USA

Copyright © 1982 by David L. Heiserman

FIRST EDITION
FIRST PRINTING—1982

All rights reserved. No part of this book shall be reproduced, stored in a retrieval system, or transmitted by any means, electronic, mechanical, photocopying, recording, or otherwise, without written permission from the publisher. No patent liability is assumed with respect to the use of the information contained herein. While every precaution has been taken in the preparation of this book, the publisher assumes no responsibility for errors or omissions. Neither is any liability assumed for damages resulting from the use of the information contained herein.

International Standard Book Number: 0-672-21809-7
Library of Congress Catalog Card Number: 81-51556

Edited by: *Jack Davis*
Illustrated by: *William Basham*

Printed in the United States of America.

Preface

I don't think there is such an animal as a perfectly contented computer programmer and operator. Such people are chronically afflicted with a desire to acquire more equipment or find ways to use existing schemes more effectively.

The matter of acquiring more equipment—more memory, more peripherals, and so on—can be an expensive route to doing more and better things with a computer system. In fact, it is often a prohibitively expensive route.

A much less expensive alternative is to learn how to use a system's existing features more effectively. It is quite surprising in many instances to discover that your own system has more computing power than you imagined. Tucked away in those ROMs and available utility tapes are a lot of features just crying to be used. Unfortunately, those bits and pieces of computing power are often overlooked, by both the user and the manufacturer who wrote the instruction manual.

This book helps you uncover some of those "hidden" features of the TRS-80 personal computer system and then shows you how to exploit them to your programming advantage. If you already have a standard Model I TRS-80 with 16K of RAM and Level II capability, your only additional expense will be tied up in two Radio Shack cassette tapes: T-BUG and Editor/Assembler. A line printer can be very helpful in the later stages of this exploration of the TRS-80, but it isn't absolutely essential.

The book is designed to stimulate your own sense of programming creativity. It shows how something can be done in a general way, illustrating the point with specific examples. It is then up to you to use the information to work out programs of your own invention.

DAVID L. HEISERMAN

Contents

CHAPTER 1

YOU, YOUR TRS-80, AND THIS BOOK 9
   Which System Do You Need?—How This Book Is Organized—How to Get the Most From This Book

CHAPTER 2

THE VIDEO ENVIRONMENT 15
   Video Data—Video Addressing—Video Control Codes

CHAPTER 3

THE KEYBOARD ENVIRONMENT 44
   The Standard INPUT Statement—The Standard INKEY$ Statement—Sensing Key Depression With PEEK(14463)—Working With the Keyboard Matrix

CHAPTER 4

THE USER'S MEMORY ENVIRONMENT 64
   Organization of the User's Memory Space—The I/O Buffer—"Disassembling" a BASIC Program—Protecting Memory Space—Some Special Memory Operations

CHAPTER 5

LINKING BASIC AND MACHINE LANGUAGE WITH USR . . . 81

Getting Set Up for a USR Operation—A Preliminary Note About Machine-Language Programming—POKEing in Machine-Language Programs From BASIC—Some Programming Examples—Passing a Value to the Machine-Language Subroutine—Passing Values From Machine Language to BASIC—Passing Values Back and Forth— Saving BASIC/Machine-Language Programs on Cassette Tape

CHAPTER 6

MANIPULATING BASIC-LOADED, USR-LINKED PROGRAMS . . 103

Specifying Entry Points for USR-Linked Programs—Deleting the Machine-Language Loader—Building Machine-Language Programs From the Bottom Up

CHAPTER 7

HEXADECIMAL PROGRAMMING WITH T-BUG 121

The T-BUG Environment—T-BUG Operations—Summary of T-BUG Operations

CHAPTER 8

EXPLORING THE TRS-80 WITH T-BUG 141

The Hexadecimal Video Environment—The Hexadecimal Keyboard Environment — Some Special Video/Keyboard Functions — T-BUG and The Memory Environment

CHAPTER 9

INTRODUCING THE TRS-80 EDITOR/ASSEMBLER 163

A Few Preliminary Notes—Bringing up EDTASM—Line Numbers, ORG, and END—Deleting and Writing Program Text—Assembling the Source Program—Working With the Object-Code Version—Other EDTASM Commands and Variations

CHAPTER 10

REAL ASSEMBLY POWER WITH PSEUDO-OPS 181

Simple EQU Pseudo-Ops—EQU Operations With Math Operations—Redefining a Label With DEFL—Leaving Memory Space With DEFS—Defining Memory Contents With DEFB and DEFW—Building Message Tables With DEFM

CHAPTER 11

PUTTING IT ALL TOGETHER 197

Building a General-Purpose FILL Routine—Applying and Refining FILL2—Building a General-Purpose MOVE Routine

APPENDIX A

NUMBER SYSTEM BASE CONVERSIONS 214

Hexadecimal-to-Decimal Conversions — Decimal-to-Hexadecimal Conversions—Decimal Address to 2-Byte Decimal Format—2-Byte Decimal to Conventional Decimal—Binary-to-Decimal Conversion—Binary-to-Hexadecimal Conversion—Hexadecimal-to-Binary Conversion—Decimal-to-Binary Conversion

APPENDIX B

Z-80 INSTRUCTION SET: OBJECT AND SOURCE CODES 222

APPENDIX C

TRS-80 ASCII CHARACTER SET: DECIMAL AND HEXADECIMAL CODES 231

APPENDIX D

TRS-80 GRAPHICS CHARACTER SET: DECIMAL AND HEXADECIMAL CODES 233

INDEX 236

CHAPTER 1

You, Your TRS-80, and This Book

Do you remember the first day you fired up your brand-new TRS-80? You probably do. For most of us that was an exciting and rewarding experience.

One of the nice things about owning your own home computer is that the feeling of having first-time adventures doesn't have to wear off; there is always something new to learn and try. Learning something new, trying it, and making it work can be just as much fun as turning on the computer the first time.

Oh sure, there are times when things don't go right and you feel like throwing the whole system across the room. Things can go wrong, they don't always work out as expected, and the frustration level can grow to disheartening proportions. But that happens to everyone who works with computers and computer programming, no matter how much or how little experience they have and no matter how sophisticated or modest the computer system is.

Home computer programming, however, still retains all the potential for being a continuously rewarding experience. All you have to do is learn what you need to know as you go along, applying the newfound knowledge until it becomes second nature to you. Then you are ready to learn something else. There is really no end to it. And it's great fun.

The key to maintaining an ongoing love affair with your computer is thus a matter of learning to do new things or to do old things in a new and better way. Doing the same old things in the same old fashion can become boring or tedious, no matter how well they work out. But in the process of trying new things, there is always the risk of failure, disappointment, and frustration.

This sort of frustration and failure most often arises from ignorance—having an unclear grasp of certain operating details, misunderstanding some of them, or, perhaps, being unaware of them altogether. The more you know about the workings of your computer, the more likely are your chances of success with new ideas.

The primary objective of this book is to help you get more fun out of creating computer programs on your TRS-80. The idea is to make it possible for you to engage in that unending and rewarding adventure mentioned in the opening paragraphs of this chapter.

How does this book help you? It describes some powerful operating details that are usually mentioned too briefly or overlooked altogether in the current Radio Shack literature. These are the sort of operating details that make it possible for you to do new things and to do old things in new and better ways. The descriptions give you information that provides a logical next step in your computer programming experiences.

There are plenty of examples and demonstrations to illustrate the operating details under discussion, but it will be up to you to transfer the ideas to your own programming plans. In a manner of speaking, this book points the way to new programming possibilities, but you get all the fun of seeing the ideas working within the context of your programs.

WHICH SYSTEM DO YOU NEED?

TRS-80s are now available in such a wide variety of configurations that it is impractical to attempt writing a book that suits all of them equally well. It is thus necessary to draw some lines, meeting the needs of the largest number of readers and hoping others will find information that is useful to them and applicable to their system configurations.

The examples and demonstrations in this book have been worked around a Model I TRS-80 having 16K of RAM and Level II BASIC. All information provided here applies to that system configuration.

Now, that doesn't mean every other system is completely counted out. Indeed, things are going to be a bit tough for anyone working with a 4K system or one equipped with Level I BASIC. Readers in this category ought to give serious thought to upgrading their systems—not only to get the most from this book but also to get a lot more computing opportunities.

Readers with bigger systems will find that virtually all the material in this book applies to their machines. Some of the numbers will be different for Model II and Model III machines, and you will have to work out the conversions for yourself. The spirit of the presentations, however, is almost universally applicable.

In keeping with the notion of working toward the most popular

TRS-80 configuration, you will need a cassette tape machine. DOS users will be able to work all the demonstrations, too, but there is no DOS-related material presented in this book.

A line printer can be quite helpful in some of the discussions, but it is never a critical requirement. Also, an expansion interface can be used, but it isn't necessary.

Looking ahead to work in the latter part of the book, you will need a couple of Radio Shack program tapes: T-BUG (catalog No. 26-2001) and Editor/Assembler (catalog No. 26-2002).

You will also need a Z-80 programming reference book. The Z-80 instruction set is offered in Appendix B of this book, but there is no room here for spelling out the details of machine-language programming in a general sense. If you need such a book, try Radio Shack's *How to Program the Z-80* (catalog No. 62-2066).

HOW THIS BOOK IS ORGANIZED

When most people are introduced to their first home computer, they get a lot of delight from running BASIC programs listed in the programming manual and, maybe, running a few "canned" programs—usually game programs.

But we have to be honest here: running simple BASIC programs and prepared cassette tapes can wear thin after a while. Of course you can buy more elaborate and expensive prepared programs, or start entering some programs from published BASIC or machine-language listings; but even if they meet your expectations (and many of them won't), they also become old hat after a while.

One way to overcome this sagging enthusiasm for your computer is to begin writing custom programs—cutting and trying a few of your own invention. That can be a lot of fun, especially if you know what you're doing. Learning to use conventional BASIC can keep you going for a long time.

Indeed, writing custom programs in BASIC can serve a lot of personal needs; however, it usually doesn't take long to become dissatisfied with certain limitations of it. Experienced TRS-80 BASIC programmers often begin feeling straightjacketed by some of the built-in procedures. It is quite possible to know exactly what you want to do but find that BASIC—whether in the TRS-80 or not—cannot handle the job as effectively or adequately as you'd like.

Animated graphics, for instance, can fall flat in BASIC because of the long execution times for the statements involved. Or maybe you would like to assign something more than 240 characters to a single string variable. In such instances the built-in relationships between BASIC and the operating system stand in your way.

There are untold instances where the structure of the system and the way BASIC is meant to work serve as roadblocks to effective programming.

One way to tackle this particular sort of problem is by digging through the avalanche of books and magazines written for people who want to go beyond the limitations of their present know-how. If you have tried that route, you have probably been disappointed more than once. It isn't that there is anything necessarily wrong with all that available information; it can prove quite valuable in many ways.

But most of the literature dealing with new TRS-80 tricks and techniques applies only to the particular situation the author is describing. And what's more, you always run the risk of applying the idea without learning anything you can use on your own at some later time.

More often than not, the real value of a book or article lies in the gems of wisdom tucked away in the program listings or accompanying text. Specific solutions for specific problems may or may not be truly helpful, but the methods and ideas behind them can be invaluable. Therein lies the virtue of most computer books and magazine articles.

For example, an article describing how to move a spot of light across the screen by depressing a certain key might not seem all that useful or exciting to you; but the technique for sensing the key depression or drawing the moving spot can be applied in countless ways—once you grasp the main principles behind those actions.

This is a book about main principles. You won't have to dig through the program listings to uncover important ideas; they are clearly spelled out.

Yes, indeed, there are a lot of program listings in this book, but they are intended only to illustrate the workings of the principle at hand. The programs, as such, aren't all that useful or exciting; they are to-the-point illustrations and not highly refined and fully developed programs. The programs are trimmed to the bare bones so that the point they illustrate will stand out as clearly as possible. Finished programs tend to be cluttered with a lot of "whistles and bells" that obscure the finer, more important details.

It is up to you to grasp the essence of an idea presented in this book, give it a first try with an accompanying program listing, and then fit it into some programming schemes of your own.

The author hopes that you will find this book rich in ideas and short on razzle-dazzle.

Finally, you should be assured at this point that the book is not devoted exclusively to machine-language programming. Many people who feel the itch to go beyond basic BASIC are told—or at least get the impression—that the next step in their programming experience must be in the direction of machine-language programming.

That is not true. Growing up in the business of computer programming is an evolutionary process. Your knowledge ought to develop gradually and smoothly, and, for most people, moving directly from basic BASIC to pure machine-language programming is hardly a gradual and smooth process. In fact, it is a terrible mistake to drop BASIC and move fully to machine-language programming if you've had no training or experience with it. The change is too big and too abrupt.

No, machine-language programming is not the first topic offered in this book. It turns out that familiar old BASIC can become exciting again, once you know more about the internal workings of the TRS-80. You can access some very useful inner workings from BASIC and do a lot of things that will tear down some of the usual programming limitations.

And that's where this book starts.

Once you know more about the system from a BASIC viewpoint, you are ready to begin some machine-language programming. But even then it is possible to work into that sort of programming from BASIC. The idea is to let you wade into the deeper waters of machine language, while keeping a tight grasp on a familiar BASIC handle.

Toward the last part of the book, we will finally get to purely machine-language programming. By that time, though, you will be well grounded in the TRS-80's internal workings and better prepared to write successful machine-language programs of your own.

So this book is for you if you want to do more with BASIC, learn more about the internal workings of the TRS-80, ease your way gradually into machine-language programming, and learn to devise new and exciting programs of your own.

In short, if you are getting a little tired of your TRS-80 system, this book ought to serve as a shot of adrenalin.

HOW TO GET THE MOST FROM THIS BOOK

This is not really a reference book, although it might have that general appearance. The book represents a step-by-step process, and, as such, you will get more from it by working through it from beginning to end, as opposed to dipping in at some point that sounds interesting to you.

Besides working through the material in sequence and from the beginning, it is also helpful to study the material with your TRS-80 system right at hand. A program listing accompanies every new idea;

so as you read about a new idea, you should be able to try it for yourself, right on the spot. You probably already know that the learning-by-doing process is the most effective one for working with computer programs.

But as mentioned earlier, the program listings are meant only to illustrate—to emphasize—one or two key points. So not many of the programs presented here are, in themselves, very useful. The idea is to encourage you to try the new ideas in a bare-bones fashion. Once you understand a new idea and have an opportunity to see it work, you should try fitting it into a more elaborate or useful program of your own design. If things don't work out the way you think they should, go back to the book and see whether or not you have overlooked or misunderstood something.

This book is a guide—a self-teaching guide. You will get the most from it by attempting to apply the new ideas in your fashion. It is really based on the old notion that you can keep a man alive for a day if you give him a fish, but you can keep him alive for a good many years if you give him some fishing equipment and show him how to use it.

You have all the equipment, and here come some ideas about how to use it in more effective ways.

CHAPTER 2

The Video Environment

The crt screen is the most-often used output device for most TRS-80 systems, and it turns out that this video feature has a level of versatility that matches up fairly well with its importance. Understanding how the video system is set up and knowing how to use it can go a long way toward building some fine video-oriented programs.

The purpose of this chapter is to explore the main features of the TRS-80 video system in detail, expanding on the points that are merely suggested or implied in the *Level II BASIC Reference Manual*. Some of the video features are better implemented in BASIC, while others are more suited to machine-language treatments. The format used throughout this chapter is BASIC oriented; later chapters illustrate some of the same principles in machine language.

A few of the principles are of questionable value, appearing to be rather awkward in BASIC and machine language. These principles are described here for the sake of exploring some unusual ideas. Even these points of questionable value will at least serve to build your understanding of the TRS-80 video system and its potential applications.

VIDEO DATA

The information flowing around inside a computer consists of two parts: addresses and data. The address portion of that information specifies *where* something is to be placed, and the data portion specifies *what* is to be placed there.

In the context of the TRS-80 video system the addressing is usually related to some position on the crt screen, and the data concerns what is to be done at that point. This section deals with the video data. The next section of this chapter introduces some details of the video memory addressing.

The video data is carried as a 1-byte (8-bit) binary code, which means there are 256 possible combinations of things that can be done at a given point on the crt screen.

In the TRS-80 system those 256 video-related data codes can be divided into four categories:

- control codes—data codes 0 through 31
- alphanumeric character (ASCII) codes—32 through 127
- TRS-80 graphic codes—128 through 191
- TRS-80 tab codes—192 through 255

This list accounts for all 256 video data codes. Some of the functions are redundant (do the same thing as others), and a few of the codes do nothing at all. But, even so, there is a lot that can be done with the video data set.

It would be nice if we could investigate the video data set in a systematic fashion, beginning with control code 0 and progressing, one step at a time, through TRS-80 tab code 255. Unfortunately, the control codes and tab codes do not lend themselves to very convincing demonstrations at this point in the discussion.

So, for the sake of avoiding undue confusion in the early going, those control and tab codes will be explained later in this chapter. Of immediate interest, then, are the alphanumeric character codes and the TRS-80 graphic codes.

Alphanumeric Character Codes

The entire TRS-80 alphanumeric character set is represented by data codes 32 through 127. For the most part this code follows the well-established convention developed as the American Standard Code for Information Interchange (ASCII). The exceptions are the lack of special line, brace, and bracket symbols that appear on ASCII code charts but not on the TRS-80 keyboard.

Table 2-1 summarizes the TRS-80 alphanumeric character set, and if you want to see the characters on your own screen, try this short program:

```
10  REM ** ALPHANUMERIC CHARACTER SET DEMO **
20  CLS
30  FOR C=32 TO 127
40  PRINT CHR$(C);
50  NEXT C
60  END
```

This program prints the entire alphanumeric character set (charac-

Table 2-1. TRS-80 ASCII Character Set

Code (Decimal)	Character	Code (Decimal)	Character
32	space	80	P
33	!	81	Q
34	"	82	R
35	#	83	S
36	$	84	T
37	%	85	U
38	&	86	V
39	'	87	W
40	(	88	X
41	)	89	Y
42	*	90	Z
43	+	91	↑
44	,	92	↓
45	-	93	←
46	.	94	→
47	/	95	—
48	0	96	@
49	1	97	a
50	2	98	b
51	3	99	c
52	4	100	d
53	5	101	e
54	6	102	f
55	7	103	g
56	8	104	h
57	9	105	i
58	:	106	j
59	;	107	k
60	<	108	l
61	=	109	m
62	>	110	n
63	?	111	o
64	@	112	p
65	A	113	q
66	B	114	r
67	C	115	s
68	D	116	t
69	E	117	u
70	F	118	v
71	G	119	w
72	H	120	x
73	I	121	y
74	J	122	z
75	K	123	↑
76	L	124	↓
77	M	125	←
78	N	126	→
79	O	127	—

ter codes 32 through 127) in about 1½ lines across the top of the screen.

If you do not have the lowercase modification for your system, you will see the alphabetical characters (A–Z), four arrows, and a dash printed at two places in the display. The standard system cannot distinguish uppercase and lowercase characters, and codes 64 through 95 do the same thing as codes 96 through 127. With the lowercase modification, the alphabet appears in a lowercase format the second time through. So there is some redundancy here, unless you happen to have the lowercase character generator installed.

The CHR$(n) statement gives you access to the TRS-80 character generator in BASIC and with decimal code numbers. If you would rather tinker around with the character generator on a one-at-a-time basis, try this program:

```
10  REM ** CALL A CHARACTER **
20  CLS
30  INPUT "WHAT ASCII CHARACTER CODE (32-127)";C
40  IF C<32 OR C>127 THEN 30
50  PRINT CHR$(C)
60  PRINT
70  GOTO 30
```

Line 30 in this program requests an ASCII character code in the range 32 through 127. If you happen to respond with a number outside that range, line 40 returns the program to line 30, thus preventing you from tinkering with character or control codes outside the range of immediate interest here.

If you are still in the mood for playing around with this character set, it can be instructive to reverse the operation: writing a program that lets you specify an alphanumeric or any other ASCII character by typing it on the keyboard, and letting the computer print the character code, itself.

```
10  REM ** CALL-A-CODE **
20  CLS
30  C$=INKEY$:IF C$="" THEN 30
40  C=ASC(C$)
50  IF C>=32 AND C<=127 THEN 70
60  PRINT "THAT IS A CONTROL CHARACTER":GOTO 30
70  PRINT C$;" —";C
80  GOTO 30
```

On running CALL-A-CODE, you can type away on the keyboard, and with every valid character entry you will see the character linked with its ASCII code number. Since some of the keys generate control codes, line 50 is necessary to avoid some FC ERROR messages that stop the program. Whenever you strike one of those control keys, this program responds by printing THAT IS A CONTROL CHARACTER and letting you try another key.

While you are studying the alphanumeric character set with the CALL-A-CODE program, be sure to try it while the SHIFT key is depressed—that will give you the uppercase version of some of the special symbols and the lowercase codes for the alphabetical characters. Striking the A key with the SHIFT key *not* depressed, the program shows the letter A linked to character code 65. Striking that same key while the SHIFT key *is* depressed prints an A, followed by character code 97.

Also try the arrow keys with the CALL-A-CODE routine. This gives you code numbers for arrow characters that can be useful for writing graphics programs having arrow figures in them.

TRS-80 Graphic Codes

Video data codes 128 through 191 hold graphic patterns that are unique to the TRS-80. There are 64 of them in that family, and they are all different from one another. See Fig. 2-1.

The rationale behind the structure of these figures is not really very obvious until they are described in terms of the binary versions of their code numbers—a task that will be handled later. But with a table of these figures available, you don't have to be concerned about any discernible relationship between the code numbers and the graphic figures they call to the screen. It is entirely possible to build up some elaborate graphics from the decimal versions of the graphic-code numbers.

The graphic character set can be called to the screen just as the ASCII characters are, using PRINT CHR$(*n*) statements, where *n* is the character code number between 128 and 191, inclusively.

To illustrate the point, try this program:

```
10  REM ** GRAPHIC CHARACTER SET DEMO **
20  CLS
30  FOR C=128 TO 191
40  PRINT CHR$(C);CHR$(128);
50  NEXT C
60  END
```

This program prints out the entire graphic character set, separating each character with a space that is called by the CHR$(128) statement in line 40. Thus the graphics can be called to the screen just as the ASCII characters are, and that should come as no surprise, considering the graphics are generated by the same sort of read-only-memory (ROM) device.

If you want to link the graphic characters with their decimal code numbers in a clearer fashion, try this selection program:

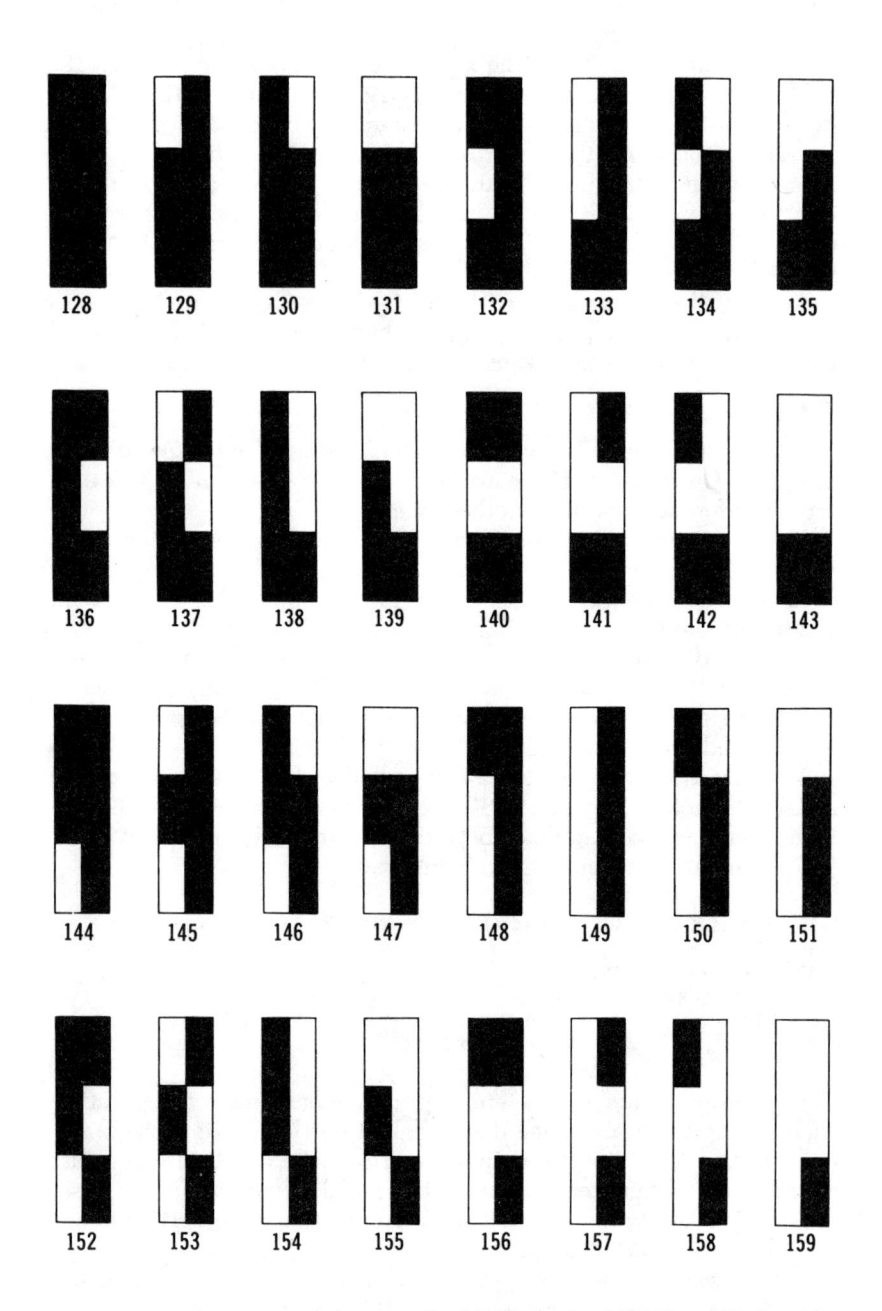

Fig. 2-1. The family of TRS-80 graphic characters

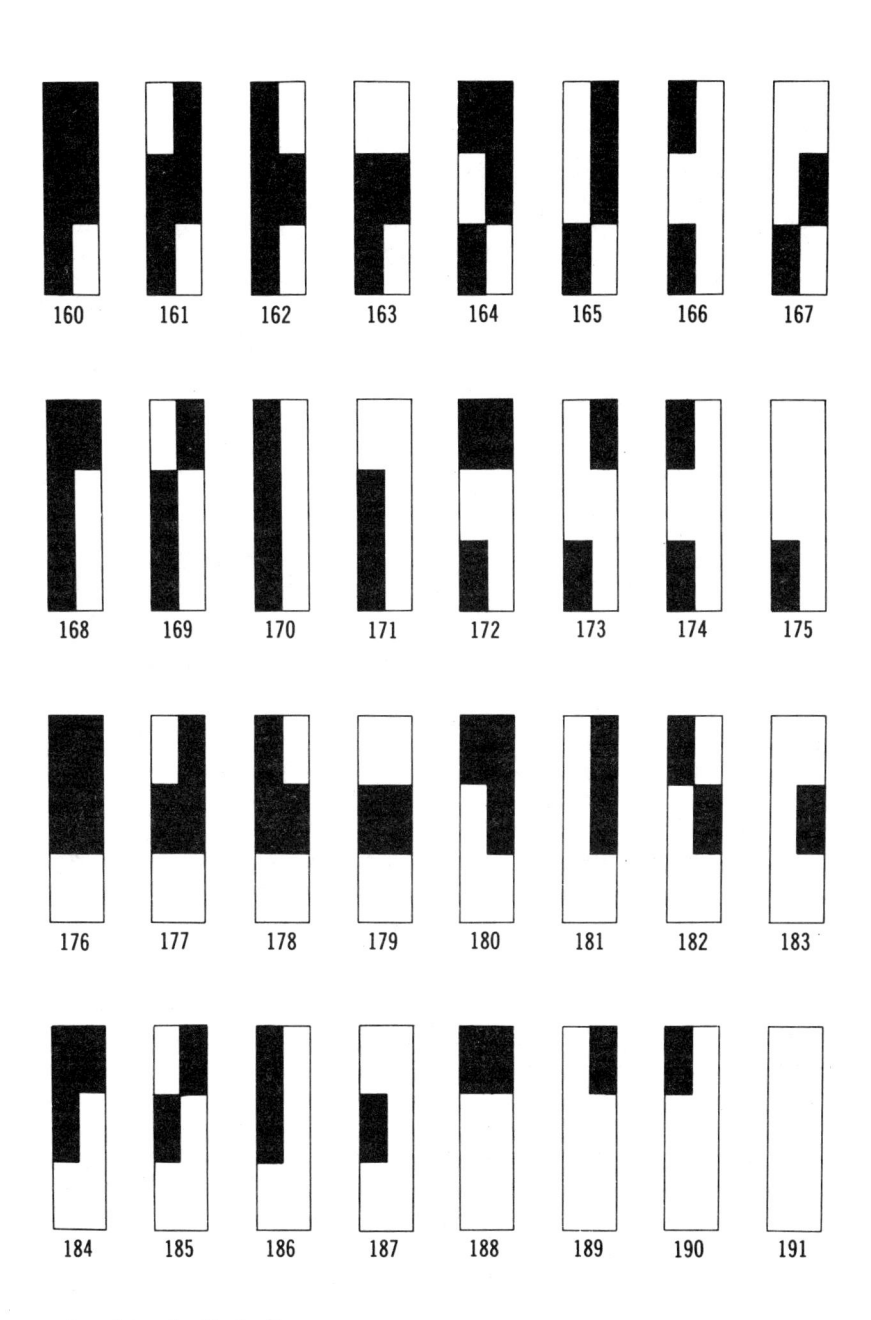

and graphic codes (decimal).

21

```
10 REM ** PICK A GRAPHIC **
20 CLS
30 INPUT "SPECIFY A GRAPHIC CODE (128-191)";C
40 IF C>=128 AND C<=191 THEN 60
50 PRINT "NOT A GRAPHIC":GOTO 30
60 PRINT CHR$(C)
70 PRINT:GOTO 30
```

Now you can specify and view the graphic characters one at a time.

To get a better appreciation for what is going on here, compare Fig. 2-1 and Fig. 2-2. For graphic purposes each character space on the screen is divided into a set of six smaller rectangles, labeled a through f in Fig. 2-2. A given rectangle, or *pixel*, within the character space is either lighted or darkened, depending on the code number being used.

| 1 | 0 | f | e | d | c | b | a |

- A 0 IN A GRAPHIC CODE BYTE DARKENS ITS PLACE IN CHARACTER SPACE.
- A 1 IN A GRAPHIC CODE BY LIGHTS ITS PLACE IN THE CHARACTER SPACE.

(A) Geometry of the graphic character space.

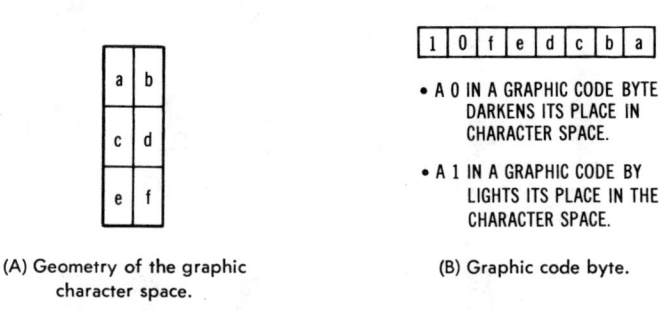

(B) Graphic code byte.

Fig. 2-2. Graphic character format and character-code layout.

Graphic code 129, for example, lights the little rectangle in the upper left-hand corner of the character space. In Fig. 2-2 that means pixel a is lighted by a binary 1 in the a-bit space of the character code. Code 130, on the other hand, lights the pixel in the upper right-hand corner of the current character space, and code 131 lights both of the top pixels (both a and b).

This process goes on through the entire 64-character graphic set, incrementing bits a through f in a binary counting sequence.

As mentioned previously, it is possible to use CHR$ statements to call the graphic characters, and thus compose some fairly elaborate graphic images on the crt. Of course, you have to know more about the video memory in order to position the individual graphic characters on the screen, and that is the next topic of discussion.

If you plan to compose any special graphic images, you will do well to pick up a pad of Radio Shack's Video/Programming Worksheets (catalog No. 26-2105). Those worksheets divide the screen addresses into character spaces and graphic pixels for you. All you have to do is sketch your graphics on the worksheet, then use

Fig. 2-1 to select the graphic character code required for each character space in the figure.

VIDEO ADDRESSING

If you consult a memory map for the TRS-80 system, you will find that the video memory occupies addresses 15360 through 16383, inclusively. That means 1024 different memory locations.

It is important to realize that those numbers represent address locations for random-access memory (RAM) built deep inside the TRS-80 keyboard/computer unit. The addresses refer to locations of data within a set of those RAM chips.

It just so happens that Radio Shack engineers linked each of those video memory addresses to a specific point on the crt screen. Tinkering around with the data in the video memory is thus tantamount to tinkering around with the video display. In fact, you cannot print any sort of character on the screen without placing the appropriate character data into some address location in the video memory.

The correspondence between video memory addresses and geometric locations on the video screen is very systematic and straightforward. Not all home computers use schemes that are so systematic and straightforward.

Whenever a program places some character data into video memory location 15360 (the lowest video memory address), the character appears at the extreme upper left-hand corner of the screen. And by putting some valid character data into memory location 16383 (the highest video memory address) the character appears in the extreme lower right-hand corner of the screen.

The video memory occupies 1024 RAM addresses, running sequentially from 15360 through 16383. The video screen is arranged with a 16-line, 64–characters-per-line format—which also is 1024 character locations. There is a nice one-for-one correspondence between those addresses and character positions on the screen.

The first 64 video memory addresses are linked to the first line on the screen; the second 64 memory addresses are linked to the second line on the screen; and so on through all 1024 addresses/locations.

Fig. 2-3 is a rough representation of the TRS-80 video screen format: the 16-line, 64–characters-per-line format. The numbers down the left-hand column show the video memory addresses for the first character position in each line, and the numbers down the right-hand column show the memory addresses for the last character position in each line.

Suppose that you want to print an X character near the middle

```
15360 ----------------------|  |---------------------- 15423
15424 ----------------------|  |---------------------- 15487
15488 ----------------------|  |---------------------- 15551
15552 ----------------------|  |---------------------- 15615
15616 ----------------------|  |---------------------- 15679
15680 ----------------------|  |---------------------- 15743
15744 ----------------------|  |---------------------- 15807
15808 ----------------------|  |---------------------- 15871
15872 ----------------------|  |---------------------- 15935
15936 ----------------------|  |---------------------- 15999
16000 ----------------------|  |---------------------- 16063
16064 ----------------------|  |---------------------- 16127
16128 ----------------------|  |---------------------- 16191
16192 ----------------------|  |---------------------- 16255
16256 ----------------------|  |---------------------- 16319
16320 ----------------------|  |---------------------- 16383
```

Fig. 2-3. POKE screen address format.

of the screen, which means putting the ASCII data for character X into a video memory location that is halfway between 15808 and 15871—the extreme ends of the middle line on the screen. Since there are 64 character spaces on the line, the midpoint is between 31 and 32 character spaces to the right, or that same number of address locations greater than 15808.

So if you POKE an X into video memory location 15808+32, or 15840, you will come very close to hitting the middle of the screen. Try it. Do a POKE 15840,88. That POKEs an 88 (ASCII code for X) into video memory address 15840.

You can POKE any ASCII character or TRS-80 graphic into any video memory address and see the character appearing at the addressed location on the crt screen.

This represents the most direct way of dealing with the video memory from BASIC. It takes advantage of the fact that each of the 1024 video memory addresses has a well-defined position on the crt screen. The same things can be done in the same general fashion in machine language, using LOAD instructions and hexadecimal addresses and data.

The technique can be summarized this way:

POKE *address, data*

where
    address is an address in video memory (an integer between 15360 and 16383),
    data is a character code (an integer between 32 and 191).

But that isn't the only way to address the video memory, putting some character data into that address and having the character appear at a well-defined spot on the screen. It's the most direct way to do the job, but Radio Shack engineers saw fit to work out some other methods for doing the same thing in a less direct but generally easier fashion.

PRINT @ Access to Video Memory

The PRINT @ statement accesses video memory very much the same way a POKE statement does. Like the POKE method just described, the PRINT @ statement includes both address and character data information, but there are some differences in the ways the addresses and data are presented.

Recall that the video memory occupies 1024 contiguous RAM locations between 15360 and 16383. When accessing the video memory via a POKE statement, you must specify an address with some integer in that address range. The PRINT @ method, however, calls for addresses between 0 and 1023.

The addressing portion of a PRINT @ statement does exactly the same thing as the addressing portion of a POKE statement, addressing the same set of 1024 locations in video memory. The only difference between the two portions is that the PRINT @ addresses have lower numbers.

```
0    ----------------------⊣  ⊢---------------------- 63
64   ----------------------⊣  ⊢---------------------- 127
128  ----------------------⊣  ⊢---------------------- 191
192  ----------------------⊣  ⊢---------------------- 255
256  ----------------------⊣  ⊢---------------------- 319
320  ----------------------⊣  ⊢---------------------- 383
384  ----------------------⊣  ⊢---------------------- 447
448  ----------------------⊣  ⊢---------------------- 511
512  ----------------------⊣  ⊢---------------------- 575
576  ----------------------⊣  ⊢---------------------- 639
640  ----------------------⊣  ⊢---------------------- 703
704  ----------------------⊣  ⊢---------------------- 767
768  ----------------------⊣  ⊢---------------------- 831
832  ----------------------⊣  ⊢---------------------- 895
896  ----------------------⊣  ⊢---------------------- 959
960  ----------------------⊣  ⊢---------------------- 1023
```

Fig. 2-4. PRINT @ screen address format.

So a PRINT @ address of 0 actually accesses video memory address 15360—the first, lowest-numbered one; and PRINT @ address 1023 actually addresses video memory location 16383 (the highest address location). Strictly speaking, then, *a PRINT @ address is simply a video memory address minus 15383.* The first line of 64 character spaces on the crt screen are thus accessed by PRINT @ addresses 0 through 63, the second line by 64 through 127, and so on.

See the screen format and corresponding PRINT @ addresses, for the extreme ends of the lines, in Fig. 2-4.

When a BASIC interpreter executes a PRINT @ address, it must add 15360 to the PRINT @ address in order to get to the actual video memory address. That bit of arithmetic, many believe, is a small price to pay for working with video address numbers that are smaller than the actual address numbers.

In all fairness it must be pointed out that there is more than the use of smaller address numbers involved in the PRINT @ statement. The data part of the statement can be much more complicated than is possible with a POKE statement.

The data portion of a PRINT @ statement must have a string character to it. POKE data must be offered in a character-code format, while PRINT @ data has to be equivalent to a string.

To illustrate this point, suppose you want to print an *A* character at the first character location on the first line of the screen. A POKE 15360,65 will do the job, and so will a PRINT @ 0,"A". So will a PRINT @ 0, ASC(65), letting the ASC function convert the character code into its string version. When the BASIC interpreter sees the data portion of a PRINT @ statement, it must convert it from a string version into a character-code version that can be effectively POKEd into video memory. This conversion, like the matter of adding 15360 to the PRINT @ address, eats up some execution time.

So the PRINT @ statement, although it has the same general format as POKE, runs much more slowly than a direct POKE does. But the PRINT @ statement is justified by the fact that it can deal with a long string (up to 255) of alphanumeric ASCII characters. The first character in the string is stored in the address indicated by the PRINT @ statement. Successive characters are then stored in successive video memory locations.

Suppose that you do a PRINT @ 0,"WHAT IS GOING ON HERE?" That string message will appear in the upper left-hand corner of the screen, because the first *W* in the message is loaded into PRINT @ address 0. The remaining characters in the message, if you care to count them, occupy PRINT @ addresses 1 through 21. The BASIC interpreter automatically increments an address counter to deposit the ASCII version of the characters into successive video memory locations. If you tried to print out that same message, using a POKE method, you would have to increment the memory addresses yourself. Look at this:

```
10 REM ** POKE STRING DEMO **
20 A0=15360:A1=16383
30 CLS
40 FOR A=A0 TO A1
50 READ C$
```

```
60   IF C$="#" THEN 60
70   POKE A,ASC(C$)
80   NEXT A
100  DATA W,H,A,T," ",I,S," ",G,O,I,N,G," ",O,N," ",H,E,R,E,?,#
```

This isn't the only way to go about writing string messages with POKE statements, but the alternatives aren't significantly simpler. Indeed, PRINT @ statements show some real promise when it comes to writing strings of characters.

Incidentally, the PRINT @ data is not limited to the ASCII character set; it can be used for displaying the TRS-80 graphic set as well. All you do is specify the graphic code (128–191) as a "string," by applying the CHR$ function. For example, PRINT @ 543,CHR$(191) prints a white rectangle near the middle of the screen—PRINT @ address 543, graphic code 191.

So as a point of interest, at least, you can see that it is possible to build some nice screen graphics using the PRINT @ statement.

Finally, the PRINT @ statement has one further advantage over its POKE counterpart: a programmer cannot inadvertently poke data into memory locations outside the video memory range. PRINT @ statements do not allow addresses outside the range of 0 to 1023. Attempting to do a PRINT @ 2000, *data*, for example, will simply result in an FC ERROR message. POKEing outside the video memory range risks a blowup of the program.

When it comes to doing video graphics and printing messages on the crt, the PRINT @ statement has a lot of advantages over its POKE counterpart. The only trade-off is the relatively slow speed of PRINT @—a feature made necessary by all the number crunching that takes place when compiling and executing a PRINT @. The following program clearly illustrates the difference in execution speed for POKE and PRINT @:

```
10   REM ** PRINT @/POKE GRAPHICS SPEED CONTEST **
20   CLS
30   PRINT "POKE RUN"
40   FOR A=15424 TO 15487
50   POKE A,191
60   NEXT A
70   PRINT:PRINT "PRINT @ RUN"
80   FOR A=192 TO 255
90   PRINT @ A,CHR$(191)
100  NEXT A
110  END
```

The first part of the program, lines 30 through 60, use POKE graphics to fill a line with solid white rectangles (character code 191). The second part, lines 70 through 100, do the same thing, but using PRINT @ graphics.

The two horizontal white bars are drawn in succession, but the differences in drawing speeds are fairly obvious.

The PRINT @ statement can be summarized this way:

PRINT @ *address, data*

where
address is a PRINT @ address between 0 and 1024,
data is a string-related character, variable, or string of characters.

Relative Video Memory Addressing With Primitive PRINTs

POKE and PRINT @ statements access the video memory in an absolute fashion. That is to say, the addresses refer directly to some specific address in the video memory. The remaining techniques for working with the video memory use relative addressing.

Using relative addressing often simplifies the task of programming the video format, but it separates the program even further from the actual video memory system, and the execution time is lengthened as a result.

For our immediate purposes here, a primitive PRINT statement is a PRINT followed by " " (quote-space-quote) or nothing at all. A primitive PRINT changes the position of the cursor on the screen; and by doing a proper selection of PRINT and PRINT " " statements, it is possible to place the cursor at any desired point on the screen.

What does this have to do with video memory addressing? Recall that every character position on the screen has a well-defined video memory address. Doing a PRINT statement changes the setting of an address counter, incrementing it to deposit data into successive video address locations. The location of the cursor on the screen is a reflection of the next video memory address to be used.

As a specific example, suppose you execute this program:

```
10 CLS
20 PRINT" ";" ";"X"
```

The CLS operation clears the screen and homes the cursor (sends it to the extreme upper left-hand corner of the screen—to video memory address 15360). Printing two spaces in succession, separated by a semicolon, moves the cursor two spaces to the right along the top line, and the X appears in the third space on the line. The character code for X ends up in video memory address 15362.

In this case you do not have to specify the exact address for the X character code—15362 for the POKE method, or 2 for the PRINT @ method. The two successive PRINT-space operations simply move the cursor two spaces from its starting position. An internal cursor counter takes care of converting this relative address change into absolute direct memory addresses.

Here is a trick that is used quite often in BASIC programs aimed at doing some screen formatting:

```
10  CLS
20  PRINT:PRINT
30  PRINT "X"
```

As in the previous example the opening CLS statement sends the cursor to the lowest video memory address location. The two successive PRINT statements in line 20 cause the cursor to skip down two lines on the screen, and the X ends up at the beginning of the third line on the screen.

Unless instructed to do otherwise, every sort of PRINT statement in BASIC is terminated by a line-feed/carriage-return operation. In terms of the video memory addresses and the screen format (see Fig. 2-3) this means setting the video memory address counter to the next address representing the beginning of a new line. Refer to the addresses in the left-hand column in Fig. 2-3.

So the CLS statement sends the cursor to video memory address 15360. The first of the two PRINT statements in line 20 sends the cursor to address 15424, and the second one sends it to address 15488. The X is deposited at that location by line 30, and that operation (being a PRINT operation) ends by setting the cursor to address location 15552. You must refer to Fig. 2-3 to appreciate this explanation.

Primitive PRINT addressing is relative addressing in the sense that you do not have to specify an exact address anywhere along the line. The cursor is moved the specified number of lines or spaces from its initial position, and that initial position can be anywhere on the screen. The addressing began at 15360 in the previous examples only because the programs began with a CLS operation—one that takes the cursor to 15360. You can actually begin anywhere you want.

Not having to reckon with absolute video memory addresses often simplifies video-oriented programming. If, for instance, you want to skip two spaces on a line before printing another character, simply do a PRINT " ";" ". That will do the trick—the BASIC compiler takes care of figuring out the absolute memory addresses to be loaded with the space code (ASCII 32).

Now, it was mentioned earlier in this discussion that every PRINT statement is followed, automatically, by a line-feed/carriage-return operation—unless instructed to do otherwise. Instructing the system to inhibit that automatic line feed/carriage return is a matter of terminating the PRINT statement with a semicolon. That is how it is possible to skip two character spaces on the same line by doing PRINT " ";" ";.

The primitive PRINT scheme allows you to view the video screen as a two-dimensional coordinate system. You can, in other words, locate a character on the screen by thinking in terms of the number of lines down and the number of character spaces to the right. So if you want to print an X near the middle of the screen, you can do that by first homing the cursor (for convenient reference), skipping down eight lines (in a 16-line format) and 31 character spaces to the right along that line (in a 64-characters-per-line format). The program looks something like this:

```
10  CLS
20  FOR L=1 TO 8:PRINT:NEXT L
30  FOR S=1 TO 31:PRINT " ";:NEXT S
40  PRINT "X"
```

More compelling applications of the primitive-PRINT scheme are offered in the next chapter. The important point here is that PRINT statements offer a relative video memory addressing scheme and the opportunity to build displays based on a vertical/horizontal coordinate system.

To be sure, this scheme eats up more BASIC programming memory and execution time than POKE and PRINT @ methods do, but, used on a small scale, the relative addressing feature of primitive PRINT formatting can simplify the original programming task.

Horizontal Addressing With PRINT TAB

PRINT TAB statements allow you to simplify the task of specifying a printing location along a given line. If you do a statement such as PRINT TAB(n)"X", where n is any integer between 0 and 63, you can place that X at any desired space location (0 through 63) along a given line on the screen.

```
10  CLS
20  PRINT TAB(31)"X"
```

This program prints the X very close to the middle of the top line on the screen. And if you want to put the X near the middle of the screen, try this:

```
10  CLS
20  FOR L=1 TO 8:PRINT:NEXT L
30  PRINT TAB(31)"X"
```

The first part of the program, lines 10 and 20, uses the line-skipping routine, described in the previous section of this chapter, to find the beginning of the middle line on the screen. The PRINT TAB statement in line 30 both runs the cursor to the middle of that line and prints the X character. Using the PRINT TAB statement represents an improvement over doing the same thing with a series of PRINT " "; primitives.

Behind the scenes, a PRINT TAB(n) statement causes an absolute video memory address counter to *increment* n counts, effectively placing the cursor n places to the right of its starting position. The data specified by the PRINT TAB statement is automatically POKEd into that newly counted video memory address location.

Incidentally, it is possible to specify PRINT TAB numbers up to 255, but it turns out that any over 63 are redundant. For instance, PRINT TAB(0), PRINT TAB(64) and PRINT TAB(128) set the character to the first character space on a line. So using PRINT TAB numbers larger than 63 changes nothing, and only adds to possible confusion on the part of the programmer.

As in the case of any PRINT statement, a PRINT TAB is automatically followed by a line-feed/carriage-return operation, unless followed by a semicolon. So if you do a PRINT TAB(31)"X", the X will appear in the middle of the current line, but the cursor will be resting at the beginning of the next line. By contrast, a PRINT TAB(31)"X"; prints the X at the middle of the current line and forces the cursor to remain at the next character space on that same line.

The fact that you can suppress the line-feed/carriage-return operation makes it possible to pull off some useful one-line tricks. Try this:

```
10  CLS
20  PRINT TAB(31)"X";
30  PRINT TAB(40)"Y"
```

This program prints the X near the middle of the first line on the screen. The semicolon at the end of line 20 inhibits the normal linefeed/carriage-return operation, so the Y appears in space 40 on the same line—nine spaces to the right of the X.

Unfortunately, it is not possible to set the absolute memory address counter backwards. It counts forward only. So, in the previous example, you will have some trouble if you print the Y at space position 40 first, and then try to print the X at space position 31. The Y will end up at position 40, but the X will appear at position 41, in spite of the fact you specify a PRINT TAB(31) for it.

In a manner of speaking, the n values in a PRINT TAB(n) statement represent a form of absolute addressing—absolute addressing with reference to character spaces on a given line on the screen. If you view a line of text as made up of locations 0 through 63, the TAB values refer absolutely to one of those 64 locations.

PRINT TAB statements can handle TRS-80 graphics as well as the standard ASCII code. If you want to print a rectangle of light at the middle of a line, just do a PRINT TAB(31)CHR$(191). Any of the graphic-code numbers (128–191) can be worked into that CHR$ data statement. You can thus use combinations of primitive PRINT statements (to select lines) and PRINT TAB statements (to select character spaces on a line) to do some graphics that combine alphanumerics and graphic symbols.

Relative Character-Space Addressing With TAB Control Codes

The upper end of the TRS-80 character/control video set includes some numbers that Radio Shack calls "space compression codes." From BASIC, these codes can be executed by a PRINT CHR$(n) statement, where n is an integer between 192 and 255, inclusively. But what do those so-called space compression codes do?

Used with PRINT CHR$(n), the space compression codes function in a manner similar to PRINT TAB(n). The codes indicate a number of spaces to be skipped (to the right) on a given line on the screen. Unlike PRINT TAB, however, the space compression codes have a relative addressing quality: the cursor is moved a given number of spaces, beginning from its current position, and not always from the beginning of a line.

There are 64 TAB control codes in the range of 192 through 255, and there are 64 character positions on each line of text on the video screen. The match of these two numbers is hardly incidental.

To see how the TAB control codes work, suppose the cursor is resting at space number 31 on a particular line on the screen—that's near the middle of the line. But then you want to skip two more spaces to the right. There are two ways to go about it: you can do a PRINT TAB(33) or a PRINT CHR$(194);. The PRINT TAB version specifies an absolute character space that turns out to be two character units to the right of the original one—really, the 33rd space from the beginning of the line. PRINT CHR$(194), on the other hand, moves the cursor two spaces to the right of its current position—there is no reference to the beginning of the line. But where did the 194 come from?

The TAB control codes allow you to move the cursor s spaces to the right, where s is an integer between 0 and 63, inclusively. The actual code number to be specified, however, is always equal to 192 (the smallest TAB control number) plus s. To move the cursor two spaces to the right of its current position, $s=2$ and the TAB control code is 192+2, or 194. That's where the 194 comes from in the previous example.

The operation can be summarized this way:

> PRINT CHR$(192+s);
>
> where
> s is the number of character spaces the cursor is moved to the right of its current position.

Specific applications of such principles are reserved for the next chapter, but one such application can serve here to illustrate the usefulness of the TAB control codes.

Suppose you want to fill the top line on the screen with asterisks, each separated from the previous one by a space. The job could be done this way:

```
10  CLS
20  FOR N=1 TO 32
30  PRINT "* ";
40  NEXT N
```

The PRINT asterisk-space combination in line 30 does the job. Or, if you are willing to sweat out some math, you could do the job with absolute PRINT TAB values:

```
10  CLS
20  FOR N=1 TO 32
30  IF INT(N/2)<>N/2 THEN PRINT TAB(N)"*"
40  NEXT N
```

Or, to take advantage of the TAB control codes, you can do this:

```
10  CLS
20  FOR N=1 TO 31
30  PRINT CHR$(193);PRINT"*";
40  NEXT N
```

To be sure, the last example is not significantly simpler than the first one, but that is only because the situation calls for skipping just one space between the asterisks. If you want to skip four spaces, PRINT CHR$(196) is more elegant than a PRINT "*   ".

Since the TAB control codes use relative space addressing, it is altogether possible to specify code numbers that will overflow a line, calling for moving the cursor more spaces than remain on a given line. The TAB control function handles that sort of situation by resuming the count on the next line. Anytime you follow a printing operation with PRINT CHR$(255), for example, the next character will be printed directly below the previous one—the cursor will advance 63 spaces to the right of the current cursor position. One might argue that the same position on successive lines are separated by 64 character spaces, and not 63. That is quite true, but bear in mind that the cursor always rests one character space to the right

33

of the last-printed character; advancing the cursor 63 spaces from that point will position the next-printed character directly under the first one.

Working Directly With the Cursor Counter

With the notable exception of the POKE method of working with the video memory, all the screen formatting techniques described thus far in this chapter take advantage of a cursor counter; a register in the Z-80 microprocessor that keeps track of the one-for-one relationship between video memory addresses and print positions on the crt. These cursor-oriented operations run more slowly than POKEs do, but they are generally easier to use.

It is possible to access that cursor counter, PEEKing at the cursor address or POKEing new cursor addresses into it. The cursor address is accessible in a section of dedicated RAM that Radio Shack calls the "video display control block." The cursor address is carried as a 2-byte number in RAM addresses 16416 and 16417. The least significant byte (lsb) of the cursor's address is saved in location 16416, and the most significant of the two bytes (msb) is in 16417.

So if you want to see the contents of that cursor-position register, you can get to it by doing something such as PRINT PEEK(16417), PEEK(16416). That will give the cursor position as it stands *after* completing that PRINT operation. (The suggested PRINT operation, you see, affects the position of the cursor and hence the contents of the registers PEEKed into.) At any rate, that operation will give you a convincing feeling that you can, indeed, get to the cursor-counting register.

Whenever you PEEK into the cursor register, you will find that the number from the msb position (address 16417) is an integer between 60 and 63. The number from the lsb position (address 16416) is an integer between 0 and 255. Those are the cursor screen coordinates in a decimal format.

The msb divides the screen into four sets of lines, each set having four lines. This accounts for all 16 lines on the video screen. The lsb divides each line into 64 character spaces: 0–63 indicates a character space on the first line of any of the four groups of lines, 64–127 indicates character spaces on the second line in each group of four lines, 128–191 is for the third line in each group, and 192–255 is for the last of the four lines in each group.

So if the cursor happens to be resting at the first character space in the first line on the screen, the msb of the cursor address is 60 and the lsb is 0. But if the cursor is at the second space on the second line, the msb is 60 and the lsb is 65.

Fig. 2-5 summarizes the cursor coordinate addresses for the beginning and end of each line on the screen.

To convert these vectors to Print @ use
*e.g. AT = PEEK (16416) + 256 * (PEEK (16417) - 60)*

MSB	LSB			MSB	LSB
60	0	┤	├	60	63
60	64	┤	├	60	127
60	128	┤	├	60	191
60	192	┤	├	60	255
61	0	┤	├	61	63
61	64	┤	├	61	127
61	128	┤	├	61	191
61	192	┤	├	61	255
62	0	┤	├	62	63
62	64	┤	├	62	127
62	128	┤	├	62	191
62	192	┤	├	62	255
63	0	┤	├	63	63
63	64	┤	├	63	127
63	128	┤	├	63	191
63	192	┤	├	63	255

THE MSB AND LSB FOR CURSOR COORDINATES ARE
STORED AT RAM ADDRESSES 16417 AND 16416, RESPECTIVELY

Fig. 2-5. Cursor-counter screen address format.

As mentioned previously, PEEKing into the cursor-position register and PRINTing the results can be a confusing operation because the PRINT operation, itself, advances the cursor position. A better way to make a convincing demonstration is by POKEing coordinates into the cursor-position register and having a PRINT operation print some well-defined character on the screen. Try this:

```
10 CLS
20 INPUT "MSB";MSB
30 IF MSB<60 OR MSB>63 THEN 20
40 INPUT "LSB";LSB
50 IF LSB<0 OR LSB>255 THEN 40
60 CLS
70 POKE 16416,LSB:POKE 16417,MSB
80 PRINT "X";
```

The program requests the msb and lsb coordinates from you. It is goofproofed to prevent you from specifying out-of-range figures. Once you have entered the coordinates, the program clears the screen and prints an X at the point you specified. You will see that the format follows Fig. 2-5 quite nicely.

This is an unusual tool for positioning the cursor on the screen. There are some fine applications for the idea of PEEKing into the cursor-address register, but they will have to await a later discussion.

There is a Level II function that does, in its own fashion, PEEK into the cursor-address register. That is the POS(x) function. POS(x) looks into the cursor-address register and returns an integer

35

between 0 and 63, indicating the horizontal position of the cursor at the moment the function is called. The x argument, incidentally, is a dummy argument and can be any alphanumeric character.

For future thinking it may be helpful to realize that *the msb and lsb numbers representing the cursor-address position are actually 2-byte versions of the actual video memory address.* The first cursor-address position, for example, is 60,0; and in terms of the video memory addresses, that first position is 15360. If you convert that 63,0 combination into hexadecimal, you get 3C00H. And by converting 3C00 hexadecimal into decimal, you get 15360. (These conversion techniques are described in greater detail in a later chapter.)

SET/RESET Video Memory Addressing

The SET(x,y) and RESET(x,y) functions are fairly well documented in the standard TRS-80 literature, and there is no real need to dwell on the general applications here. Bear in mind that x is an integer between 0 and 127, and y is an integer between 0 and 47. The SET function turns on a spot of light at its designated x,y coordinates, and RESET darkens the spot at those character coordinates.

The BASIC interpreter translates those x,y coordinates into absolute video memory address locations, inserting one of the graphic-code numbers (128–191) as appropriate to the configuration of spots of light in a given character space. See the relationships between the x,y coordinates and screen positions in Fig. 2-6. Radio Shack's Video/Programming Worksheets spell out this relationship in a clearer and more useful fashion.

It is quite possible to write a BASIC program that will print out the graphic-code number and video address for each graphic element previously generated by the SET/RESET statements. That project is left to the reader as an exercise in applying much of the material presented thus far in this chapter.

VIDEO CONTROL CODES

Data codes 0 through 31 do jobs other than print characters on the screen. They are video/line-printer function codes that call ROM subroutines for doing certain print-related tasks. See Table 2-2.

The control functions are normally generated by striking the special control keys on the keyboard, but they can be called during the execution of a BASIC program by doing a PRINT CHR$($n$) statement, where n is the control-code number from Table 2-2.

The following discussions deal only with the control codes that influence the cursor position on the crt and hence the current address of the video memory.

```
Y                                    X
0   < 0 ----------------⊣  ⊢---------------- 127 >
1   < 0 ----------------⊣  ⊢---------------- 127 >
2   < 0 ----------------⊣  ⊢---------------- 127 >
3   < 0 ----------------⊣  ⊢---------------- 127 >
4   < 0 ----------------⊣  ⊢---------------- 127 >
5   < 0 ----------------⊣  ⊢---------------- 127 >
6   < 0 ----------------⊣  ⊢---------------- 127 >
7   < 0 ----------------⊣  ⊢---------------- 127 >
8   < 0 ----------------⊣  ⊢---------------- 127 >
9   < 0 ----------------⊣  ⊢---------------- 127 >
10  < 0 ----------------⊣  ⊢---------------- 127 >
11  < 0 ----------------⊣  ⊢---------------- 127 >
12  < 0 ----------------⊣  ⊢---------------- 127 >
13  < 0 ----------------⊣  ⊢---------------- 127 >
14  < 0 ----------------⊣  ⊢---------------- 127 >
15  < 0 ----------------⊣  ⊢---------------- 127 >
16  < 0 ----------------⊣  ⊢---------------- 127 >
17  < 0 ----------------⊣  ⊢---------------- 127 >
18  < 0 ----------------⊣  ⊢---------------- 127 >
19  < 0 ----------------⊣  ⊢---------------- 127 >
20  < 0 ----------------⊣  ⊢---------------- 127 >
21  < 0 ----------------⊣  ⊢---------------- 127 >
22  < 0 ----------------⊣  ⊢---------------- 127 >
23  < 0 ----------------⊣  ⊢---------------- 127 >
24  < 0 ----------------⊣  ⊢---------------- 127 >
25  < 0 ----------------⊣  ⊢---------------- 127 >
26  < 0 ----------------⊣  ⊢---------------- 127 >
27  < 0 ----------------⊣  ⊢---------------- 127 >
28  < 0 ----------------⊣  ⊢---------------- 127 >
29  < 0 ----------------⊣  ⊢---------------- 127 >
30  < 0 ----------------⊣  ⊢---------------- 127 >
31  < 0 ----------------⊣  ⊢---------------- 127 >
32  < 0 ----------------⊣  ⊢---------------- 127 >
33  < 0 ----------------⊣  ⊢---------------- 127 >
34  < 0 ----------------⊣  ⊢---------------- 127 >
35  < 0 ----------------⊣  ⊢---------------- 127 >
36  < 0 ----------------⊣  ⊢---------------- 127 >
37  < 0 ----------------⊣  ⊢---------------- 127 >
38  < 0 ----------------⊣  ⊢---------------- 127 >
39  < 0 ----------------⊣  ⊢---------------- 127 >
40  < 0 ----------------⊣  ⊢---------------- 127 >
41  < 0 ----------------⊣  ⊢---------------- 127 >
42  < 0 ----------------⊣  ⊢---------------- 127 >
43  < 0 ----------------⊣  ⊢---------------- 127 >
44  < 0 ----------------⊣  ⊢---------------- 127 >
45  < 0 ----------------⊣  ⊢---------------- 127 >
46  < 0 ----------------⊣  ⊢---------------- 127 >
47  < 0 ----------------⊣  ⊢---------------- 127 >
```

Fig. 2-6. SET/RESET screen address format.

Table 2-2. Summary of Control Codes and Functions for the TRS-80

Decimal Code	Control Function
0–7	None
8	Backspace and erase current character
9	None
10	Line feed/carriage return
11, 12	Go to top of next form (line-printer function)
13	Line feed/carriage return
14	Turn on cursor
15	Turn off cursor
16–22	None
23	Convert to 32 characters per line
24	Backspace the cursor
25	Advance the cursor
26	Downward line feed
27	Upward line feed
28	Home the cursor
29	Cursor to beginning of current line
30	Erase to end of current line
31	Clear to end of frame

Line Feed/Carriage Return

Generally speaking, a line feed/carriage return drops the cursor down one line and then moves it to the beginning of that line. An important exception occurs when the cursor is resting on the bottom line of the crt display; doing a line feed/carriage return at that point scrolls the entire display up one line and moves the cursor to the beginning of that bottom line.

Striking the ENTER key generates a line-feed/carriage-return code (code No. 13) anytime the system is responding to characters typed on the keyboard. And when a BASIC program is running, any PRINT statement that is not terminated with a semicolon will call a line feed/carriage return.

You can insert a line feed/carriage return anywhere you wish in a BASIC program by either

PRINT CHR$(10);

or

PRINT CHR$(13);

Yes, indeed, you can accomplish the same effect with a simple PRINT primitive, but we are trying to illustrate a principle here that will prove useful later on.

Relating this line-feed/carriage-return operation to the video memory address, the line-feed portion effectively adds 64 to the current cursor address—this drops the cursor down one line. The carriage-return part of the operation then backs up the address to the point where statement POS(X) would return a 0—to the beginning of that line.

When a line feed/carriage return calls for a scrolling of the entire display, the cursor address is kept at the first space on the bottom line, but a 64 is subtracted from the addresses for all characters, except those on the top line. All characters, in other words, undergo an upward line feed, and those on the top line are lost.

Home the Cursor, Clear to End of Frame

Control codes 28 (home the cursor) and 31 (clear to end of frame) can be used separately, but one of their most useful applications use them together.

Homing the cursor sends it to the lowest video memory address: to the extreme upper left-hand corner of the screen. You can implement the function in a BASIC program by doing a

    PRINT CHR$(28);

Any successive printing operations will then be referenced to this home point. The semicolon at the end of the statement is necessary to prevent an automatic line feed/carriage return—an operation that will carry the cursor to the beginning of the second line from the top of the screen.

In terms of video memory addressing, doing a home-cursor operation simply sets the cursor address counter to 15360, or 60,0 if you want to consider the 2-byte address format.

Control code 31 is not really a cursor-moving operation, but it clears the screen from the address of the cursor to the highest video memory address. So if the cursor happens to be situated in the middle of the screen when a BASIC program encounters

    PRINT CHR$(31);

the cursor does not move, but the remainder of the line and all successive lines to the bottom of the screen are cleared.

As far as the internal working of the computer is concerned, doing a clear-to-end-of-frame operation inserts data code 32 (a space) into all address locations from that of the cursor to the highest video memory address (16383).

As mentioned earlier, control codes 28 and 31 are often used together and in that particular sequence. Insert this statement into a BASIC program:

    PRINT CHR$(28);CHR$(31);

That sequence homes the cursor and clears to the end of the frame. In this case, clearing to the end of the frame amounts to clearing the entire screen. The sequence does the same thing as the CLS statement or striking the CLEAR key when the system is in its command mode.

Move to Beginning of Line and Erase to End of Line

Control codes 29 (move the cursor to the beginning of the current line) and 30 (erase to end of current line) work just like codes 28 (home the cursor) and 31 (clear to end of frame). Codes 29 and 30 deal only with the current line of text, however, while 28 and 31 deal with the entire screen.

Whenever you want to return the cursor to the beginning of its line, without erasing any characters along the way, insert this statement into a BASIC program:

PRINT CHR$(29);

This operation sets the cursor-address counter back to an address representing the beginning of the current line. If POS(X) happens to return a 31 before the operation is executed, it will return a 0 after the operation is done.

Erasing all the characters between the cursor and the end of its line is a matter of writing this statement into a BASIC program:

PRINT CHR$(30);

This causes the computer to insert a character code 32 (space) into each address location, beginning from the cursor and ending at the extreme right end of the current line. The cursor position is not affected by that clear-to-end-of-line operation.

Erasing an entire line of text, regardless of the cursor's position on that line, is a matter of using these two codes in succession:

PRINT CHR$(29);CHR$(30);

The first part of the statement moves the cursor to the beginning of the current line, and the second part erases everything to the right of it on that same line. In effect, the statement clears the entire line. The cursor remains at the beginning of the line, perhaps giving you the opportunity to replace it with fresh characters.

Turn On/Turn Off the Cursor

When one is writing a BASIC program or working with the system in its command mode, the TRS-80 automatically turns on the cursor symbol to indicate the printing position of the next character. The cursor figure, however, is normally turned off while running a

BASIC program. Whenever you execute a program that generates a long series of alphanumeric characters, for example, you do not see the cursor figure as it buzzes along, indicating the next character-printing position.

It is possible to turn on the cursor figure and observe its position on the screen during a BASIC program by inserting the statement:

PRINT CHR$(14);

After that, you will be able to see the cursor, wherever it goes. As you might imagine, being able to see the cursor during the execution of a program can be a valuable aid in keeping track of what is going on and in editing screen graphics.

The turn-on-cursor control code can be executed just one time, and it will remain in effect until some other operation forces it off. So a PRINT CHR$(14); is normally inserted at the beginning of a BASIC program.

Turning off the cursor is a simple matter of executing the BASIC statement:

PRINT CHR$(15);

After seeing this statement, the cursor remains turned off until another turn-on operation occurs.

The next section of this chapter illustrates some important applications of the cursor turn-on control code.

One-Step Cursor Operations

Control codes 24, 25, 26, and 27 increment the cursor position back one space, forward one space, down one line, and up one line. The contents of the video memory are left unchanged in the process.

Here is a summary of these operations as implemented in BASIC:

PRINT CHR$(24);—This statement backspaces the cursor position by effectively subtracting a 1 from the cursor-position address.

PRINT CHR$(25);—This statement advances the cursor position one space, effectively adding a 1 to the current cursor address.

PRINT CHR$(26);—This statement drops the cursor position down one line, but maintains the same horizontal position. This is done by effectively adding 64 to the current cursor address. The downward line-feed operation wraps around to the top of the screen whenever the cursor is on the bottom line.

PRINT CHR$(26);—This statement moves the cursor position up one line, but maintains the same horizontal position. The cursor address, in effect, has a 64 subtracted from it. Doing this upward line feed while the cursor is already on the top line causes it to wrap around to the bottom line.

These statements can be written into a BASIC program to achieve some useful formatting effects, doing things such as reserving a portion of the screen for in-line text printing and another portion for video graphics. This is sometimes called *split-screen formatting*, but the standard Radio Shack literature says little, if anything, about it.

It turns out that the four arrow keys on the TRS-80 keyboard will generate the one-step cursor motion codes—if you strike them while depressing the SHIFT key. The keys do not generate the right cursor-control codes when the system is in the command mode, however. You must use them in a BASIC execution mode. Here is a little program to demonstrate the point.

```
10  PRINT CHR$(14);CHR$(28);CHR$(31);
20  C$=INKEY$:IF C$="" THEN 20
30  PRINT C$;
40  GOTO 20
```

Line 10 turns on the cursor symbol, sends it home, and clears to the end of the frame. Line 20 then picks up a string character from the keyboard, and line 30 executes the PRINT operation on the key character.

As long as you are striking the alphanumeric keys you will see the characters printed on the screen. The cursor symbol will be there to indicate the position of the next-printed character.

The main point of the demonstration is the use of the arrow keys, though. So depress the SHIFT key and strike one of the arrow keys. You will see the cursor responding as outlined earlier in this section. The back arrow makes the cursor move to the left, the up arrow makes it move up one line, and so on. You don't get the same sort of response if the SHIFT key is *not* depressed.

Also note that you can use this shift/arrow-key feature to move the cursor through printed text without altering it. It deletes the character at its current position, but replaces it when you move the cursor somewhere else on the screen.

This suggests some elementary word-processing operations, giving you an opportunity to edit characters in the text without messing up a whole line of them. You can replace a character with another one by setting the cursor to that character position and striking the key representing the desired character. Or you can delete the character by striking the space bar.

Backspace and Delete Current Character

Control code 8 works just like the backspace operation just described (control code 24), except that it deletes the character as it goes along. Doing PRINT CHR$(8); is the same thing as striking the back-arrow key when the system is the command mode of operation.

CHAPTER 3

The Keyboard Environment

Just as the most-used output device for the TRS-80 is its crt screen, the most-used input device is its keyboard. The keyboard environment is neither as sophisticated nor as versatile as the video environment, but understanding its operating features can go a long way toward building some especially useful programs.

In the command mode of operation the keyboard is normally linked to the video display system. Every keystroke produces a well-defined response on the screen—printing characters, spacing, line feeding, and so on. See the SPECIAL NOTE on page 45 for an exception to this general idea.

There are two BASIC statements that let you interact with an ongoing program from the keyboard: INPUT and INKEY$. Both statements are well documented in the standard TRS-80 literature, but the first two sections of this chapter consider them in more detail, illustrating some applications that can be quite useful.

As you might suspect, there are some more subtle ways to deal with the keyboard, PEEKing around in the so-called keyboard memory part of the TRS-80 memory map. As in the case of such schemes in the video environment, some of these PEEK-keyboard routines will appear a bit cumbersome when used in BASIC, but understanding the principles will make it easier for you to grasp the essence of some keyboard operations in machine language. The latter part of the chapter is devoted to some of these unconventional keyboard-input notions.

THE STANDARD INPUT STATEMENT

The INPUT statement allows in-line interaction with a program, halting the execution of that program until the user strikes the

> **SPECIAL NOTE**
>
> It is possible to link the keyboard directly to a standard Radio Shack line-printer system by doing:
>
> **POKE 16414,141:POKE 16415,5**
>
> Doing this, all PRINT and LIST statements and commands affect the line printer instead of the video display. In effect, it replaces the video display with the line printer.
>
> Since the line printer responds only after seeing the end of a line of text, it prints nothing until you strike the ENTER key or it finds the end of a program line.
>
> Unfortunately, this scheme doesn't always work with nonstandard line-printer systems—those using printer-driving software. In such instances, doing the suggested POKEs sends the system "into outer space," and the only way to recover is by switching the computer off and on again.
>
> If the scheme works for your line-printer system, you can always return to the normal video link by doing:
>
> **POKE 16414,88:POKE 16415,4**

ENTER key. The main purpose of INPUT is to allow the operator to enter some necessary numerical or string values.

Nature of the INPUT Statement

The *BASIC* INPUT statement has the general form:

INPUT *"message";variable*

The *message* portion of the statement is optional, so it can be expressed as:

INPUT *variable*

The *message* option lets you prompt the operator, spelling out the nature of the *variable* to be entered from the keyboard. You can, however, accomplish the same sort of thing with this sequence of statements:

PRINT *"message";:*INPUT *variable*

On encountering an INPUT statement the system prints a question-mark prompt symbol, followed by the cursor symbol. The question mark indicates that the system is expecting data from the keyboard, and the cursor symbol marks the point on the screen

45

where that data will appear as the user types it in. The prompt and cursor symbols are generated in ROM, and there is nothing you can do to change their configuration, but you do have some options regarding their position on the screen.

When using the INPUT *"message";variable* format, the prompt and cursor symbols always appear in the two character spaces following the end of the *message*. The semicolon is responsible for this business of inhibiting a line feed/carriage return that would otherwise place the prompt and cursor symbols at the beginning of the next line on the screen. Try as you might, however, you cannot link a *message* with a *variable* in an INPUT statement without using the semicolon—a SYN ERROR message shows up every time.

But if you leave out the *"message";* part of the INPUT statement, you do have some choice in the matter of placing the prompt and cursor symbols. Compare these two sets of operations:

PRINT *"message";*:INPUT *variable*

and

PRINT *"message"*:INPUT *variable*

In the first instance, the prompt and cursor symbols appear on the same line as the *message*. The semicolon inhibits the line feed/carriage return that normally follows a PRINT statement. In the second case the prompt and cursor appear at the beginning of the line below the *message*.

While the PRINT *"message"*/INPUT *variable* combination is more cumbersome than a simple INPUT *"message";variable* statement, the former allows for a lot of different kinds of screen formatting. Suppose, for instance, you want the prompting message to appear at the upper left-hand corner of the screen, but, for some reason, you want the keyboard entry for *variable* to appear near the bottom, left-hand corner.

```
10  PRINT @ 0, "INPUT YOUR VALUE";
20  PRINT @ 832,"";
30  INPUT V
```

Line 10 PRINTs the prompting message in the upper left-hand corner of the screen and inhibits the line feed/carriage return. Line 20 prints nothing at PRINT @ location 832 (double quotes with no space between them is a nonprinting "null" character) and inhibits the line feed. The prompt and cursor for the INPUT statement in line 30 thus appear at PRINT @ location 832.

The nice feature here is that you can prompt an input and accept it at two different places on the screen without affecting any text or graphics that might be situated in between. The same sort of thing can be done with many of the cursor-moving video operations described in Chapter 2.

Just bear in mind that an INPUT statement is not fully executed until the user ends the input operation by striking the ENTER key. And striking the ENTER key causes a line feed/carriage return that will scroll the display if the INPUT cursor is on line 14 or 15.

The *variable* portion of the INPUT statement specifies the variable type and assigns the keyboard input data to it. The variable can be either a numeric or string variable, the former expressed without a dollar sign and the latter with a dollar sign. In either case the keyboard entry operation is not complete until the user strikes the ENTER key.

It is possible to use a single INPUT statement to enter values for more than one variable; simply separate the variable names/types by a comma:

INPUT NL$,I$,A

That INPUT statement will expect three different variables from the keyboard: two strings, followed by a numerical variable. The values for the variables can be entered one at a time or in a sequence.

To illustrate the point consider an example. Suppose that NL$ represents a person's last name, I$ is the middle initial, and A is his or her age. If you decide to enter these variables one at a time, the screen format shows a single question-mark prompt symbol when it is time to enter the first variable:

```
? JONES     <ENTER>
??_
```

Typing in the name and striking the ENTER key, you note that the double question-mark prompt appears at the beginning of the next line. The system is expecting the second variable.

```
? JONES     <ENTER>
?? F        <ENTER>
??_
```

On entering the second variable, the prompt and cursor symbols for the third one appear at the beginning of the next line. The number of question marks does not increase beyond two, however. At this point the machine is expecting a numerical variable—the "age" variable in this example.

```
$ JONES     <ENTER>
?? F        <ENTER>
?? 23       <ENTER>
```

Now the INPUT operation is done, and the program goes about its business.

The user can respond to the INPUT statement in a different, and perhaps simpler, fashion. Instead of doing an ENTER after typing each variable, it can be done this way:

? JONES,F,23   <ENTER>

Separating the variables by a comma does the same thing as ending each variable-entry with an ENTER. Here the user does just one ENTER; and, what's more important in some graphic formats, the whole entry operation takes up just one line.

A complete INPUT statement for this example ought to look like this:

INPUT "LAST NAME, MIDDLE INITIAL, AGE";NL$,I$,A

This way, everything, including the prompting message, appears on the same line.

Some Special Applications of INPUT

The INPUT statement is a program stopper. Once the system encounters an INPUT statement, everything comes to a halt until the user enters the proper kinds of variables and at least one ENTER keystroke. It is possible to take advantage of the program-stopping feature, using INPUT as a control operation rather than a data-entry operation.

Suppose you have a program that prints out a very long list of data—a list containing more lines than the video display can accommodate at one time. The real problem is that the user probably cannot read and interpret the information as it scrolls up the screen so rapidly.

There are a couple of ways to handle this sort of situation, both using the INPUT statement. To see how they work, suppose you want to inspect the content of addresses 0 through 1023 in your TRS-80 ROM. That represents a lot of lines of information, but here are some programs for doing the job.

```
10  CLS
20  A=0
30  PRINT A,PEEK(A)
40  A=A+1
50  IF A>1023 THEN END
60  GOTO 30
```

This program will print out the addresses and data for ROM locations 0 through 1023, but too quickly to be meaningful. So you might try this:

```
10  CLS
20  A=0
30  INPUT S$
40  PRINT A,PEEK(A)
50  A=A+1
60  IF A>1023 THEN END
70  GOTO 30
```

In this program the system does not print out the next line of information (address and data) until you strike a key on the keyboard. The INPUT statement in line 30 brings everything to a halt until a string variable is entered. It makes no difference what that variable is, because it is not used anywhere else in the program.

The point is that an INPUT statement used in this way lets you display the text one line at a time, giving you plenty of time to inspect the data on the screen. To make the display look a little neater, try putting a semicolon at the end of the PRINT statement in line 40. That way, the information appears on successive lines, and not on alternate ones.

Another way to handle the situation is to let the screen fill with 15 lines of text before the program calls for a keystroke to show the next 15 lines. Try this:

```
10  A=0
20  CLS
30  FOR L=1 TO 15
40  PRINT A,PEEK(A)
50  A=A+1
60  IF A>1023 THEN END
70  NEXT L
80  INPUT S$
90  GOTO 20
```

Now the FOR...NEXT loop between lines 30 and 70 prints 15 lines of information before the INPUT statement in line 80 brings the action to a halt. At that point you can inspect the data at your leisure and then strike any key to view the next 15 addresses.

As nice as the INPUT statement might be in many instances, the fact that it interrupts the program can be a real nuisance in other kinds of situations. That's where the INKEY$ statement comes into play.

THE STANDARD INKEY$ STATEMENT

The INKEY$ statement causes the computer to scan the keyboard, detecting any keystroke that might occur during the scanning, or strobing, interval. And using a BASIC statement such as C$=INKEY$, a string version of the key that is depressed will be assigned to that string variable, C$.

The nice thing about INKEY$, compared with INPUT, is that INKEY$ does not necessarily interrupt the execution of the program. It sidetracks the program during the keyboard-strobing interval, but it doesn't have to bring everything to a halt as the INPUT statement does.

Used as intended, INKEY$ can be a useful and powerful BASIC statement. Some programmers, however, attempt to use INKEY$ outside its intended realm, and they get into trouble as a result. Perhaps that accounts for some of the nasty comments that writers sometimes publish about the TRS-80 INKEY$ function.

One of the first things to bear in mind about INKEY$ is that it is a string-related statement. An ever-present reminder of that fact is the presence of the dollar-sign symbol at the end of the expression. Getting numerical values into the system via an INKEY$ function calls for an accompanying VAL(*string*) statement.

Another important feature is that INKEY$ allows the entry of just one character at a time. Inputting multiple-character values into the system via INKEY$ calls for executing the statement more than one time and assembling the individual characters as appropriate.

Finally, the system executes the keyboard strobing operation in a very short period, and any program calling for doing a single keystroke during that strobing interval is bound to cause some trouble—making it necessary to tap the key an undetermined number of times before the keystroke and strobe happen to take place simultaneously.

Programmers who neglect any of these three basic notions about INKEY$ find themselves having some problems with it. Others, who understand these notions, can use the statement quite effectively.

Dealing With the String Nature of INKEY$

Here is a continuous, integer-counting program that uses an INKEY$ function to adjust the time delay between successive counts—without having to interrupt the execution of the program:

```
10  CLS
20  N=0
30  C$=INKEY$:IF C$="" THEN 50
40  C=VAL(C$)
50  FOR T=0 TO 10*C:NEXT T
60  PRINT N
70  N=N+1
80  GOTO 30
```

The statements in line 50 generate the time delay between counts, and you can see that the delay interval depends on the numerical value of variable C. The larger is the value of C, the longer the delay between successive counts.

The value of C is determined by the statements in lines 30 and 40. Line 30 uses an INKEY$ statement to pick up a character (a string character) from the keyboard. If that character happens to be a null string (no key depressed), the program jumps down to line 50, allowing no change in the value of C. But if INKEY$ turns up a numerical string character (0 through 9), the statement in line 40 converts it to a numerical quantity. That value has to be converted to a numerical quantity so that it can be mathematically manipulated in the time-delay loop, line 50.

The main point of this illustration is to show that it is necessary to convert a string-related INKEY$ variable into a numerical value before it can be treated as a number. Any single-digit number can be inserted into an ongoing program this way, and there is no interruption of the kind that characterizes an INPUT statement.

Beginning programmers sometimes get into trouble with the idea because they forget to account for the null-string condition; they forget the conditional statement in the second part of line 30. Hack off the second statement in line 30, and you will not see the program running as it is supposed to run.

Now, here is another counting program that uses the INKEY$ statement to adjust the direction of count. Once the program is operational, you can strike the F key to count forward, the R key to count in reverse, the S key to stop and hold the current count, and the X key to reset the count to zero and stop it. A rather straightforward decoding sequence translates the INKEY$ string characters into counting-interval numbers.

```
20   N=0:I=0
30   C$=INKEY$:IF C$="" THEN 80
40   IF C$="F" THEN I=1
50   IF C$="R" THEN I=-1
60   IF C$="S" THEN I=0
70   IF C$="X" THEN 20
80   PRINT @ 0,USING "####";N
90   N=N+I
100  GOTO 30
```

In the next example the INKEY$-input string characters are converted into their ASCII codes before they are decoded as counting direction/speed parameters. The ASC function in line 35 converts a valid INKEY$ character into ASCII form, and lines 40 through 75 set up the counting parameters—the I variable takes care of the direction of count, and variable D sets the delay between successive counts.

```
10   CLS
20   N=0:I=0:D=0
30   C$=$INKEY$:IF C$="" THEN 80
35   C=ASC(C$)
40   IF C=70 OR C=102 THEN I=1
50   IF C=82 OR C=114 THEN I=-1
60   IF C=83 OR C=115 THEN I=0
70   IF C=88 OR C=120 THEN 20
75   IF C<95 THEN D=0 ELSE D=100
80   PRINT @ 0,USING "####";N
85   FOR T=0 TO D:NEXT T
90   N=N+I
100  GOTO 30
```

The program takes advantage of the fact that the ASCII codes for uppercase and lowercase characters are different. As far as the alphabetical characters are concerned, the lowercase versions are separated by their uppercase counterparts by decimal 32. Consequently, line 40, for example, is sensitive to ASCII 70 (uppercase F) or ASCII 102 (lowercase F).

So you can control the direction of count by striking the F or R keys (for forward and reverse, respectively). As in the previous example, striking the S key (ASCII 83 or 115) stops and holds the current count, and striking the X key (ASCII 88 or 120) stops the count and resets it to zero.

In any event the conditional statement in line 75 is sensitive to lowercase characters—those entered while the SHIFT key is depressed. That being the case, variable D is set to 100, and this inserts a noticeable time delay in the counting operation at line 85. Otherwise, the count runs at full speed.

It is also possible to write routines that convert INKEY$-entered keystrokes into screen-control operations. You are free to assign single-character control codes as you choose. Look at this example:

```
10   C$=INKEY$:IF C$="" THEN RETURN          <to calling program>
20   C=ASC(C$)
30   IF C=96 THEN DT=8
40   IF C=97 THEN DT=31
50   IF C=100 THEN 70
60   PRINT DT;:RETURN                        <to calling program>
70   PRINT CHR$(28);CHR$(31);
80   RETURN                                  <to calling program>
```

This routine, written as a subroutine that is called by some mainline program, allows the user to strike the <SHIFT> B key to backspace and erase the current character on the screen (line 30), strike the <SHIFT>C key to clear the screen to the end of the frame (line 40), and strike the <SHIFT>N key to home the cursor and clear the entire screen (lines 50 and 70). The routine can be expanded to cover all sorts of control functions, all specified by single keystrokes dreamed up by the programmer.

Putting Together Multiple-Character Values From INKEY$

One of the not-so-nice features of the INKEY$ statement is that it permits the entry of just one keyboard character at a time. Single-character INKEY$ inputs can be quite useful, as demonstrated in the previous discussion, but there are instances where it is more desirable and, perhaps, absolutely necessary to input variable values having more than one character. This is a bit troublesome when using the INKEY$ function, but it often beats the program-stopping feature of an INPUT statement.

It is somewhat easier to enter multiple-character string values via INKEY$ than it is to enter multiple-digit numerical values; so let's consider the easier part first.

The following program uses the INKEY$ function to build up a string value, W$, from individual keystrokes. The characters are entered one at a time and then assembled (concatenated) to build a single multiple-character string. The string is limited to five characters, and it will truncate the string beyond that point. Limiting the string to five characters is an arbitrary choice, however; the string can be as long as desired.

There are a couple of special features built into this program that are incidental to the main point of the discussion. While these "whistles and bells" add to the complexity of the program, they help make a convincing case for the overall usefulness of the main idea—inputting multiple-character strings from INKEY$ statements.

```
10   REM ** INKEY$ STRING DEMO **
20   CLS:LN=0:PRINT @ 50,"#"
30   GOSUB 100
40   REM (PUT YOUR REGULAR PROGRAMMING HERE)
50   IF LN>15 THEN 20
60   GOTO 30
70   REM
80   REM
100  REM ** INKEY$ INPUT SUBROUTINE **
110  C$=INKEY$:IF C$="" THEN RETURN
120  C=ASC(C$)
130  IF C=8 THEN 180
140  IF C=13 THEN 200
150  IF LEN(W$)>=5 THEN 170
160  W$=W$+C$
170  PRINT @ 50,"#"+W$;:RETURN
180  FOR CP=50 TO 55:PRINT @ CP,CHR$(32);:NEXT CP
190  W$="":PRINT @ 50,"#";:RETURN
200  PRINT @ 0+LN*64,W$;
210  LN=LN+1
220  GOTO 180
```

On running this program, you will see a pound sign symbol near the right end of the top line on the screen. This is one of those "whistles-and-bells" features; it is a homebrewed prompt symbol for entering the string characters.

Now, type up to five alphanumerics—combinations of letters and numbers. If you don't like the string that is being built up to the right of the pound sign, strike the left-arrow key (←) to clear it. This clearing operation is another one of those optional features that are built into the program.

When you are satisfied with the appearance of your multiple-character string entry, strike the ENTER key. That operation clears your entry, resets the pound-sign cursor and, more importantly, prints your entry as a single string "message" at the left-hand side of the screen.

Now you can type in and ENTER another string of characters. As you do that, the list of strings builds downward along the left side of the screen. When the list reaches the bottom of the screen (after entering 15 strings), the list clears and begins again from the top.

The main point of the demonstration is that you can, indeed, enter multiple-character strings with the INKEY$ function. Now it is time to dig into the program and see how the job is done.

The program is written with the keyboard-entry operations residing as a subroutine, beginning at line 100. The mainline program (the one that calls the INKEY$-input subroutine) occupies lines 10 through 80.

After initializing the line counter (LN), clearing the screen, and printing the initial # prompt symbol, the mainline program calls the INKEY$ subroutine at line 30. If you had some additional programming that called for in-line interaction with your input expressions, it would fit between lines 30 and 50.

Basically, the mainline program loops endlessly between lines 30 and 60, calling the INKEY$ subroutine and doing any program operations you might enter in the area of line 40.

Turning to the subroutine itself, notice that the INKEY$ characters are carried as variable C$. The C$ variable represents the single-character input. In line 160 this character is concatenated with string W$. This is the point where the individual INKEY$ characters are assembled into a single multiple-character string. In fact, that is the critical operation—the point of the demonstration. The rest is intended to make things run smoother for the operator.

The statement in line 120, for instance, converts the INKEY$ input into an ASCII code number. And if C=8 (left-arrow key code), the program jumps to line 180, where the entry is cleared from the screen, W$ is nulled, and the pound-sign prompt symbol is replaced on the screen. This simply means that striking the left-arrow key erases the current entry, making it possible to correct any typing errors.

If C=13 in line 140, it means the user has hit the ENTER key. The response in that instance is determined by operations beginning at line 200. Those operations print the assembled string, W$, on the next line of text along the left side of the screen, increment the line counter (LN), and go back to 180 to erase the entry version of the string.

This notion of concatenating single-keystroke characters from INKEY$ to make multiple-character strings can lead to some powerful in-line keyboard operations. It allows you to make up multiple-character control expressions that can influence the ongoing activity. Try this program, making just a few additions to the original version (lines 52, 53, and 55).

```
10   REM  ** INKEY$ STRING DEMO **
20   CLS:LN=0:PRINT @ 50,"#"
30   GOSUB 100
40   REM (PUT YOUR REGULAR PROGRAMMING HERE)
50   IF LN>15 THEN 20
52   IF W$="DONE" THEN END
53   IF W$<>"CLEAR" THEN 60
55   W$="":GOTO 20
60   GOTO 30
70   REM
80   REM
100  REM ** INKEY$ INPUT SUBROUTINE **
110  C$=INKEY$:IF C$="" THEN RETURN
120  C=ASC(C$)
130  IF C=8 THEN 180
140  IF C=13 THEN 200
150  IF LEN(W$)>=5 THEN 170
160  W$=W$+C$
170  PRINT @ 50,"#"+W$;:RETURN
180  FOR CP=50 TO 55:PRINT @ CP,CHR$(32);:NEXT CP
190  W$="":PRINT @ 50,"#";:RETURN
200  PRINT @ 0+LN*64,W$;
210  LN=LN+1
220  GOTO 180
```

Now the program is uniquely sensitive to the strings DONE and CLEAR. On entering DONE, the program immediately ends. Entering CLEAR clears the accumulated lines of text and starts everything from scratch.

This technique ought to suggest some intriguing program-control formats and, indeed, the possibility of making up custom programming languages—interactive ones, at that.

Inputting multiple-digit numerical values via INKEY$ follows the same general scheme. The point of departure is where the string version is converted into decimal numbers, and that calls for some math operations. See lines 200 through 230.

```
10   REM ** INKEY$—ENTERED NUMBERS **
20   CLS:LN=0:PRINT @ 50,"#"
30   GOSUB 100
40   REM (PUT YOUR REGULAR PROGRAMMING HERE)
50   IF LN>15 THEN 20
60   GOTO 30
70   REM
80   REM
100  REM ** INKEY$ INPUT SUBROUTINE **
110  C$=INKEY$:IF C$="" THEN RETURN
120  C=ASC(C$)
130  IF C=8 THEN 180
140  IF C=13 THEN 200
145  IF C<48 OR C>57 THEN RETURN
150  IF LEN(W$)>=5 THEN 170
160  W$=W$+C$
170  PRINT @ 50,"#"+W$;:RETURN
180  FOR CP=50 TO 55:PRINT @ CP,CHR$(32);:NEXT CP
190  W$="":PRINT @ 50,"#";:RETURN
200  W=0
210  FOR CP=LEN(W$)−1 TO 0 STEP−1
220  W=W+VAL(MID$(W$,LEN(W$)−CP,1))*10[(CP)
225  NEXT CP
230  PRINT @ 0+LN*64,W;
240  LN=LN+1
250  GOTO 180
```

The program develops string W$ as before, but it is no longer enough to simply concatenate the new keystrokes to get the final result—the finished string has to be converted into a legitimate decimal format.

The decimal version of the number is first set to 0 at line 200. Variable W is the current decimal value of the number. Line 210 picks up the number of characters in the number and, one at a time, assigns them a power-of-10 value that is appropriate to their place in the numeric expression. By the time the program gets to line 230, W is equal to the number entered from the keyboard. It is a true numerical value, as suggested by the fact it is PRINTed as a numerical, rather than a string, variable.

A further modification in line 145 prevents the operator from entering nonnumerical figures.

As you might imagine by now, this technique can be useful for entering the values of numerical variables while some program is running. You can, for instance, change the parameters in a graphing program while the graph, itself, is being generated.

It is very difficult to imagine a more powerful interactive programming technique in BASIC. The INKEY$ statement is perhaps the most powerful interactive tool in BASIC, but one of the most maligned. It's too bad so many programmers miss the opportunity to use it.

The Loop Requirement for INKEY$

An INKEY$ statement must be placed within a looping operation. If you inspect all the programs suggested thus far for the INKEY$ statement, you will find it is in a loop of some sort.

INKEY$ must be placed into a loop to make its operation reliable. The keyboard strobing operation that is called by an INKEY$ statement runs so quickly that there is very little chance a keystroke will occur at the precise instant INKEY$ is scanning the keyboard.

Here is an example of a very tight INKEY$ loop:

```
10  C$=INKEY$:IF C$="" THEN 10
```

In this instance the program "buzzes" on line 10 until a keystroke occurs. It is the same thing as inserting an INPUT statement into a program. The program effectively comes to a halt until the system senses a keystroke.

SENSING KEY DEPRESSION WITH PEEK(14463)

While INPUT and INKEY$ serve most keyboard input functions quite nicely in BASIC, there are a couple of useful operations that are foreign to those two statements. Some of those operations can be utilized by working with the so-called keyboard memory.

The keyboard memory is a section of the memory map, between 14336 and 15359, inclusively. One of these addresses that is of particular importance is 14463. That address location carries data zero unless one or more keys are depressed. Set up this simple demonstration program, and try things for yourself:

```
10  CLS
20  C=PEEK(14463)
30  PRINT C;
40  GOTO 20
```

When you start this program, you will see strings of zeros being printed across the screen—until you depress a key. The moment you depress a character key (some control keys do not affect 14463), you will see some number other than zero being printed.

What is of special interest here is the fact that the program continues printing those numbers as long as the key is depressed. By contrast, the INPUT and INKEY$ statements are "stroke" operated. Unless your system is suffering from keybounce, INPUT and

INKEY$ are one-shot operations; they can tell a key has been depressed, but the duration of a key depression is not relevant.

So a PEEK (14463) gives you a control function that is not described in the standard TRS-80 literature. In effect, the entire keyboard becomes a set of normally open push-button switches. Try this:

```
10  CLS
20  C=PEEK(14463)
30  IF C=0 THEN 20
40  PRINT CHR$(191);
50  GOTO 20
```

This little routine draws a white bar as long as a key is depressed. Release the key, and the drawing stops. It isn't quite so easy to do such a thing with a togglelike INKEY$ statement. This kind of routine is invaluable whenever you want some action to take place while a key is depressed.

There are some other features of PEEK(14463) that could prove useful as well. Whenever you do a PRINT PEEK(14463) and depress a single key, you see one of the following numbers: 1, 2, 4, 8, 16, 32, 64, or 128. Several different keys produce the same number in this particular family of numbers. PEEK(14463) turns up a 2, for example, whenever you depress A, I, Q, Y, or 2. On the other hand, it turns up a 4 whenever you depress B, J, R, Z, or 3. Table 3-1 summarizes the content of address 14463 for all of the useful key functions.

The code numbers picked up at address 14463 can be decoded and used for specific control applications. Suppose, for example, you want to move a "paddle" figure up and down on the screen, in response to depressions of the up-arrow or down-arrow keys. Depressing the up-arrow key ought to make the figure move up the

Table 3-1. Decimal Content of Address 14463 While a Specified Key Is Depressed

Contents of 14463	Key Depressed
0	(No key depressed)
1	@ H P X 0 (8 ENTER
2	A I Q Y ! 1) 9 CLEAR
4	B J R Z " 2 * : BREAK
8	C K S # 3 + ; ↑
16	D L T $ 4 < , ↓
32	E M U % 5 = − ←
64	F N V & 6 > . →
128	G O W ' 7 ? / SPACE

NOTE: <SHIFT> @ produces a 1 on alternate key depressions. An alphabetical character with SHIFT produces the same value as its non-SHIFT version.

screen, and depressing the down-arrow key should make the figure move downward.

The basic idea in this case is to PEEK(14463) and take appropriate action if that PEEK turns up an 8 (up-arrow depression) or a 16 (down-arrow depression). The following example is becoming a classic demonstration for the PEEK(14463) operation:

```
10  BL=15360:TL=16383:P=15557
20  CLS:POKE P,191
30  M=PEEK(14463):IF NOT(M=8 OR M=16) THEN 30
40  IF M=8 THEN PT=P-64 ELSE PT=P+64
50  IF PT<BL OR PT>TL THEN 30
60  POKE P,32
70  P=PT:POKE P,191
80  GOTO 30
```

Line 30 looks at address 14463 and loops around on that same line until it turns up a value of 8 or 16. At that time line 40 sets the next position for the paddle figure, and line 50 checks for the possibility of running the figure out of video memory range.

Line 60 then erases the old paddle position (replacing it with a space), line 70 draws the figure in its new position, and line 80 loops the whole program back up to line 30, where it looks for the key depression again.

So depressing the up-arrow key develops an 8 at address 14463, and depressing the down-arrow key develops a 16. You will find, however, that some other keys work equally well with the paddle demonstration program. From Table 3-1 you will find a lot of other keys generating 8s and 16s. Those will cause the same action as the up-arrow and down-arrow keys.

The basic problem is that the key-depression sensing activity of address 14463 does not completely decode the keyboard. Rather, it decodes the keys into eight groups. Coupling a PEEK(14463) with an INKEY$ statement, however, lets you reap the benefits of both: sensing continuous key depression with PEEK(14463) and completely decoding the character code with INKEY$.

So here is a demonstration program that works as a REPEAT KEY operation. Depress any key listed in Table 3-1, and you will find it being repeatedly written on the screen as long as that key is depressed. The program is fun if you first fill the screen with arbitrary characters, and then "edit" the display by means of the cursor controls (working the arrow keys while depressing SHIFT).

```
10  CLS:PRINT CHR$(14);
20  IF PEEK(14463)=0 THEN 20
30  C$=INKEY$
40  IF C$<>"" THEN R$=C$
50  PRINT R$;
60  GOTO 20
```

In this program, line 10 clears the screen and turns on the cursor. Line 20 looks for a key depression—any key depression. That is half the job. On detecting a key depression, the INKEY$ statement in line 30 decodes the key, and line 40 sets the value of R$ so that the program continues drawing that same character long after the INKEY$ function has reset itself. The program, in other words, continues generating the R$ character as long as its key is depressed.

The keyboard can thus be completely decoded and yet respond in a push-button fashion that is lacking in either the INKEY$ or INPUT functions, alone.

The PEEK(14463) operation has one more special feature that can prove useful. Table 3-1 indicates the content of address 14463 whenever *one* key is depressed. But when you depress more than one key at a time, address 14463 tends to show the sum of the basic key codes. Normally, depressing the A key turns up a 2 in address 14463, and depressing the B key generates a value of 4 in that location. Depress both of those keys at the same time, however, and you will find a value of 6 in address 14463. Depress A, B and C, and you will find 2+4+8, or 14, in that address.

So, by depressing more than one key at a time, address 14463 shows the sum of the individual key-depression codes—all the way up to 255 (you cannot get a number larger than 255, no matter how many keys you depress). That leads to some potential applications: setting the speed of an animated figure by depressing more than one control key simultaneously, for instance.

SUMMARY

PEEK(14463) will return an integer between 1 and 255 as long as any key, or combination of keys, is depressed.

Table 3-1 shows the content of address 14463 when *one* key is depressed. Depressing more than one key returns the sum of those numbers, up to 255.

WORKING WITH THE KEYBOARD MATRIX

The TRS-80 keyboard is set up with an 8×8-key format. It at least has the potential for working with eight columns of keys, each having eight keys in them. Not all the rows are filled, however. See Fig. 3-1.

When your TRS-80 is in its command mode of operation some ROM programming routinely scans, or strobes, the keyboard, looking for a possible key depression. And while a program is running in BASIC, the INPUT and INKEY$ functions also call for a keyboard-strobe operation.

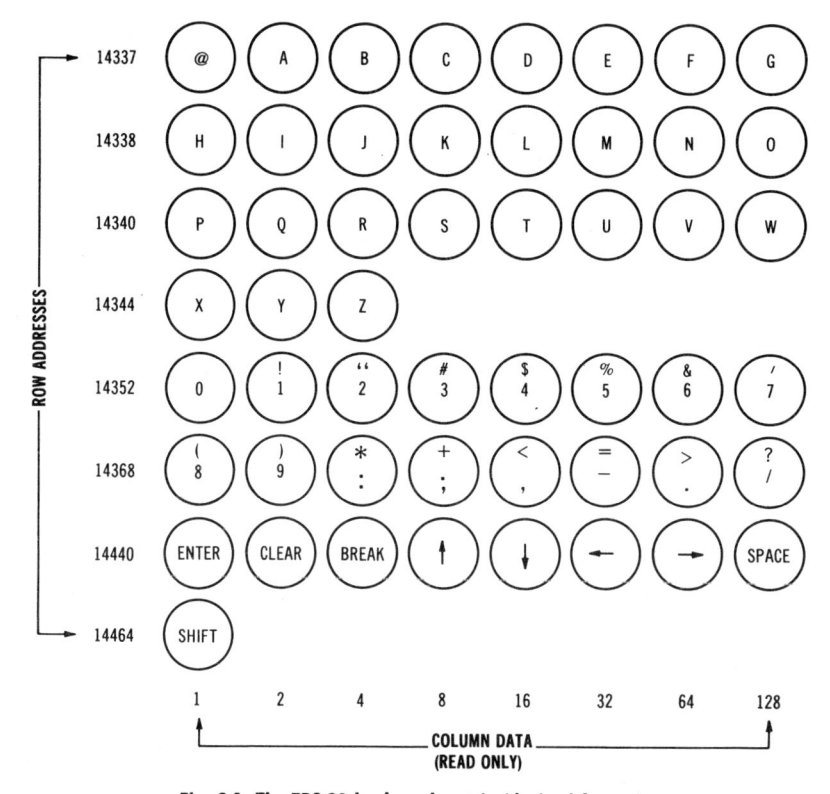

Fig. 3-1. The TRS-80 keyboard matrix (decimal format).

 The system, in either case, scans the keyboard one row at a time. If a key in a given row is depressed, the system generates a code number representing that key. This is how the scheme works in a general sense.

 The system PEEKs at the row addresses, in sequence and one at a time. Each PEEK returns a zero (if no key is depressed in that row) or a number representing the key that is depressed in that row.

 Referring to Fig. 3-1, suppose that you are depressing the A key when the strobing action begins. When the system does a machine-language version of PEEK(14337) it will find a 2 in that location. All subsequent row addresses will turn up zeros. As another example, you might be depressing the P key. This being the case, PEEKs at 14337 and 14338 (addresses of the first two rows) will turn up zeros, but the system will find a 1 when it does a PEEK (14340)—the first bit in the third row.

 Now, this strobing scheme can turn up key data that is the same for a number of different keys. The numbers in this case are identical with those listed in Table 3-1. The system keeps everything straight, however, by keeping track of which row is being addressed at the moment. A and *I* keys both turn up a 2, but the system will see that 2 in row address 14337 only when the *A* key is depressed, and it will see the 2 in row address 14338 only when the *B* key is depressed.

To test your understanding of this idea, see if you can answer this question: Which key is being depressed if a 64 turns up in row address 14340? Answer: The *V* key is being depressed.

The machine-language keyboard strobing/decoding routine goes through the same procedure you used to answer that question. The strobing routine runs through all eight row addresses, whether it finds some data along the way or not. This is important because the two SHIFT keys generate a 1 at address 14464 whenever one of them is depressed. So if you are doing a SHIFT while holding down the *A* key, the system finds a 2 at address 14337 and a 1 at address 14464. If the SHIFT key is *not* depressed, address 14337 holds a 0.

The following program lets you interrogate the keyboard matrix. It is essentially a BASIC version of the ROM-based keyboard strobing operation.

```
10  REM ** KEYBOARD MATRIX DEMO **
20  IF PEEK(14463)=0 THEN 20
30  CLS
40  A=14337:PRINT A,PEEK(A)
50  FOR N=0 TO 6
60  P=2↑N
70  A=A+P:PRINT A,PEEK(A)
80  NEXT N
90  IF PEEK(14463)<>0 THEN 90
100 GOTO 20
```

Run the program, then depress a key. The program then scans the keyboard and prints the row addresses and corresponding data as it goes along. Depress the keys in any sequence you choose, including some while the SHIFT key is depressed. Just make sure you hold down the key until the display is completely generated. What you observe on the screen should line up with the information you can glean from Fig. 3-1.

Try depressing more than one key at a time, and see if you can figure out why the display responds the way it does. Compare the results with the discussion of the PEEK(14463) operation in the previous section of this chapter.

Incidentally, you will note from Fig. 3-1 that the row addresses grow successively larger, but the intervals between them are not identical. The row addressing follows a binary/hexadecimal sequence; thus there appears to be a lot of wasted "memory space" between row addresses 14400 and 14464.

The row addresses shown in Fig. 3-1 are necessary for addressing just one row at a time. If you PEEK any address between a pair of those row addresses, you are going to address more than one row at a time.

If you do a PEEK(14339), for example, you will address rows 14337 and 14338 at the same time. The result will be the sum of whatever keys might be depressed in those two rows. And what do you suppose happens if you do a PEEK(14463)? This addresses all rows (except the SHIFT row) at the same time, and that is a special case you have already studied in the previous section of this chapter.

Under normal operating conditions the keyboard routine has two phases: it first strobes the keyboard as described here, and then it decodes the information to generate a unique ASCII code for the key being depressed. The decoding is done in ROM, but it is difficult to get at that decoding routine from BASIC. You will be able to access the key-decoding routine rather easily from machine-language programs, thus saving yourself a lot of needless programming—programming aimed at decoding the keyboard.

CHAPTER 4

The User's Memory Environment

Every TRS-80 system has a certain memory capacity: 4K, 16K, 32K, or 48K. These figures refer to the amount of RAM space—the number of bytes—available for working BASIC programs or any other kind of memory operations.

In all cases the RAM available to the user begins at address 17129. The top address, however, depends on the system's memory capacity. See Table 4-1.

Table 4-1. User's Available RAM Space

System Capacity	Lowest Address	Highest Address
4K	17129	20479
16K	17129	32767
32K	17129	49151
48K	17129	65535

If you figure the difference between the lowest address and the highest address in Table 4-1, you won't come up with the number representing system capacity. These extremes indicate the range of RAM addresses that are available for user's programs.

The RAM space actually begins at 16384 in all Level II machines. The memory space between 16384 and 17129 is devoted to internal operations: restart vectors 1–7, device control blocks, the i/o buffer, and so on. See any of the memory maps supplied by Radio Shack for details.

Some of the demonstrations in Chapters 2 and 3 involved working in that lower part of the RAM space. The real working memory, however, begins at 17129, and that's the starting place for the discussions in this chapter.

The first part of the chapter looks into the i/o buffer and shows how BASIC statements are assembled in the user's memory space. The second part deals with the matter of the so-called protected memory—a section of the user's memory that is set aside for special applications through the MEMORY SIZE? entry routine.

ORGANIZATION OF THE USER'S MEMORY SPACE

Fig. 4-1 is a general memory map of the memory space available for writing and executing programs. The range of this memory space is clearly defined for every machine, but the space devoted to the various categories of information stored there is not.

To be sure, BASIC program text always begins at address 17129 and builds upward from there. Program text is an almost-literal listing of a BASIC program; so the longer the program is, the farther it builds up into the user's memory space.

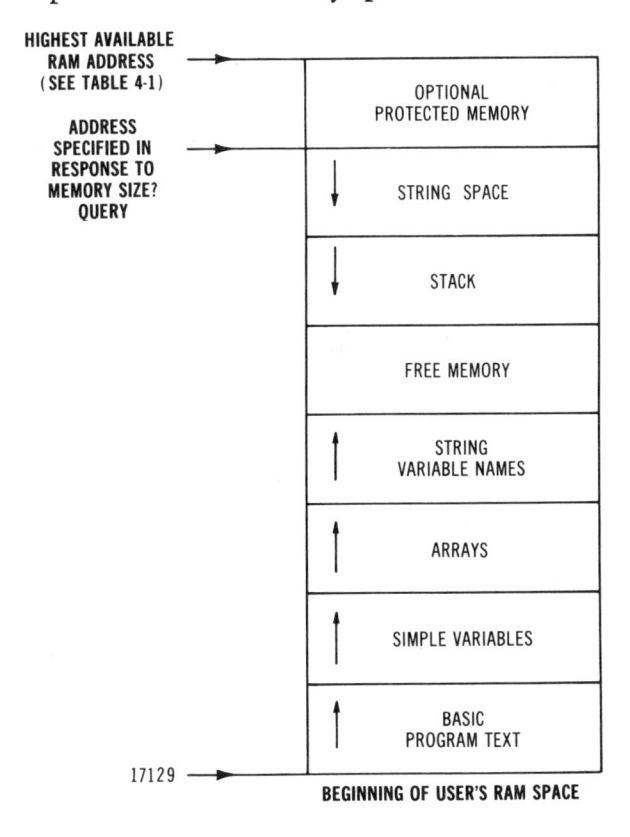

```
HIGHEST AVAILABLE
  RAM ADDRESS      ────►┌─────────────────────┐
  (SEE TABLE 4-1)       │                     │
                        │      OPTIONAL       │
     ADDRESS            │  PROTECTED MEMORY   │
   SPECIFIED IN    ────►│                     │
   RESPONSE TO          ├─────────────────────┤
   MEMORY SIZE?         │         ↓           │
     QUERY              │     STRING SPACE    │
                        │                     │
                        ├─────────────────────┤
                        │         ↓           │
                        │        STACK        │
                        │                     │
                        ├─────────────────────┤
                        │                     │
                        │     FREE MEMORY     │
                        │                     │
                        ├─────────────────────┤
                        │         ↑           │
                        │       STRING        │
                        │   VARIABLE NAMES    │
                        ├─────────────────────┤
                        │         ↑           │
                        │       ARRAYS        │
                        │                     │
                        ├─────────────────────┤
                        │         ↑           │
                        │   SIMPLE VARIABLES  │
                        │                     │
                        ├─────────────────────┤
                        │         ↑           │
                        │        BASIC        │
                        │    PROGRAM TEXT     │
        17129      ────►└─────────────────────┘
                         BEGINNING OF USER'S RAM SPACE
```

Fig. 4-1. Memory map for BASIC programs.

But there's more in the user's memory space than the program text. As the BASIC program is entered and executed, simple variables, arrays, and string variable names are appended to the top of the BASIC program text. A memory map cannot specify the starting address of simple variables, for example, because that address varies with the size of the program text. The same is true for the array and variable-name addresses.

The best we can do is illustrate their relative positions on the memory map.

There is also some of this dynamic sort of memory space allocated for strings and a stack. (The stack is responsible for keeping track of things while a BASIC program is running nested arithmetic, logic, and GOSUB routines.) These two memory spaces are not appended to the others, however. As indicated in Fig. 4-1, string space and stack begin at a high address and build downward. The more complex the string and stack operations become, the farther they grow down toward the lower end of the user's RAM space.

Incidentally, the starting address for the string-space allocation depends on the computer's memory capacity and any reply the user might make to the MEMORY SIZE? query. There's much more to say about that later in this chapter.

The main point of the present discussion is that during the entry and execution of a BASIC program, some of the program elements load upward into the user's memory space, and some begin at the top and grow downward.

It figures, then, that there is a no-man's land in between. This is the user's memory space that is commonly called *free memory*. There's no telling exactly where that free memory is located; all we know for sure is that it stands between the upward-growing variable-name space and downward-growing stack.

Even though it is pointless to figure the exact location of the free memory, you can always determine how large it is—how many bytes of memory are left in that space. To do this, simply ENTER a PRINT MEM. That's the purpose of the MEM statement.

The term "free memory" isn't really a misnomer, but it is often misunderstood. It must not be interpreted as a section of memory you are free to use as you wish; it is a bad idea to tinker around in the free memory. It isn't *free* in the sense that you are free to use it for your own purposes (the protected memory plays that role for you). Rather, its size indicates how much memory remains for entering and executing BASIC programs.

As the program text and stack grow, they decrease the free memory space. And that amount of free memory doesn't necessarily remain constant after a program is fully entered. It can vary during the execution of a program, especially if that program has a lot of stack-related operations—nested math and logic operations or nested GOSUBs. Try this little demonstration program:

```
10   PRINT MEM
20   GOSUB 40
30   PRINT MEM:END
40   GOSUB 60
50   PRINT MEM:RETURN
60   GOSUB 80
70   PRINT MEM:RETURN
80   GOSUB 100
90   PRINT MEM:RETURN
100  PRINT MEM:RETURN
```

This program contains a number of nested subroutines, and each one of them prints out the amount of available free memory. You will see very clearly that the size of the free memory space changes during the execution of a stack-related program.

The practical significance of this demonstration becomes apparent when writing very long and complicated BASIC programs—programs that occupy nearly all available memory space. When you are through entering the program and do a PRINT MEM to check on the amount of free memory still available, you might get a comfortable figure. That can lull you into thinking that you did, indeed, manage to get that nasty program into your available memory. But then you might get a rude awakening to stack operations when you try running the program, and the stack space collides with the variable-names space—the program crashes for a lack of available memory.

Understanding the significance of the free memory space, and making certain that a long program leaves a generous amount of it can save some real disappointments.

The "protected memory" is an optional part of the user's memory space. It is always situated at the very top of the available RAM space, beginning from an address specified during the MEMORY SIZE? power-up routine. If you respond to that power-up query by simply striking the ENTER key, there will be no reserved memory, and the string space and stack will grow downward from the highest available RAM address—addresses specified for you in Table 4-1.

But if you respond to MEMORY SIZE? with a valid RAM address, the string and stack spaces will begin building downward from that address; all available memory above that point will be reserved for things such as machine-language programs and any other memory tinkering you may want to do.

After running through the previous discussion of the free memory space, you ought to see the value in reserving as little protected memory as possible. If you are overly generous and protect too much memory, you will leave little space for entering and executing programs in BASIC. In effect, every byte you reserve for protected memory steals a byte from the free memory; and we have already discussed what can happen when the system runs out of free memory.

In actual practice, however, a programmer rarely runs out of free memory because he or she has reserved some protected memory space. Usually, the purpose of reserving protected memory is to provide space for machine-language programs. When using machine-language programs any BASIC programming used in conjunction with them is generally rather short and unsophisticated. In fact, a purely machine-language program can occupy the entire user's memory space, because there will be none of the memory-gobbling BASIC operations involved.

A BASIC program will never run into any protected memory for the simple reason that the built-in BASIC entry and execution routines never specify addresses larger than the upper string-space address entered in response to MEMORY SIZE? Of course you can write BASIC programs that POKE into the protected memory space, and we will be doing that in a later section of this chapter. But the BASIC routines, themselves, never get into that upper-address area—if it has been specified.

THE I/O BUFFER

In all Level II systems the i/o buffer occupies RAM addresses 16870 through 17127. All keyboard-entry operations take place through this memory space. Whenever you are typing in a line of BASIC programming, for example, it first goes into that buffer, and it is transferred to the program text space only after you strike the ENTER key. During the execution of a BASIC program the keyboard response to INPUT, INKEY$, and any other kinds of in-line entry operations go to the buffer first.

Strings and lines of BASIC text are limited to 255 characters because they must pass through the i/o buffer first; the buffer isn't much larger than that.

If you want to take a look at the sort of data that goes into the i/o buffer, try this program from the command mode (do not use a line number):

```
A=16870:FOR I=0 TO 63:PRINT PEEK(A+I);:NEXT I
```

As you type in this line of text the information goes into the i/o buffer; and when you end the operation by striking the ENTER key

Chart 4-1. I/O Buffer Contents

65	213	49	54	56	55	48	58	129	32	73	213	48	32	189
32	54	51	58	178	32	229	40	65	205	73	41	59	58	135
32	73	0	0											

the program displays itself as it appears in the i/o buffer. The resulting display resembles the sequence of numbers in Chart 4-1.

There will be more to your display than shown here, but, as you will see shortly, anything following a pair of zeros in succession is irrelevant—it's just bits and pieces of data left over from previous i/o operations.

If you compare that string of numbers in Chart 4-1 with an ASCII character table and the command-level program you entered, you can see something of a pattern in the whole thing.

The first number in the i/o listing, for example, is 65. It is no mere coincidence that 65 is the ASCII code for the letter *A* and that the first character in the program is an *A*. Skip the second number, 213, for a moment, and look at the third number in the i/o printout: it's a 49. This is the ASCII code for numeral *1*—the next alphanumeric character in the program.

Running through this process on your own, you will find the i/o buffer containing the ASCII code numbers for all variable names, constants, and punctuation in the program.

But command words and operators are not represented in an ASCII form in the i/o buffer. Rather, they are shown as special *compression code* numbers. The equal sign, for example, appears as a 213 everywhere in the i/o buffer. The FOR part of the FOR... NEXT command shows up as a 129.

> Variable names and values appear in the i/o buffer in a literal, ASCII code format.
>
> Command words and arithmetic/logic operators appear in the i/o buffer as single-number *compression* codes.

Of course, the point of loading command words and operators as single-number compression codes is to make more room in the i/o buffer (and, ultimately, the program memory space) for more BASIC operations.

Table 4-2 is a complete listing of command words and operators that have special compression codes. This table will help you "disassemble" the i/o listing in Chart 4-1. Now you should be able to see how that one-line program appears in the buffer.

Table 4-2. Compression Codes for BASIC Commands and Operators

Command	Compression Code	Command	Compression Code	Command	Compression Code
ABS	217	INKEY$	201	RND	222
AND	210	INP	219	RSET	172
ASC	246	INPUT	137	RUN	142
ATN	228	INSTR	197	SAVE	173
AUTO	183	INT	216	SET	131
CDBL	241	KILL	170	SGN	7
CHR$	247	LEFT$	248	SIN	226
CINT	239	LEN	243	SQR	205
CLEAR	184	LET	140	STEP	204
CLOAD	185	LINE	156	STOP	148
CLOSE	166	LLIST	181	STR$	244
CLS	132	LOAD	167	STRING$	196
CMD	133	LOC	234	SYSTEM	174
CONT	179	LOF	235	TAB(	188
COS	225	LOG	223	TAN	227
CSAVE	186	LPRINT	175	THEN	202
CSNG	240	LSET	171	TIME$	199
CVD	232	MEM	200	TO	189
CVI	230	MERGE	168	TROFF	151
CVS	231	MID$	250	TRON	150
DATA	136	MKD$	238	USING	191
DEF	189	MKI$	236	USR	193
DEFDBL	155	MKS$	237	VAL	255
DEFINT	153	NAME	169	VARPTR	192
DEFSNG	154	NEW	187	+	205
DEFSTR	152	NEXT	135	−	206
DELETE	182	NOT	203	*	207
DIM	138	ON	161	/	208
EDIT	157	OPEN	162	[	209
ELSE	149	OR	211	>	212
END	128	OUT	160	=	213
EOF	233	PEEK	229	<	214
ERL	194	POINT	198	&	38
ERR	195	POKE	177	'	251
ERROR	158	POS	220		
EXP	224	PRINT	178		
FIELD	163	PUT	165		
FIX	242	RANDOM	134		
FN	190	READ	139		
FOR	129	REM	147		
FRE	218	RESET	130		
GET	164	RESTORE	144		
GOSUB	145	RESUME	159		
GOTO	141	RETURN	146		
IF	143	RIGHT$	249		

"DISASSEMBLING" A BASIC PROGRAM

When you are writing in a line of BASIC program text the information first goes into the i/o buffer, and it accumulates there until you strike the ENTER key. As explained in the previous discussion the text in the buffer shows ASCII character codes for all numbers and variable names, but special compression codes for the commands and operators.

As shown in the i/o "disassembling" program information in Chart 4-1, the line ends with a double-zero marker. Those zeros are added automatically to the end of a line of program text in the i/o buffer, and they carry over to the program memory as the line is transferred there.

Here is a program that makes the point:

10 A=17129:FOR I=0 TO 63:PRINT PEEK(A+I);:NEXT I

This program is very similar to the one used for looking at the contents of the i/o buffer. There are just two differences. First, this program is entered with a preceding line number. That line number has to be present in order to make the transfer from the i/o buffer to the program text space in the user's memory. Second, the starting location for the searching operation is different. Instead of starting at the beginning of the i/o buffer (A=16870), this one starts at the beginning of the BASIC program text space (A=17129).

Do a RUN on this program, and you will see the contents of the first 64 locations in the BASIC program text memory. It should look like the data in Chart 4-2.

Chart 4-2. Contents of BASIC Program Text Memory Space

14	67	10	0	65	213	49	54	56	55	48	58	129	32	73
213	48	32	189	32	54	51	58	178	32	229	40	65	205
73	41	59	58	135	32	73	0	0						

Again, there will be more text on the screen than shown in this table, but anything past the double-zero point is irrelevant. Now compare Charts 4-1 and 4-2. They represent the same program, but the former is pulled from the i/o buffer and the latter as it appears after being transferred to the BASIC program text space.

The only significant difference between those two printouts is the presence of 4 extra bytes of information at the beginning of the program-text version in Chart 4-2. Skip those first four numbers, and the printouts are identical.

Indeed, the data set up in the i/o buffer is transferred to the BASIC text memory as ASCII characters and BASIC compression codes.

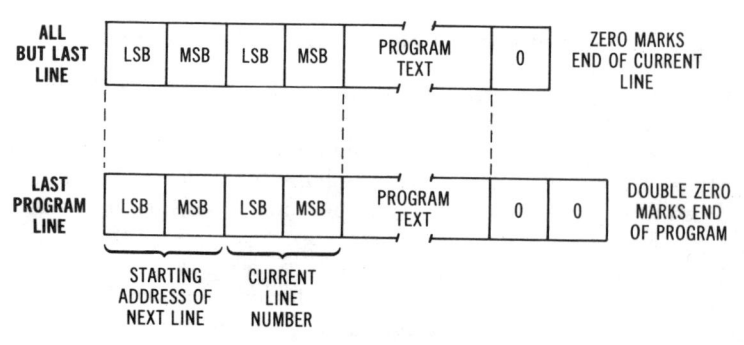

Fig. 4-2. BASIC text format.

What are those first 4 bytes in the program text listing? Well, they represent the program line number and the memory address of the next program line. Every line of BASIC text stored in the program memory starts out this way: 2 bytes for the address of the beginning of the next program line, and 2 bytes indicating the line number of the current line. See Fig. 4-2.

Interpreting the information in these first 4 bytes of each program line is a bit messy, because they are formatted as decimal versions of 2-byte numbers. So if you are confused by the discussion that follows, you should consult Appendix A to see the rationale behind it.

The first 2 bytes in Chart 4-2 indicate the address of the next line of text in the program. Those numbers are 14, 67. Converting them to a hexadecimal format, they are 0E, 43. Turning them around so that the msb is in its loading position, the hexadecimal address of the next program line is 430E. If you don't like working in hex, this number converts to decimal 17166. So whenever a second line is added to this program, it will begin at user's memory address 17166.

Any BASIC program begins at address 17129, and the line under discussion happens to end at 17165 (remembering that 17166 is the starting address of the next line). If you take the difference between the two numbers and add 1, you end up with the number of bytes that program line occupies in program memory: 37 bytes. Count the number of bytes in the listing of Chart 4-2, remembering to exclude the second of the two zeros marking its end. Sure enough, there are 37 bytes in that line.

Of course the number of bytes in a BASIC program line varies with the number of characters and commands you put into it. This one just happens to use 37 bytes of BASIC program memory.

Perhaps the discussion is getting a bit off the track here. The main point is that the first 2 bytes of any line of BASIC text that is stored in program memory represent the starting address of the next line—the actual memory address.

The second 2 bytes reflect the current line number, as indicated in Fig. 4-2. In this particular case the line number is 10, and that shows up clearly in the third and fourth bytes of the listing in Chart 4-2.

A program made up of more than one line of text, as most BASIC programs are, will have a zero at the end of each one. The zero marks the end of a program line, and that's what the BASIC compiler looks for when executing a BASIC program. The last line of program text also ends with a zero, but there is a second zero to mark the end of the program. And that's how the BASIC interpreter knows it has reached the end of a program, whether the END statement is used or not.

As noted in an earlier demonstration, every line of text from the i/o buffer concludes with that double-zero, end-of-program marker. In a sense the i/o buffer assumes that every line you ENTER is the last one. But as you ENTER additional lines of program text, the line just ENTERed begins at the address of the second zero attached to the end of the previously entered line. So no matter how long or short your BASIC program might be, single zeros separate the lines of text in the program memory, and the last-entered line of text ends with two zeros.

Here is a program that searches the user's memory and displays the data for each program line. It ignores any zeros appearing in the first 4 bytes of each line but begins a new line of printout after seeing a single zero at the end of a line. The program stops under two conditions: whenever it sees a double-zero combination that marks the end of all the programming in the BASIC program text memory, and when it sees an END command—compression code 128.

If this is the only programming in the BASIC program text memory, it "disassembles" itself for you, showing you all the BASIC

```
1000  REM ** BASIC 'DISASSEMBLER' **
1010  CLS
1020  A=17128
1030  FOR B=1 TO 4
1040  A=A+1
1050  PRINT PEEK(A);
1060  NEXT B
1070  A=A+1
1080  PRINT PEEK(A);
1090  IF PEEK(A)=0 AND PEEK(A+1)=0 THEN 1150
1100  IF PEEK(A)=0 THEN 1140
1110  IF PEEK(A)=128 THEN 1130
1120  GOTO 1070
1130  A=A+1:PRINT PEEK(A):INPUT S$:GOTO 1030
1140  PRINT:GOTO 1030
1150  PRINT PEEK(A+1)
```

text information for each line. But if you enter a short BASIC program, using line numbers smaller than 1000, you can "disassemble" that program by doing a RUN 1000. Just be sure to end your custom program with an END statement. Otherwise the program will run through itself.

This discussion of how the BASIC program is formatted in the user's memory space ought to suggest some utility programs. You can, for instance, write a program that will search another program, looking for the occurrence of certain functions or variable names. The program can list the line numbers for you or count the number of occurrences.

Probably the most sophisticated and useful utility program is one that renumbers the BASIC lines for you. While such a program is beyond the scope of this book, you might be able to see how it would work. You can write a utility that will search out the line numbers (the second 2 bytes from the beginning of each line) and modify them in any way you choose. The tricky part of a renumbering utility is keeping track of line-number changes for GOTO, GOSUB, ON...GOTO, and ON...GOSUB statements. Finding such statements is easy; just look for their compression codes (Table 4-2), but keeping track of how the line numbers should change is another matter.

In any event, bear in mind that a BASIC program always begins loading at address 17129 and builds upward from there.

PROTECTING MEMORY SPACE

The only section of the user's memory space that is available for any sort of non-BASIC tinkering is the optional protected memory. The amount of protected memory depends on your response to the system's MEMORY SIZE? query at power-up. The number ENTERed at that time sets the lowest available address for the protected memory, and it runs from that point to the highest memory address available on your system. See Table 4-1 for those top addresses.

As an example, suppose you want to save 1024 bytes (1K) for protected memory. If you have a 16K system, subtracting 1024 from 32767 yields the lowest address of the protected memory: 31743. Respond to the MEMORY SIZE? query by entering 31743, and you will have 1024 bytes reserved for your own memory operations; a space running from address 31743 to 32767.

There are occasions when it is necessary to save more than one block of protected memory. A user, for instance, might want 512 bytes for one kind of job, 64 for another, and maybe 1024 for yet another application. The MEMORY SIZE? query allows only one

> SA=MA−BS
>
> where
> SA = the starting address of the protected memory space,
> MA = the highest memory address available (Table 4-1),
> BS = the number of bytes to be protected.

response. What will it be? Simply add up the byte sizes for the individual blocks, and subtract the results from the highest available address. In this case the total amount of protected memory required is 512+64+1024=1600 bytes. If the system has a 16K memory, 32767−1600=32167 gives the starting address of the protected memory space. That's the number to ENTER in response to MEMORY SIZE?

The same situation sometimes arises in a different light. The writer's line-printer system, for example, operates from a machine-language driver program. That program must be entered into the system before it will respond to LPRINT and LLIST commands. Now, the literature supplied with that software driver calls for responding to MEMORY SIZE? by entering 32512. Apparently that is the starting address of the driver routine in the protected memory space.

But for the sake of doing some special experiments with protected memory, I have to set aside some additional space, say 1024 bytes. Remembering that I cannot use any addresses from 32512 and up, the additional protected memory cannot have addresses exceeding 32511—otherwise my memory tinkering might mess up the line-printer program. So with 32511 being the highest address to be used, I subtract the additional bytes of reserved memory (1024) from 32511. That turns up the number 31487. Thus I should respond to MEMORY SIZE? with 31487. That being the case, I can begin my special memory projects at address 31487, and as long as I do not tinker around in memory addresses greater than 32511, the line-printer driver program will remain intact.

Unfortunately, there is no way to protect blocks of memory within the protected memory area. The programmer simply has to be very careful about the matter, perhaps writing BASIC programs that do not allow things to be POKEd into certain blocks of protected memory.

SOME SPECIAL MEMORY OPERATIONS

Most TRS-80 literature refers to protected memory in the context of machine-language programs: specifically, machine-language programs that are used in conjunction with BASIC programs. This is a common situation and this book deals with it later on, but it isn't the only reason for reserving some protected memory. Protected memory can be used as a repository for information that has nothing at all to do with machine-language programming. And that is the point of the following discussions.

Saving One-Line Text in Memory

The following BASIC program, PUTTING STUFF IN, lets you type some text on the screen and save it in memory. Every character is loaded into memory as you enter it, and the entering operation ends only as you strike the pound-sign key (#).

The program assumes that the characters will be entered into successive memory locations, beginning at 31487. This means you have to save some protected memory by answering MEMORY SIZE? with that number. Of course, you are free to change that starting point of the protected memory; but if you do, be sure to change the initial value of variable A in line 1010 accordingly.

The program further assumes you will not wish to enter more than 1000 characters. That limit is set by IM=1000 in line 1010. That, too, can be changed if you wish.

```
1000  REM ** PUTTING STUFF IN **
1010  A=31487:I=0:IM=1000
1020  CLS:PRINT CHR$(14);
1030  C$=INKEY$:IF C$="" THEN 1030
1040  IF I>IM THEN 1110
1050  PRINT C$;:POKE A+I,ASC(C$)
1060  IF C$="#" THEN 1090
1070  I=I+1
1080  GOTO 1030
1090  PRINT:PRINT "TEXT ENTERED"
1100  END
1110  PRINT:PRINT "MEMORY FULL"
1120  END
```

So, get to the MEMORY SIZE? query by turning the TRS-80 off and on, and respond by entering the beginning address of some protected memory—31487 in this example. Then do a RUN.

You will see the cursor on the screen, because the PRINT statement in line 1020 turns it on for you. Then type in some text, anything you want to enter into the protected memory space. When you are done, strike the # key.

Striking the # key signals the end of the test-writing operation, and the program will confirm that condition by printing TEXT ENTERED.

Looking through some of the other lines, note how the current character, carried as string C$, is both PRINTed on the screen and

POKEd into protected memory at line 1050. Variable I, initialized at zero in line 1010, is the character counter. It is incremented after every character operation at line 1070.

If the value of I should ever exceed IM, the program brings up a MEMORY FULL message and stops everything. The value of IM (the maximum number of characters to be written into the protected memory space) is set to 1000 in line 1010.

So this program, PUTTING STUFF IN, gets up to 1000 characters loaded into successive memory locations in the protected memory space. Just be sure to end the operation by striking the # key. Now the problem is to get to that saved text material and print it out on the screen again. This will confirm that the program works.

The next program, GETTING STUFF OUT, runs through the protected memory, printing out saved characters until it sees the pound-sign character.

```
2000  REM ** GETTING STUFF OUT **
2010  A=31487:I=0:IM=1000
2020  C$=CHR$(PEEK(A+I))
2030  IF C$="#" THEN END
2040  PRINT C$;
2050  I=I+1
2060  IF I>IM THEN 2080
2070  GOTO 2020
2080  PRINT:PRINT "OUT OF MEMORY"
2090  END
```

On doing a RUN 2000, *GETTING STUFF OUT* PEEKs at successive addresses in the protected memory (line 2020) and prints the characters contained therein (line 2040). The reading and printing operation continues until it turns up the pound-sign character (line 2030) at the end of the text or it runs out of memory (lines 2060 and 2080).

With those two programs entered into your system, check out the operation of the scheme by writing in some text, making sure you don't strike the # key until you want to end the text-entering phase. Then do a RUN 2000 to see the message you saved in protected memory.

It is possible to slick up the operations a bit, using PUTTING STUFF IN and GETTING STUFF OUT as subroutines for a nice mainline program. Here, then, is 1-LINE TEXT MEMORY DEMO:

```
100  REM ** 1-LINE TEXT MEMORY DEMO **
110  CLS
120  INPUT "READ OR WRITE";F$
130  IF LEFT$(F$,1)="W" THEN 150
140  IF LEFT$(F$,1)<>"R" THEN 120 ELSE 170
150  GOSUB 1000
```

```
160   GOTO 120
170   CLS:GOSUB 2000
180   END
190   REM
200   REM
1000  REM ** PUTTING STUFF IN **
1010  A=31487:I=0:IM=1000
1020  CLS:PRINT CHR$(14);
1030  C$=INKEY$:IF C$="" THEN 1030
1040  IF I>IM THEN 1110
1050  PRINT C$;:POKE A+I,ASC(C$)
1060  IF C$="#" THEN 1090
1070  I=I+1
1080  GOTO 1030
1090  PRINT:PRINT "TEXT ENTERED"
1100  RETURN
1110  PRINT:PRINT "MEMORY FULL"
1120  END
1130  REM
1140  REM
2000  REM ** GETTING STUFF OUT **
2010  A=31487:I=0:IM=1000
2020  C$=CHR$(PEEK(A+I))
2030  IF C$="#" THEN END
2040  PRINT C$;
2050  I=I+1
2060  IF I>IM THEN 2080
2070  GOTO 2020
2080  PRINT:PRINT "OUT OF MEMORY"
2090  END
```

If PUTTING STUFF IN and GETTING STUFF OUT are already resident in your BASIC memory space, all you have to do is enter the mainline program (lines 100 through 200) and change line 1100 to RETURN instead of END. The program gives the option of reading or writing into the protected memory.

If you choose to write, respond to the READ OR WRITE message with a W and enter your text, ending with a pound sign. The program immediately returns to the READ OR WRITE message and, at that point, if you want to see a printout of the text, respond with a R. After printing out the message saved in the protected memory space, the program ends.

Incidentally, the text remains in the protected memory space, even after the BASIC program ends. You can confirm that fact by doing another RUN and specifying a READ operation right away.

Saving a Whole Screen of Text/Graphics in Memory

It isn't always easy to compose elaborate graphics on the TRS-80 screen. The SET/RESET feature eases the task a bit, however, by saving you the trouble of building graphics out of the graphic character set and doing the appropriate sequence of POKE statements.

But no matter how you choose to go about composing a graphic, it is possible to dump the finished product into some user's memory space and call it back to the screen, rather quickly, whenever you want.

The following demonstration uses some SET statements to draw the face with a "have-a-nice-day" smile on the screen. As soon as the drawing operation is done, the entire screen—the video memory—is transferred to user's memory space, beginning at address 19454. After that, this message appears on the screen: GRAPHIC IS DRAWN AND SAVED/ ENTER X TO GET IT FROM MEMORY. When you respond to the message by entering an X, the graphic is duplicated from user's memory to the video memory. Note that this transfer takes place quite a bit faster than the original drawing operation.

Once the graphic is drawn and saved (program lines 20 through 180) you can recall it to the screen at any later time by doing a RUN 200. This assumes, of course, you have done nothing that will disturb the contents of the memory space where it is saved.

```
10   REM ** SCREEN TRANSFER DEMO **
20   CLS
30   FOR A=0.02 TO 6.28 STEP 0.02
40   X=COS(A):Y=SIN(A)
50   SET(34*X+64,16*Y+23):SET(4*X+48,2*Y+18):SET(4*X+80,2*Y+18)
60   NEXT A
70   FOR A=0.02 TO 3.14 STEP 0.02
80   SET(16*COS(A)+64,8*SIN(A)+25)
90   NEXT A
100  V=15360:M=19454
110  FOR I=0 TO 1024
120  POKE M+I,PEEK(V+I)
130  NEXT I
140  CLS
150  PRINT"GRAPHIC IS DRAWN AND SAVED"
160  PRINT "ENTER X TO GET IT FROM MEMORY"
170  INPUT S$
180  IF S$="X" THEN 200 ELSE 170
200  V=15360:M=19454
210  CLS
220  FOR I=0 TO 1024
230  POKE V+I,PEEK(M+I)
240  NEXT I
```

You can replace program lines 10 through 90 with any text or graphic-drawing routine you choose. Just work things out so that your program goes to line 100 when it is time to transfer the screen material to user's memory.

Of course, you can change the location of the graphic storage space by changing the value of the M variable in lines 100 and 200. This variable represents the starting address for the storage area, and the routine occupies 1024 bytes from there.

Then, too, you can change the line numbers if you find you do not have enough space for your drawing routine. Just bear in mind that lines 100 through 180 transfer the screen information to user's memory, and lines 200 through 240 bring it back.

This is not really the most efficient sort of graphic-storage technique; a better one would use some space compression techniques to eliminate the storage of long strings of spaces. But this technique does illustrate one powerful use for user's RAM space.

CHAPTER 5

Linking BASIC and Machine Language With USR

Any protected memory can be used as a repository for data—data being used in conjunction with some BASIC programming. This notion was described and demonstrated in the latter part of Chapter 4.

But that same sort of protected memory can also be used as a place for storing machine-language programs. And those programs, like the data that could be stored there as well, can be used in conjunction with some BASIC programming. This is the main topic of this chapter.

Using BASIC and machine-language programs together can be useful at times and, certainly, instructive at any time. The idea is especially useful when you are writing special utility programs that manipulate the character of a resident BASIC program; and when it comes to writing BASIC programs that call for some high-speed graphics, a machine-language subroutine can be invaluable.

As far as being instructive, the idea of using BASIC and machine-language at the same time can be a useful learning tool, especially in cases where the user is fairly well acquainted with BASIC but knows little about machine-language programming.

When using BASIC and machine language at the same time, the BASIC programming always resides at the lower end of the user's memory space. Not much can be done about changing that position for the BASIC, because it is automatically established by some TRS-80 ROM programming. (See the details of this particular matter in Chapter 4.)

The machine-language part of the scheme always resides in a portion of user's memory that is above all the BASIC—in some protected memory space. You, the user, must establish the size, or starting address, of that protected memory by making an appropriate response to the MEMORY SIZE? query. Again, the details for this operation are outlined for you in Chapter 4.

In a practical sense, then, the first thing you must always do when combining BASIC and machine-language programming is to set aside some protected memory space for the machine-language part. And you must keep track of the number you specify in response to the MEMORY SIZE? query, because it marks the lowest possible address you can use for storing the machine-language program.

Suppose the BASIC is automatically set to the lower part of the user's memory, and you establish the starting point for the machine-language programming in the upper part of the user's memory. Now, how do you get a BASIC program to call the machine-language program, and vice versa? Answer: Use the BASIC USR statement.

The USR statement is your link between BASIC and any machine-language programming. Actually, the USR statement works much like a GOSUB; whenever the computer is running a BASIC program and encounters a USR, operations are sent to a specified starting address for a machine-language program. Just how that starting address is specified will be discussed in a moment.

So a USR statement gets operations from BASIC to machine language. But how, if you want, do you get back from a machine-language program to BASIC? How, if USR works like a GOSUB, do you carry out the RETURN part of the call?

Returning from a machine-language program to BASIC is a matter of ending the machine-language subroutine with a machine-language version of a RETURN statement. There are several different kinds of machine-language RETURN instructions, and it is up to you, the machine-language programmer, to select the right one for the job at hand. But the point is that a machine-language version of a RETURN sends control back to the BASIC line that follows the USR statement.

GETTING SET UP FOR A USR OPERATION

While the TRS-80 system automatically initializes a great many different operations, it does not initialize the USR function. You have to prepare the way yourself.

First, you must set aside some useful amount of protected memory for the machine-language programming. As described in Chapter 4, that is a matter of responding to the MEMORY SIZE? query with an address that marks the beginning of the protected memory space.

Keep track of that number, because it represents the lowest address you can call from BASIC.

The next step is to prepare some critical parts of the BASIC routine. Schemes that combine BASIC and machine language always begin operation in BASIC; and one of the critical BASIC operations is to establish the starting address of the machine-language subroutine. USR works like a GOSUB, but, just as you must specify a line number for a GOSUB statement, you must also specify a starting address for a USR-called machine-language subroutine.

Now, that starting address can be the lowest-available address in protected memory—the same address you entered in response to the MEMORY SIZE? query. But it can be any address within the protected memory space.

That starting address is specified as a 2-byte decimal number that is POKEd into addresses 16526 and 16527. The lsb of the 2-byte version of the starting address goes into 16526 and the msb goes into 16527. Suppose, for example, you want to begin a BASIC-called machine-language subroutine at 31404. Converting that decimal number to a 2-byte decimal format (as described in Appendix A), it comes out to be 122 172—msb and lsb, respectively.

To call a machine-language subroutine that begins at address 31404, the BASIC program must include the following:

POKE 16526,172:POKE 16527,122

Whenever the computer encounters a USR statement, it first looks to addresses 16526 and 16527 to find out where the machine-language routine is to begin. Those two "magic numbers" never change. It is up to you, however, to specify the 2-byte version of the starting address in those memory locations.

To initialize a machine-language subroutine from BASIC, you must:

POKE 16526,*lsb*:POKE 16527,*msb*

where *lsb* and *msb* are the least significant and most significant bytes of a 2-byte version of the starting address.

Anytime after specifying the starting address of the machine-language subroutine, you are free to write in a USR statement to call it. POKEing the starting address does not actually call the subroutine; the USR statement does that.

Most programmers who use BASIC and machine language together specify the starting address—with the two POKE statements—rather early in the BASIC program. That way they can be sure the subroutine is properly initialized when they are ready to write in the USR statement.

So far in this discussion you have seen how to set aside some protected memory space for a machine-language program and then specify the starting address of a machine-language subroutine. The final step in the operation is to specify the USR statement itself.

The expression USR is not a complete statement, but it must be presented as a complete statement if the BASIC program is to execute it—to call the machine-language subroutine you have specified.

A complete USR statement can take on several forms, depending on what you want it to do:

1. Call a machine-language subroutine and return to BASIC without passing any values in either direction.
2. Carry a value from BASIC to the machine-language subroutine but return to BASIC without passing a value.
3. Call a machine-language subroutine without passing a value but return to BASIC, carrying a value.

There are several variations that combine a couple of these basic kinds of USR-oriented operations, but these are the fundamental ones.

In the first case, passing no values between the two kinds of programs, the USR in BASIC simply calls a machine-language subroutine that does a job that does not generate any numbers that are useful to the BASIC program. Perhaps the machine-language program generates some high-speed animation graphics and does nothing to generate any numbers that are useful to later BASIC operations. The USR statement that calls the subroutine is likewise lacking in any numerical information that is useful to the animation sequence.

Calling a machine-language subroutine, without passing any values, can be done with a statement such as

X=USR(X)

where the Xs are dummy variables—variables arbitrarily chosen simply to fit the USR function into a complete BASIC statement. A statement such as A=USR(B) would accomplish exactly the same thing.

Assuming that a machine-language program is already loaded into protected memory, beginning at address 31488, a typical BASIC sequence could look like this:

```
10   POKE 16526,0:POKE 16527,123
20   CLS
30   X=USR(X)
40   PRINT "IT'S DONE"
50   END
```

84

Line 10 in this example establishes the calling address at 31488, line 20 simply clears the screen, and the USR statement in line 30 calls the machine-language program. And when the system is through with the machine-language subroutine (and assuming that subroutine ends with a RETURN-like instruction), operations return to BASIC at line 40, printing the IT'S DONE message and coming to an END at line 50.

No numerical values are passed from BASIC to the machine-language subroutine, and none return to BASIC when the subroutine is done.

The second major class of USR calls passes some value from BASIC to the machine-language subroutine. Maybe you would like the machine-language subroutine to print some characters on the screen, with those characters being specified from the keyboard while the BASIC part of the program is still running. That is just one sort of operation that calls for passing a variable value from BASIC to machine language.

Calling a machine-language subroutine, and passing a value to it from BASIC, can be done with a statement such as:

```
X=USR(Y)
```

where X is still an arbitrarily chosen dummy variable, but Y is some integer between −32,768 and 32,767. The dummy variable, X, is necessary only to fit the USR function into a complete BASIC statement. A statement such as X=USR(65), for example, will carry decimal number 65 to the machine-language program, where it will be used for some particular purpose.

Here is a program that passes an ASCII character code, in decimal, to a machine-language program:

```
10  POKE 16526,0:POKE 16527,123
20  CLS
30  INPUT S$
40  S=ASC(S$)
50  X=USR(S)
60  PRINT "DONE"
70  GOTO 30
```

The program assumes that some sort of machine-language program is in protected memory and begins at address 31488. That starting address is specified by the POKE statements in line 10. Line 20 clears the screen, and line 30 allows you to input some value for S$ from the keyboard. Line 40 assigns the ASCII version of that variable to S, and line 50 calls the machine-language subroutine, passing the value of S to it. When the system is through executing the machine-language subroutine, operations return to line 50 of the

BASIC program, PRINTing a DONE message and looping back up to line 30, giving you a chance to pass another ASCII character code to the subroutine.

The argument in the USR statement—the term enclosed in parentheses—can be a function as well as an integer value. Taking advantage of this feature, the previous example can be shortened somewhat: omit line 40, and replace line 50 with X=USR(ASC(S$)).

Recall that any value passed from the USR to the machine-language program must be an integer value. If you are doing some mathematical operations in BASIC that might pass a value that isn't an integer, you can goofproof the system by doing something such as X=USR(INT(Y)), where Y can be any value—integer or otherwise—between $-32{,}768$ and $32{,}767$.

Finally, you can always pick up a numerical value from a machine-language program and pass it back to the BASIC programming. Perhaps your machine-language programming does some math or logic operations for you, and you want to return the results to BASIC.

Calling a machine-language program and bringing back a value when it returns to BASIC can be done with a statement such as

Y=USR(X)

where X is a dummy variable used to make a complete BASIC statement, and Y is the value returned from the machine-language program. That value returned from machine language will be some integer between $-32{,}768$ and $32{,}767$.

Here is a program that picks up a value from a machine-language program that it calls:

```
10  POKE 16526,0:POKE 16527,123
20  CLS
30  Y=USR(X)
40  PRINT Y
50  END
```

This one assumes a machine-language program begins at address 31488, a point specified by the POKEs in line 10. Line 20 clears the screen, and line 30 calls the machine-language subroutine. When the system returns from that subroutine, line 30 has called for assigning the numerical result to variable Y. Line 40 then prints that value for you.

It is possible to shorten the BASIC program in this case by omitting line 40 and rewriting line 30 this way:

```
30  PRINT USR(X)
```

This modification bypasses the need for variable Y, and it illustrates the fact that a USR function can be used in more than one sort of complete BASIC statement. The USR function *is* a function, and it can be used as such—just as ABS, INT, SQR, and a whole host of BASIC functions are used.

This completes the discussion of the three fundamental USR operations, at least from the BASIC point of view. Much of the material remaining in this chapter considers the same sorts of things from the machine-language viewpoint.

Before getting down to the machine-language view of things, consider an important variation of two kinds of USR operations: combining those passing a value from BASIC with those passing a value back from the machine-language program. Such a scheme can look like this in BASIC:

```
10  POKE 16526,0:POKE 16527,123
20  INPUT S$
30  PRINT USR(ASC(S$))
40  GOTO 20
```

Assuming once more that a machine-language program is resident and beginning at address 31488 (as specified by line 10), the BASIC program picks up a value for S$ from the keyboard at line 20. Line 30 then passes the ASCII value of that string to the machine-language program, and after the machine-language program has presumably done some manipulations with that value, line 30 also brings back the result to BASIC and prints it on the screen.

So line 30 actually does three things: it calls a machine-language subroutine, passes an ASCII version of S$ to it, and then brings back the result from machine language, printing it on the video display.

A PRELIMINARY NOTE ABOUT MACHINE-LANGUAGE PROGRAMMING

Machine-language instructions are stored in memory as 1-byte binary numbers. Every instruction that the Z-80 microprocessor (the one used in your TRS-80) can perform is represented by one of those 1-byte *op codes*.

Appendix B is a complete listing of the Z-80 instruction set, including the op codes and almost-plain-English source-code mnemonics. Every machine-language instruction used in this book can be found somewhere in that listing.

So you can find the complete instruction set for Z-80 machine-language programming in this book, but you will find no details concerning the actions of these instructions nor any special discussions of fundamental machine-language programming. All of that sort of thing is beyond the scope of this book. Indeed, it is unfortunate that it is impractical to write a single volume that both spells out the special features of the TRS-80 system and teaches beginners how to handle machine-language programming. It is simply too much for one book.

The emphasis of this book is on *what* can be done with your Level II TRS-80. The *how* of the matter is described in general terms and does not (cannot) get down to the finer details of machine-language programming.

You can certainly work the examples and demonstration programs without having any knowledge of machine-language programming, but you have to learn that sort of programming on your own if you want to extend the examples and demonstrations to suit your needs.

Any good book on the Z-80 microprocessor and its instruction set will do. Learn that sort of thing from another source, and this book will help you fit it into the context of your TRS-80 machine.

POKEING IN MACHINE-LANGUAGE PROGRAMS FROM BASIC

When linking BASIC and machine-language programs with the USR function, the BASIC program generally performs two functions. It calls the machine-language program as outlined in several different ways earlier in this chapter. But it also loads the machine-language program into protected memory for you.

Thus there are at least two phases to the BASIC part of the scheme: loading the machine-language program and calling it when the loading is done.

After you have written a machine-language program on paper it must be POKEd into its memory space, one byte at a time and in the proper sequence.

The simplest possible machine-language program in a USR-linked scheme is one that does nothing more than return operation to the BASIC program. The instruction code for an unconditional RETurn is decimal 201. So if a 201 is POKEd into the starting address of the machine-language program, a USR function will call it from BASIC, and it will return control immediately back to the BASIC program. Here is a complete example that you can run on your machine:

```
10  POKE 16526,0:POKE 16527,123
20  POKE 31488,201
30  X=USR(X)
40  CLS:PRINT "IT WORKED!!"
50  END
```

It isn't a very exciting program, but it serves as an example of the discussion at hand.

Line 10 establishes the starting point of the machine-language program at 31488. The 0 and 123, you recall, are 2-byte versions of the starting address. The purpose of that line is to tell the USR function where it is supposed to begin execution of the machine-language program.

Line 20 represents the main point of this discussion. That statement POKEs the one-instruction machine-language program into memory address 31488. The 201 is a decimal version of the Z-80's unconditional RETurn instruction.

Now, it is no coincidence that line 10 sets the starting point at address 31488 and line 20 pokes the first (and only) machine-language instruction into that same address. The first instruction and the starting point of the USR-called subroutine must be the same.

By the time the system completes its execution of line 20 the BASIC program has loaded the machine-language program. The next step is to execute that machine-language program, and that is done by the USR statement in line 30.

It should be apparent that the machine-language program must be entered before it is called by the USR function. The statement in line 20 must occur sometime before the statement in line 30.

The statement in line 10—establishing the calling address for the USR function—must occur before USR does but not necessarily before the machine-language-loading operation. Line 10, for example, could be moved to, say, line 25, and things would work just as well. It is a fairly well established convention, however, to specify the starting address of the machine-language programming very early in the BASIC routine.

So line 20 calls the one-instruction machine-language program. And when control returns to BASIC, things pick up at line 40, clearing the screen and printing IT WORKED!!.

Incidentally, if you failed to POKE the right instruction into memory at line 20, the system might not return at all. It would most likely go "into outer space," making it necessary to do a RESTART (depressing the RESTART push button on the back of your TRS-80 unit) or a total power-up.

Seeing the IT WORKED!! message in this case confirms the proper function of that one-instruction subroutine.

*When loading a machine-language program from BASIC POKE statements, the op codes must be entered in a decimal format. TRS-80 BASIC, you see, is a decimal-oriented language. This poses a minor difficulty, because the Z-80 instruction set specifies the op codes in a hexadecimal format. So an unconditional RET in Appendix B is shown as C9. This is a hexadecimal number. But the same instruction is represented as a 201 in that last example. Where does the 201 come from? It is the decimal version of hexadecimal C9.

The moral of the story is this: *hexadecimal op codes from the Z-80 instruction set must be converted to decimal before they can be entered into memory by way of POKE statements.* See Appendix A, Table A-1, to make the necessary conversion.

Most machine-language programs have more than one instruction in them—a lot more. Each one of them has to be loaded into memory by a POKE statement; if you have a lot of instructions, you can end up with a whole lot of POKE statements.

Things are generally simplified, however, by enclosing the instruction-POKEing statement within a FOR... NEXT loop. And if that FOR... NEXT loop also contains a READ statement, the instructions can be written in their proper sequence in some DATA lists.

Here is a working example:

```
10   POKE 16526,0:POKE 16527,123
30   FOR I=0 TO 5:READ D:POKE 31488+I,D:NEXT I
40   CLS
50   X=USR(X)
60   PRINT:PRINT
70   END
100  DATA 62,65,50,0,60,201
```

Line 10 sets the starting point of the machine-language program at 31488. This assumes, of course, you have previously set aside some protected memory that includes that address. The program is loaded into protected memory by the statements in line 30.

Line 30 includes a READ statement that references the DATA list in line 100. Line 100, incidentally, is the machine codes to be entered. In this case it is a 6-byte program. So as variable I is incremented from 0 to 5, the READ statement picks up the DATA items in sequence, and the POKE statement inserts them into successive memory locations, beginning at 31488—the place already specified as the starting point in line 10.

Once the system completes the execution of line 30 the machine-language program is completely loaded, and the next series of BASIC operations clears the screen, executes the machine-language program (line 50), does a couple of PRINTs, and then ENDs.

We'll discuss the machine-language program, itself, shortly. What is more important now is the way the BASIC program loads the machine-language program.

The statements shown here in line 30 have a form that is almost universally accepted as the general procedure for loading a machine-language program from BASIC. The features thus call for a detailed analysis.

The first part of the line reads, in general:

FOR i=0 TO n

where

i is any numerical variable name,
n is the number of machine-language bytes to be loaded, minus 1.

There are six items in the DATA list in the previous example, so the first part of the loading sequence should read: FOR I=0 TO 5. If there happened to be 25 items in the DATA list, you would write FOR I=0 to 24.

The second part of the loading sequence reads:

READ d

where d is any valid numerical variable name.
The third part looks like this, when presented in a general form:

POKE a+i,d

where

a is the starting address of the machine-language program,
i is the same variable used in the first phase of the loading operation,
d is the same variable READ in the previous statement.

The value of address a in this statement must be a conventional decimal version of the starting address specified in a 2-byte decimal format at the beginning of the program. In this case, address 31488 is the conventional decimal form of 123 0.

Putting it all together, the line for entering a machine-language program from BASIC looks like this:

FOR i=0 TO n:READ d:POKE a+i,d:NEXT i

where
i and d are any convenient numerical variable names,
a is the starting address of the machine-language program,
n is the number of bytes in the machine-language program, minus 1.

This entire scheme for loading a machine-language program from BASIC assumes you have listed the instructions and data as decimal numbers in a DATA list. In the previous example the DATA list read: 62,65,50,0,60,201. A disassembled version is shown in Table 5-1.

Table 5-1. A Typical Decimal-Oriented Machine-Language Program

Address	Op Code	Mnemonic	Comment
123 0	62 65	LD A,65D	;LOAD ASCII "A" INTO REGISTER A
123 2	50 0 60	LD (15360D),A	;LOAD A TO THE VIDEO MEMORY
123 5	201	RET	;RETURN TO BASIC

Table 5-1 is a formal, assembly-language version of the program executed by a USR function in line 50 of the previous BASIC program. It prints the letter A at the first video memory location.

The assembly-language program in that table has some features that are common to any sort of Z-80 source and op-code listing. One difference is that the op codes are presented in a decimal, rather than hexadecimal, format. The addresses are also in a decimal format—a 2-byte decimal format, to be exact. The justification for using addresses in this peculiar 2-byte decimal format will become clear in a later section of this chapter. The mnemonics are standard Z-80 mnemonics, and the comments are typical of those used with any machine-language programming.

If you are totally confused by the listing in Table 5-1, you will have to consult a Z-80 assembly-language book or manual (e.g. look at Radio Shack's *TRS-80 Assembly-Language Programming*).

When you get tired of seeing this program do nothing but print a single *A* in the upper left-hand corner of the screen, change the number in the second item of the DATA list to some other number between 33 and 191. Then run the program again.

That little exercise, incidentally, suggests how easy it is to modify a machine-language program that is loaded from BASIC; just change the item or items in the DATA list and, if necessary, adjust the value of *n* in the FOR *i*=0 TO *n* part of the loading routine.

SOME PROGRAMMING EXAMPLES

The following examples of USR-called programs are intended to illustrate the range of interaction that is possible between a BASIC program and a machine-language program that it can call. In every instance the BASIC program not only controls the calling of a machine-language program but loads it into a specified section of protected memory as well. All examples assume you have responded to MEMORY SIZE? with a number no greater than 31488.

A Simple Calling Routine From BASIC

Here is a decimal-oriented, machine-language program that simply draws a wide white bar across the top line of the screen:

```
;WIDE BAR ROUTINE
123 0      33 0 60      START:   LD HL,15360D    ;POINT TO START OF VIDEO
123 3      62 63                 LD A,63D        ;END OF COUNT TO A
123 5      54 191       AGAIN:   LD (HL),191D    ;SET GRAPHIC CHARACTER
123 7      189                   CP L            ;LOOK FOR END
123 8      200                   RET Z           ;RETURN IF AT END
123 9      35                    INC HL          ;NEXT VIDEO POINT
123 10     195 5 123             JP AGAIN        ;DRAW AGAIN
;END
```

Basically, the program loads character code 191 (full rectangle) into the 64 character locations across the top of the screen. Here is a BASIC program for loading and executing it:

```
 0   REM ** CALL A WHITE BAR **
10   POKE 16526,0:POKE 16527,123
20   FOR I=0 TO 12:READ D:POKE 31488+I,D:NEXT I
30   CLS
40   X=USR(X)
50   PRINT:PRINT
60   END
100  DATA 33,0,60,62,63,54,191,189,200,35,195,5,123
```

The BASIC program loads the machine-language program from the DATA list in line 100, using the procedure in line 20. After that, it clears the screen (line 30), calls the machine-language program, and does a couple of PRINTs before coming to an END. Of course the white bar is drawn the moment the BASIC program calls the machine-language program via a USR statement. The RET Z instruction in the machine language ensures that the operations return to BASIC when the line-drawing operation is done.

Conditioning a Call at the BASIC Level

In some actual applications you might not want to execute the machine-language portion of a program unless certain conditions are met at the BASIC level. Using the same machine-language program—the one that draws a white bar across the top of the screen—you can make the drawing of the line contingent on striking the B key. Here's the revised BASIC program:

```
 0   REM ** CONDITIONAL CALL FROM BASIC **
10   POKE 16526,0:POKE 16527,123
20   FOR I=0 TO 12:READ D:POKE 31488+I,D:NEXT I
25   C$=INKEY$:IF C$="" THEN 25
30   IF C$="B" THEN 40
35   PRINT "NOT YET":GOTO 25
40   CLS:X=USR(X)
50   PRINT:PRINT
60   END
100  DATA 33,0,60,62,63,54,191,189,200,35,195,5,123
```

This BASIC program still loads the machine-language subroutine. See lines 20 and 100. Doing the USR function, however, is contingent on striking the *B* key. Until that happens, striking any other key yields a NOT YET message.

Conditioning the call of a machine-language subroutine can be a rather sophisticated operation. For example, you might work out a BASIC program of this sort, allowing it to execute the USR function (and hence the machine-language program) only on typing the string CALL BAR, or something like that.

Repetitive Calling

The following program draws a solid bar of light across the top of the screen. Everything remains unchanged until you depress the *F* key. At that time the bar begins flashing on and off, and it remains flashing until you release the *F* key.

The BASIC program is responsible for sensing the depression of the *F* key and calling a machine-language program that first turns off the light, and then turns it on again. After completing that one cycle, control returns to BASIC, where the *F* key is checked again. If that key is still depressed, the control returns to the machine-language program for another off/on cycle. But when control returns to BASIC and at that time the *F* key is no longer depressed, the program continues looping in BASIC until the *F* key is depressed again.

This is an example of looping around and around between a BASIC and machine-language program. Such loops have some powerful applications, especially when it comes to doing some real-time, animated graphics.

The flashing effect, by the way, is far less satisfactory if it is generated—if the bar is alternately erased and drawn—in purely BASIC terms. Even POKE graphics do not run fast enough to create a good flashing effect of such a long bar on the screen. Machine-language graphics certainly does the job, as you will see when running this program.

Here is the BASIC part of the program:

```
0   REM ** FLASHING BAR WITH BASIC CONTROL **
10  POKE 16526,0:POKE 16527,123
20  FOR I=0 TO 37:READ D:POKE 31488+I,D:NEXT I
30  CLS:PRINT @ 64,"DEPRESS THE F KEY TO GET A FLASHING BAR OF
    LIGHT..."
40  IF PEEK(14463)=0 THEN 40
50  C$=INKEY$
60  IF C$<>"" THEN R$=C$
70  IF R$<>"F" THEN 40
80  X=USR(X)
90  GOTO 40
```

```
100  DATA  6,128,205,11,123,6,191,205,11,123,201
100  DATA  33,0,60,62,63,112,189,202,25,123,35,195,16,123
120  DATA  22,225,14,225,13,194,29,123,21,194,27,123,201
```

Line 10 sets the starting address of the machine-language program at 31488, and line 20 loads that program from DATA lines 100, 110, and 120. That is a 38-byte program there.

Line 30 simply clears the screen and prints a prompting message at the second line on the screen.

The real looping action, the main point of the demonstration, begins at line 40. This line, working together with lines 50 and 60, views the keyboard as a big set of normally open push-button switches. Line 70, however, maintains the key-searching loop until you depress the *F* key.

Line 80 uses the USR function to call the machine-language subroutine—a routine that flashes the white bar off and on one time. After completing just one flashing cycle in machine language, control returns to BASIC at line 90.

Now, line 90 restarts the key-sensing loop; and if the *F* key is still depressed, line 80 is executed again, and the bar of light flashes. As long as that *F* key is depressed, the USR function and the machine-language subroutine become part of a loop. Line 80 is removed from the loop only when the *F* key is not depressed.

So, indeed, machine-language programs can be written into a BASIC program loop.

In passing, notice the short time delay between the time you do a RUN for the program and the appearance of the prompting message. That delay will occur only when you start this program from scratch, and it is caused by the time required for POKEing the machine-language op codes into your protected memory space.

The machine-language program, itself, is justified in its hand-assembled form in Table 5-2. The number of jumps and calls'in the routine clearly demonstrates the value of specifying the addresses as 2-byte numbers. Note that only the lsb of those addresses changes. The same msb is good for up to 256 memory locations.

PASSING A VALUE TO THE MACHINE-LANGUAGE SUBROUTINE

As stated earlier in this chapter the statement X=USR(Y) will pass the value of the argument, the Y, to the subroutine it calls, provided Y is an integer between $-32,768$ and $32,767$. This is stating the case in a very general way, however. It is more precise to say that the X=USR(Y) statement makes the value of the argument *available* to the machine-language program it calls.

Table 5-2. Machine-Language Progam Called by the BASIC Program FLASHING BAR WITH BASIC CONTROL

Address	Op Code		Mnemonic	Comment
123 0	6 128	START:	LD B,128D	;SET B FOR OFF
123 2	205 11 123		CALL DRAW	;DRAW "OFF"
123 5	6 191		LD B,191D	;SET BE FOR ON
123 7	205 11 123		CALL DRAW	;DRAW "ON"
123 10	201		RET	;RETURN TO BASIC
123 11	33 0 60	DRAW:	LD HL,15360D	;START OF VIDEO MEMORY
123 14	62 63		LD A,63D	;SET END IN A
123 16	112	AGAIN:	LD (HL),B	;DRAW CHARACTER OF B
123 17	189		CP L	;LOOK FOR END
123 18	202 25 123		JP Z,TIME	;IF END, DO TIME DELAY
123 21	25		INC HL	;ELSE SET FOR DRAW AGAIN
123 22	195 16 123		JP AGAIN	;JUMP TO DO AGAIN
123 25	22 255	TIME:	LD D,255D	;SET MSB OF TIME DELAY
123 27	14 255	SETC:	LD C,255D	;SET LSB OF TIME DELAY
123 29	13	DECC:	DEC C	;COUNT DOWN LSB
123 30	194 29 123		JP NZ,DECC	;DO AGAIN IF NOT DONE
123 33	21		DEC D	;COUNT DOWN MSB
123 34	194 27 123		JP NZ,SETC	;DO AGAIN IF NOT DONE
123 37	201		RET	;RETURN AT END OF TIME

Whenever a value is to be passed from BASIC to a machine-language program, the first step in the machine-language program must be a CALL 2687D. The value passed from BASIC, in other words, has to be pulled from somewhere else by another subroutine—one executed by doing the CALL 2687.

And after that CALL is executed, the value of the argument will appear in the Z-80's HL register pair. It is then up to the programmer to do something with it.

A machine-language CALL 2687D places the value of a passed term into the HL register pair.

Here is a machine-language program and its BASIC calling program that illustrate the point:

123 0	205 127 10	CALL 2687D	;GET THE PASSED VALUE
123 3	125	LD A,L	;LOAD LSB TO A
123 4	33 0 60	LD HL,15360D	;POINT TO START OF VIDEO
123 7	119	LD (HL),A	;PUT VALUE ONTO SCREEN
123 8	201	RET	;RETURN TO BASIC

```
 0 REM ** CARRY A CHARACTER TO SUBROUTINE **
10 POKE 16526,0:POKE 16527,123
```

```
20   FOR I=0 TO 8:READ D:POKE 31488+I,D:NEXT I
30   CLS
40   C$=INKEY$:IF C$="" THEN 40
50   X=USR(ASC(C$))
60   GOTO 40
100  DATA 205,127,10,125,33,0,60,119,201
```

The BASIC portion of the scheme loads the machine-language program, then looks for a character string from the keyboard. On finding one, line 50 both converts the character string to its ASCII value and calls the machine-language subroutine. And after the machine-language routine does its job—to be described shortly—the BASIC program simply loops back to line 40, giving you a chance to enter another character.

Now look at the machine-language part of the project. The BASIC program passes ASC(C$) to the machine-language subroutine, and the first instruction in that subroutine calls the value from its mysterious place in the TRS-80 memory. On completing execution of that instruction the value passed from BASIC resides in the Z-80's HL register pair.

The second line in the machine-language program loads the content of register L into register A. The lsb of the value passed to the subroutine is thus saved in that register. There is no need to save the content of the H register in this particular case, because ASCII values cannot exceed 255 and are thus completely specified in a single, 1-byte register—the L register in this case.

So the second line saves the ASCII character code in register A. That is an important step, because the next instruction uses the HL pair for another purpose—to point to the beginning of the video memory. Then the ASCII code is moved from register A to the video memory, where the character appears on the screen.

The last line in the machine-language program simply returns operations to BASIC.

Not a very exciting program, perhaps, it simply prints whatever character is entered from the keyboard. But the entry operation is done in BASIC and the printing is done in machine language; and that illustrates the main point of this discussion: passing a value from BASIC to machine language.

The next BASIC/machine-language routine is another example of passing a value from BASIC. Unlike the previous example, this one has the potential for working with numbers that occupy a register pair—passing numbers that may be larger than 255.

The BASIC program loads the machine-language subroutine, then enters a loop that allows you to enter decimal numbers between 0 and 1023. For the purposes of this demonstration, those numbers represent the range of plotting positions on the crt. The numbers are

```
123 0     205 127 10            CALL 2687D         ;GET THE PASSED VALUE TO HL
123 3     235                   EX HL,DE           ;GET PASSED VALUE TO DE
123 4     33 0 60               LD HL,15360D       ;POINT TO VIDEO
123 7     175                   XOR A              ;CLEAR A REGISTER
123 8     54 131                DRAW:LD(HL),131D   ;DRAW LINE SEGMENT
123 10    187                   CP E               ;LOOK FOR END OF LSB VALUE
123 11    194 16 123            JP NZ NEXT         ;JUMP IF NOT DONE
123 14    186                   CP D               ;LOOK FOR END OF MSB VALUE
123 15    200                   RET Z              ;IF DONE, RETURN TO BASIC
123 16    27                    NEXT:DEC DE        ;COUNTDOWN VALUE
123 17    35                    INC HL             ;SET NEW VIDEO POINT
123 18    195 8 123             JP DRAW            ;DRAW AGAIN

  0  REM ** PRINT @ LINE DRAW **
 10  POKE 16526,0:POKE 16527,123
 20  FOR I=0 TO 20:READ D:POKE 31488+I,D:NEXT I
 30  CLS
 40  INPUT Y
 50  IF Y<0 OR Y>1023 THEN 40
 60  CLS
 70  X=USR(INT(Y))
 80  PRINT:GOTO 40
100  DATA 205,127,10,235,33,0,60,175
110  DATA 54,131,187,194,16,123,186,200
120  DATA 27,35,195,8,123
```

comparable to those used for doing PRINT @ operations in BASIC.

Instead of printing a character at a single point, however, the machine-language part of the program draws a continuous white line, beginning at point 0 on the screen and running to the value passed from the BASIC program.

The endpoint-coordinate of the line is INPUT at line 40. The conditional in line 50 goofproofs the system from numbers outside the video-memory range. Line 70 calls the machine-language subroutine, but also goofproofs the system against any fractional numbers the user might try to enter. Recall that numbers passed to a machine-language subroutine must be integer values. (Things will happen if you attempt to pass a noninteger value, but there will seem to be no rational correspondence between the specified number and the response of the machine-language program.)

Notice that the machine-language program begins with the manditory CALL 2687. The step is mandatory, at least, if you want to work with the value passed from the BASIC part of the scheme. That operation always puts the passed value into the HL pair, but this writer wanted to use the HL pair as a video-memory pointer; so the next step is to exchange the HL and DE register contents. That effectively moves the passed value to the DE pair.

The remainder of the machine-language program simply plots character code 131 onto the screen, counts down the value passed from BASIC, and moves to the next character space on the screen. The machine-language routine continues looping in this fashion until the value passed to it is counted down to zero. Then the control is returned to BASIC, where you have a chance to enter another endpoint number between 0 and 1023.

The main points demonstrated by these two programs are:

1. A value passed from BASIC to machine language must be picked up at the machine-language level by executing a CALL 2687 (decimal).
2. A value picked up by a CALL 2687 will appear in the Z-80's HL register pair.
3. You are free to manipulate that value as it is passed to the HL register pair.

PASSING VALUES FROM MACHINE LANGUAGE TO BASIC

A BASIC statement such as Y=USR(X) will call a machine-language subroutine and return to BASIC with a value assigned to the Y variable. An alternate form is PRINT USR(X): a statement that will immediately print the value returned from the machine-language routine.

But in order to pass a value from a machine-language routine to BASIC, that value must be residing in the Z-80's HL register pair, and there is a very special, mandatory technique for returning to BASIC.

Whenever you want to pass a value back to BASIC, the machine-language program must end with this instruction:

```
195 154 10    JP 2714D    ;RETURN TO BASIC WITH VALUE
```

Such a routine does not return to BASIC with one of the usual sorts of RETurn instructions. Technically speaking, that mandatory JUMP instruction sends operations to a place in TRS-80 ROM that does the RETurn job for you, and in the meantime it takes care of the operations involved in assigning the value in the HL register pair to the USR function in the BASIC listing.

So when you are ready to get out of a machine-language subroutine and return a value to BASIC, you must make sure the value to be passed is in the HL pair, and then you must execute the special JUMP instruction, JP 2714D.

The following BASIC/machine-language program illustrates the point. This one counts and prints integer values. The counting operation, however, is done at the machine-language level, while the PRINTing is done in BASIC. That sort of scheme calls for passing the current count from machine language to BASIC.

```
123 0    42 10 123    LD HL,(COUNT)    ;FETCH COUNT TO HL
123 3    35           INC HL           ;COUNT BY ONE
123 4    34 10 123    LD (COUNT),HL    ;SAVE COUNT AT END OF PROGRAM
123 7    195 154 10   JP 2714D         ;RETURN VALUE TO BASIC

0    REM ** COUNT AT MACHINE LEVEL **
10   POKE 16526,0:POKE 16527,123
20   FOR I=0 TO 11:READ D:POKE 31488+I,D:NEXT I
40   PRINT USR(X);
50   FOR T=0 TO 10:NEXT
60   GOTO 40
100  DATA 42,10,123,35,34,10,123,195,154,10,0,0
```

The BASIC portion of the program loads the machine-language program and then enters an endless loop between lines 40 and 60. That loop calls and prints a value from the machine-language subroutine and then does a short time delay at line 50. The time delay simply slows down the operation so you can observe it better. The only way to end the program is by striking the *BREAK* key.

The most important part of the machine-language routine is the last line. This is the mandatory instruction—the one that makes it possible to assign the number in the HL pair to the USR function and return to BASIC.

The count, itself, is saved at two bytes of memory just above the main program listing. Saving the count in that fashion is absolutely necessary, because most of the Z-80 registers are affected by the return to BASIC, and a count residing in them will be lost. The two zeros at the end of the DATA listing initialize that "counter" to zero but only when the program is first RUN. After that, the "counter" carries the current count.

In summary:

1. A value to be passed from machine language to BASIC must reside in the Z-80's HL pair at the moment the return occurs.
2. When carrying a value back to BASIC, the return must be carried out by executing a JP 2714 (decimal).
3. The value assigned to the USR function may be treated as any BASIC value.

PASSING VALUES BACK AND FORTH

Some of the most useful kinds of BASIC/machine-language programs are those that pass one value from BASIC, perform some mathematical or logic operations on the value, and return the result to BASIC. The back-and-forth process is really just a matter of combining the principles described in the two previous sections of this chapter: passing values from BASIC to machine language, and passing values from machine language to BASIC.

The following program illustrates the point. This program allows you to enter any integer between −32,768 and 32,767. The integer is passed to the machine-language part of the program and a 2-byte version of the number is returned. In other words, the program carries out the tedious task of converting a standard decimal number into its 2-byte decimal form—something that frequently troubles programmers who are working with BASIC and machine language together.

```
123  0    205 127 10    START:  CALL 2687D      ;VALUE TO HL PAIR
123  3    17 25 123             LD DE,PHASE     ;SET PHASE ADDRESS
123  6    26                    LD A,(DE)       ;FETCH CURRENT PHASE
123  7    254 0                 CP 0            ;ZERO PHASE?
123  9    194 17 123            JP NZ,MSB       ;IF NOT, THEN MSB
123 12    60                    INC A           ;SET FOR PHASE 1
123 13    18                    LD (DE),A       ;SAVE PHASE
123 14    195 20 123            JP DONE         ;AND JUMP TO DONE
123 17    61            MSB:    DEC A           ;SET FOR PHASE 0
123 18    18                    LD (DE),A       ;SAVE PHASE
123 19    108                   LD L,H          ;MSB TO L REGISTER
123 20    38 0          DONE:   LD H,0          ;CLEAR H REGISTER
123 22    195 154 10            JP 2714D        ;RETURN TO BASIC
                                                ;WITH VALUE
```

```
  0  REM ** CONVERT TO 2-BYTE DECIMAL **
 10  POKE 16526,0:POKE 16527,123
 20  FOR I=0 TO 25:READ D:POKE 31488+I,D:NEXT I
 40  CLS:INPUT "ENTER STANDARD DECIMAL (−32768 TO 32767)";N
 50  IF N<−32768 OR N>32767 THEN 40
 60  PRINT N"=";
 70  FOR PH=0 TO 1:PRINT USR(N);:NEXT PH
 80  PRINT:PRINT
 90  INPUT"STRIKE ENTER KEY TO DO AGAIN";S$:GOTO 40
100  DATA 205,127,10,17,25,123,26,254,0,194,17,123
110  DATA 60,18,195,20,123
120  DATA 61,18,108,38,0,195,154,10,1
```

As in all previous examples the BASIC portion of this program both loads the machine-language portion of the program and performs some important i/o operations in its own right. The machine-language program is loaded by line 20, calling on the DATA items in lines 100, 110, and 120. The actual working part of the program begins at line 40 and loops endlessly between that line and line 90. The machine-language subroutine is called by the PRINT USR(N) statement in line 70.

The general idea of the program is to enter a decimal integer in response to the INPUT statement ENTER STANDARD DECIMAL (−32768 TO 32767). Line 50 goofproofs that entry, making sure the value passed to the machine-language subroutine is within its acceptable range (a matter described earlier in this chapter).

For the sake of doing some tidy formatting, line 60 reprints your entry and inserts an equal sign. The semicolon preceding the equal sign suppresses the usual line-feed/carriage-return operation, allowing the results of the machine-language program to be printed on that same line.

The FOR...NEXT statements in line 70 imply a two-phase operation, as far as the execution of the machine-language program is concerned. This two-phase operation allows PRINTing of the msb of the result on the first pass and PRINTing of the lsb on the second pass.

The same value is passed to the machine-language program in both phases—the value of N entered in response to the INPUT message. The machine-language program passes back a value two different times. The first value passed back to BASIC is the msb of the 2-byte decimal number, and the second value in the sequence is the lsb of that number.

So if you respond to the INPUT message with a 15360, the PRINTed results on the screen look like this: 15360=60 0. And, sure enough, the 2-byte decimal version of 15360 (the beginning address of the TRS-80 video memory) is 60 0, a figure used in several previous demonstrations.

The main point of the demonstration lies in the first and last lines of the machine-language portion of the program. The first line does the CALL 2687 (decimal) to insert a value passed from BASIC into the Z-80's HL pair. And the last line does the JP 2714 (decimal) to carry a value from machine language to BASIC.

SAVING BASIC/MACHINE-LANGUAGE PROGRAMS ON CASSETTE TAPE

One of the advantages of using BASIC and machine-language programs together is that they are so easy to save on cassette tape. Since the machine-language part of the scheme is loaded from BASIC, the entire program can be saved on tape via the usual CSAVE command. Likewise, the programs can be loaded into the TRS-80 by means of the usual CLOAD command.

In short, there is no need to fool around with SYSTEM commands. As far as the TRS-80 is concerned, the programs are purely BASIC programs, and they can be treated as such.

There is much more to be said about this matter of linking BASIC and machine-language programs with the USR function. This chapter has presented the most fundamental parts of the matter. The next chapter deals with special procedures and applications.

CHAPTER 6

Manipulating BASIC-Loaded, USR-Linked Programs

The USR function allows the user to link together BASIC and machine-language programs. Chapter 5 describes the process in general terms, and the demonstrations show how values can be passed between the BASIC and machine-language portions of the program.

This chapter, like Chapter 5, deals with BASIC-loaded, USR-linked programs, but from a somewhat more sophisticated point of view. Here, for instance, you will see how it is possible to enter the machine-language portion of a program at any desired point, and not just from the lowest address. This principle then leads to the notion of calling any one of a number of different machine-language programs.

To put some finishing touches on the subject you will see how to delete the loader portion of a BASIC program, leaving behind just the operational part of BASIC and the machine-language subroutines.

SPECIFYING ENTRY POINTS FOR USR-LINKED PROGRAMS

When writing the BASIC portion of a program that links BASIC and machine language via the USR statement, it is necessary to specify the starting address of the machine-language routine before executing the USR function. That starting address is POKEd into 16526 and 16527 as a 2-byte version of the address. See Chapter 5 if you have any doubts about the meaning of this important principle.

The POKE statements, however, do not necessarily have to point to the very beginning of a machine-language subroutine. They can point to any valid *entry point*—any valid point in the subroutine that will execute a set of instructions without causing confusion.

The practical significance of this notion is that you can write machine-language subroutines that do a number of different tasks and you can call from BASIC any one you choose. It's all a matter of setting the desired entry point at addresses 16526 and 16527.

Before getting into the details of a program that illustrates this point, it is instructive to view it from a general angle. The program you will enter is a rather simple counting program. It uses a 46-byte machine-language routine to count upward or downward between 0 and 9. It can also preset the count to 0 or 9. All operations are under the control of the BASIC portion of the program—the machine-language portion simply carries out the decisions made at the BASIC level.

Table 6-1 summarizes the four entry points for the machine-language program. The first column describes the operation, the second specifies the starting address of that operation in standard decimal form, and the third column specifies the starting addresses in a 2-byte decimal format.

Table 6-1. Summary of the Entry Points for the Machine-Language Program in Table 6-2

Function	Entry-Point Address Standard Decimal	2-Byte Decimal MSB	LSB
ZERO the counter	31488	123	0
Preset to NINE	31493	123	5
Count UP	31501	123	13
Count DOWN	31513	123	25

Getting to any one of the four valid entry points of the machine-language program is a matter of first setting the entry-point address and then doing the USR function. To zero the counter, for example, the BASIC program should include the sequence: POKE 16526,0: POKE 16527,123. A USR function appearing anytime after that will cause the system to enter the machine-language program at address 31488, thus causing the counter to reset to zero.

Presetting the counter to 9 is a matter of specifying the entry point for that particular operation: POKE 16526,5:POKE 16527,123. A USR function appearing anytime after that will call the preset-to-9 operation at the machine-language level.

In a similar fashion, doing a POKE 16526,13:POKE 16527,123 sets the entry point for counting upward, and doing a POKE 16526,25: POKE 16527,123 sets up a down-counting operation.

The standard Radio Shack literature says that Level II BASIC can call just one machine-language subroutine from the USR function.

It might be more precise to say that Level II BASIC allows the assignment of just one USR-linked operation at any given time. There is nothing to prevent you from specifying different starting points as the program progresses, thus achieving the effect of accessing any number of machine-language entry points you choose.

Table 6-2 is the machine-language portion of this counting program. The entry points are at ZERO, NINE, UP, and DOWN. It is a rather tightly structured program that shares two other routines with each of the four entry points: NEXT and DOIT.

Referring to the machine/assembly program in Table 6-2, the NEXT routine saves the current count from the accumulator in memory location 31535, then does a jump to routine DOIT. DOIT converts the count to an ASCII character code, prints the result in the screen upper left-hand corner, and returns operations to BASIC.

NEXT and DOIT are accessed from all four of the program's main entry points: ZERO, NINE, UP, and DOWN. ZERO sets the accumulator to 0, NINE sets it to 9, UP either increments the accumulator or resets it to 0 after showing a 9, and DOWN either decrements the accumulator or resets it to 9 after showing a 0.

Enter the machine-language program at ZERO, and you will see a 0 printed on the screen. Enter at NINE, and you will see a 9. Enter at UP or DOWN, and you will see the character increment or decrement within the counting range of 0 through 9.

The BASIC portion of this program must do two things: it must enter the machine-language portion of the program and control the selection of the entry point. The most important feature, as far as the present discussion is concerned, is the adjustment of the entry point just prior to executing a USR function. Here is the BASIC program:

```
10    FOR I=0 TO 47:READ D:POKE 31488+I,D:NEXT I
20    DATA 62,0,195,7,123
22    DATA 62,9,50,47,123,195,37,123
24    DATA 58,47,123,254,9,210,0,123,60,195,7,123
26    DATA 58,47,123,254,0,202,5,123,61,195,7,123
28    DATA 33,0,60,58,47,123,198,48,119,201,48
100   RL=16526:RH=16527
110   CLS
120   IF PEEK(14463)=0 THEN 120
130   C$=INKEY$
140   IF C$<>"" THEN R$=C$
150   IF R$="Z" THEN L=0
160   IF R$="N" THEN L=5
170   IF R$="U" THEN L=13
180   IF R$="D" THEN L=25
190   IF NOT(R$="Z" OR R$="N" OR R$="U" OR R$="D") THEN 120
200   POKE RL,L:POKE RH,123
210   X=USR(X)
220   FOR T=0 TO 10:NEXT T
230   GOTO 120
```

Table 6-2. Machine-Language Program for the Controlled Counter Routine

Address	Op Code				Mnemonic		Comment
123 0	62	0		ZERO:	LD A,0		;ZERO THE ACCUMULATOR
123 2	195	7	123		JP NEXT		;JUMP TO DO NEXT
123 5	62	9		NINE:	LD A,9D		;LOAD 9 IN THE ACCUMULATOR
123 7	50	47	123	NEXT:	LD (COUNT),A		;LOAD ACC. TO COUNT
123 10	195	37	123		JP DOIT		;JUMP TO DOIT
123 13	58	47	123	UP:	LD A,(COUNT)		;COUNT TO ACCUMULATOR
123 16	254	9			CP 9D		;MAXIMUM COUNT?
123 18	201	0	123		JP NC ZERO		;IF SO, JUMP TO ZERO
123 21	60				INC A		;INCREMENT ACCUMULATOR
123 22	195	7	123		JP NEXT		;JUMP TO NEXT
123 25	58	47	123	DOWN:	LD A,(COUNT)		;FETCH CURRENT COUNT
123 28	254	0			CP 0		;MINIMUM COUNT?
123 30	202	5	123		JP Z NINE		;IF SO, JUMP TO NINE
123 33	61				DEC A		;ELSE DECREMENT ACCUMULATOR
123 34	195	7	123		JP NEXT		;JUMP TO NEXT
123 37	33	0	60	DOIT:	LD HL,VIDEO		;POINT TO START OF VIDEO
123 40	58	47	123		LD A,(COUNT)		;FETCH CURRENT COUNT
123 43	198	48			ADD A,48D		;CONVERT TO ASCII
123 45	119				LD (HL),A		;PRINT CHARACTER
123 46	201				RET		;RETURN TO BASIC

106

Lines 10 through 28 make up the machine-language loader. The procedure is identical with the one described in Chapter 5, with line 10 doing the actual loading operation and the DATA in lines 20 through 28 carrying the instruction bytes that are justified in Table 6-2.

So the loading of the machine-language portion of the program is completed at line 28.

Line 100 points to the USR entry-point registers. Those points, here assigned variable names RL and RH, are the same ones used for all USR-linked programs. Note, however, that the address they are to specify is not indicated—not yet, anyway.

Lines 120 through 140 make up a key-depression sensing operation: one that responds as long as a key is being depressed. Recall the details from Chapter 3. Whenever a key is being depressed, its string value is assigned to variable R$ at line 140.

Lines 150 through 180 decode four different key depressions, assigning some numerical values to variable L. As long as the Z key is being depressed, for instance, variable L takes on the value of zero.

Those values of L represent the lsb of the entry-point address for the machine-language subroutines; and they are assigned to the USR's entry-point register at line 200. So if you are depressing the Z key, line 200 performs this operation for you: POKE 16526,0:POKE 16527,123. This is precisely the set of operations required for starting the USR-called machine-language routine at address 31488—the entry point for presetting the counter to zero. Depressing the *N, U,* or *D* keys set up things in the same way, pointing to the entry points for NINE, UP counting, and DOWN counting, respectively.

It is not only important to set up the proper entry points to be assigned at line 200, but in a program of this sort it is equally important to eliminate key depressions that will provide other, unwanted values for L. You certainly do not want to specify some undetermined entry points, and that is the purpose of line 190.

Without line 190, you could depress any other key and end up specifying an entry point having an lsb of some undetermined value; and that could be disastrous, sending the program to some strange point in the system and, most likely, crashing the whole program out of existence.

IMPORTANT

BASIC programs that call multiple entry points in a machine-language program must be structured in such a way that unwanted entry points cannot be specified.

Line 210 calls the specified machine-language routine. When the routine is completed, line 220 does a short time delay. The delay simply makes it easier for you to watch the counting operation. Line 230 returns operations to the key-entry point at line 120.

Summarizing the main points of this discussion:

1. Write a machine-language program, keeping close track of the addresses of all possible entry points.
2. Write a BASIC program that:
    a. Loads the machine-language portion.
    b. Controls the entry-point addresses before doing the USR function.
    c. Eliminates the possibility of specifying undetermined machine-language entry points.

Once this is done, you can enter the machine-language portion of the program at any desired point, creating the effect of having a system that can call any number of entry points or machine-language subroutines.

DELETING THE MACHINE-LANGUAGE LOADER

Through all of the BASIC/machine-language programs presented thus far, the machine-language portion is loaded from BASIC (via DATA lists). Once the machine language is loaded, the loader line and DATA lists perform no useful function—all subsequent operations at the BASIC level involve doing some controls and implementing the USR function to call the machine-language subroutines that are stored in protected memory space.

Once the machine-language portion of the program is loaded from BASIC, the lines of the BASIC program devoted to that process can be deleted. In the example offered in the previous section of this chapter, for example, you can do a RUN to get it loaded; and once it begins running, you can do a BREAK, and then DELETE 10-28. That DELETE command will eliminate the loading portion of the BASIC program, leaving the operational part intact. And as long as the machine-language program still resides in its place in protected memory, the program can be run at your heart's content.

It is a good idea to retain the loading portion of a BASIC/machine-language program until you have a chance to test and debug it. But once you are confident it is running as it is supposed to run—and the machine-language portion is loaded into protected memory space—you can wipe out the loading portion of the BASIC program without altering the operation of the program in any way.

Suppose that you have worked out the program presented in the previous example. It is working to your satisfaction, but you'd like to tidy up the matter by deleting the loading portion. RUN the full program one more time, just to make sure the machine-language program is, indeed, properly loaded into protected memory, then do a BREAK to interrupt the program at the BASIC level.

Next, CSAVE the entire program on cassette tape (or disk), and then DELETE 10-28. A LIST will show that the loading part of the program is gone; but when you do a RUN you will find the program running just as well as it did before. (The idea of saving the program on tape before deleting the loader makes it possible for you to enter the entire program—including the machine-language loader—at any later time.)

Doing those BREAKs and DELETEs as described here is rather inelegant, however. An elegant way to get rid of the loader at the BASIC level is to write an appropriate DELETE statement right into the BASIC program. Write in a line that will delete the machine-language loader immediately after that loading operation is done.

In the previous example you can insert a new line:

30 DELETE 10-30

Insert that statement into the program, and it will delete the loader and line 30 as well, after the loading operation is done. Try it.

Get the loader back into your system. (Hopefully, you have saved it on tape or disk as suggested earlier; otherwise you will have to type in the loading line and DATA lines again.) Then insert the suggested DELETE 10-30 at line 30.

Save on tape or disk, then do a RUN. After a short delay, caused by the loading operation, the system will return a READY? and, indeed, the program is ready to run. From that point on, the loader will be missing from the BASIC program, but the whole thing does its intended job quite nicely.

In fact, you can do a NEW, and the machine-language portion of the program will be unaffected. It will still be residing there in protected memory space, and you can write another BASIC program that calls it.

DELETEing the machine-language loader, either manually from the keyboard or automatically by a built-in DELETE statement, creates a much neater BASIC program. But there are certainly some more compelling reasons for doing the DELETE.

One good reason for DELETEing the machine-language loader is to make more room in the BASIC text memory for elaborate BASIC operations. This is especially desirable in cases where the machine-language portion of the program is a rather extensive one as well. Why bother keeping all those DATA lists in BASIC memory after they have performed their intended task?

Another reason for getting rid of the BASIC-level, machine-language loader is that some machine-language programs are intended to manipulate any kind of BASIC program you might want to enter. A line-renumbering utility, for example, can be loaded as a machine-language subroutine from BASIC. The program you want to renumber, however, will be an entirely different one. So the idea is to write a machine-language loader in BASIC, do the loading operation, and then completely DELETE the BASIC portion of the program. After that, any USR-oriented set of operations will call up the subroutine for you, presumably doing things such as renumbering the resident BASIC program.

Finally, the ability to DELETE BASIC-level, machine-language loaders makes it possible to create some rather elaborate machine-language programs in a bottom-up fashion. Machine-language routines can be loaded and tested piecemeal, moved around in the protected memory at will, and merged with other machine-language routines. This feature is the subject of the next section in this chapter.

BUILDING MACHINE-LANGUAGE PROGRAMS FROM THE BOTTOM UP

For a beginner, writing machine-language programs can be a difficult and emotionally trying task. It takes a whole lot of experience to feel at ease with this sort of programming, and anyone not feeling at ease ought to use as many programming aids as possible.

The idea of writing USR-called, decimal-oriented programs can be of some help for beginners. And one way to take advantage of USR-called machine-language programming is to write and test basic elements of the routines in a piecemeal fashion, working on one element until it is working and then moving to another element. Once the elements are all entered and tested, they can be strung together to make up one large program—a machine-language program that might appear far too imposing to tackle in one shot.

The following operations demonstrate this particular approach to building a machine-language program. The general idea is to compose a USR-called subroutine that draws a large rectangle on the crt screen. The procedure will be to write, enter, and test the drawing operations for the four sides separately, and then assemble things to come up with one machine-language program for doing the job.

Drawing the Top of the Rectangle

Here is a machine-language and BASIC program for drawing a white line across the top of the screen:

```
123 0      33 0 60     BORDER:   LD HL,15360D    ;POINT TO START
123 3      62 63                 LD A,63D        ;SET END
```

```
123  5   189          TOP:    CP L            ;AT END?
123  6   202 20 123           JP Z,NEXT1      ;JUMP IF SO
123  9   54 131               LD (HL),131D    ;ELSE DRAW LINE
123 11   44                   INC L           ;SET NEXT SPOT
123 12   195 5 123            JP TOP          ;DO MORE DRAWING
123 20   201          NEXT1:  RET             ;RETURN TO BASIC

  0  REM ** BORDER-DRAWING DEMO **
 10  DATA 33,0,60,62,63,189,202,20,123,54,131,44,195,5,123
 50  REM ** LOADER FOR TOP **
 55  FOR I=0 TO 14:READ D:POKE 31488+I,D:NEXT I
 57  POKE 31508,201
100  REM ** CALLING PROGRAM **
110  POKE 16526,0:POKE 16527,123
120  CLS
130  X=USR(X)
140  GOTO 140
```

Referring to the machine-language portion of the program, it begins by loading the lowest video memory address into the HL register pair. This points to the upper left-hand corner of the screen, the starting point of the line marking the top of the rectangular figure to be drawn.

Decimal 63, marking the endpoint of the TOP line, is loaded into the accumulator, and then the content of the L register is compared with that number. If the numbers do not match, presumably because the content of L is less than that of the accumulator (and the drawing operation isn't done), graphic code 131 is drawn on the screen at the point indicated by the HL pair. Then the L register is incremented one space, and control returns to the TOP routine.

The routine continues drawing graphic 131 until the L register is incremented to 63. At that point the TOP-line drawing is done, and control is sent to memory location 31508 (or 123 30 as expressed as a 2-byte decimal address).

That NEXT1 location contains a RETurn instruction, but only temporarily. When it is time to add a routine to draw the bottom of the rectangular figure, it will begin at that point. For testing purposes, however, this address returns control to the BASIC calling program.

Note that there are some unused bytes between the last instruction in the TOP routine and the beginning of NEXT1. It is generally considered good programming procedure to allow a few unused bytes between the various elements of a machine-language program. The same idea applies to designating line numbers for BASIC programs. In either case the rationale is to allow some room for expanding the routine without having to adjust addresses (or line numbers in BASIC) from that point through the end of the program.

So it is advisable to leave some unused memory locations in a machine-language program. Just be sure, however, to use an appropriate JUMP instruction to pass over those blank spaces. That's done in this case with the JP Z, NEXT1 instruction.

The BASIC part of the program shows the object codes as a DATA line. Those codes are entered into protected memory space by line 55. Note that the loading begins at address 31488 (or 123 0 in a 2-byte decimal format).

Line 57 is necessary in order to answer the jump-over-blank-places operation. You could add a bunch of zeros to the DATA list, and adjust the FOR. . .NEXT statement in line 55 accordingly. But that would place an unnecessary burden on the DATA list. The statement in line 57 is thus added separately.

Lines 100 through 140 execute the program. If all is going well to this point, doing a RUN will load the machine-language segment and execute it, drawing a clean line across the top of the screen. Because of the tight loop built into line 140, you have to strike the BREAK key to get something else going.

Anything wrong with your program will show up right away. If the program blows up, it is short enough to enter again from scratch —after, of course, you work out the bug that caused the blowup. Or you can save the program on tape *before* doing a RUN. That way you can reload it in a few moments, make the fix and give it another try—all in a fairly short period.

Drawing the Bottom of the Rectangle

After entering and debugging the first element of the program, it is possible to move to the second phase without disturbing the good stuff that is already in place. Here are the machine-language and BASIC routines for drawing the bottom portion of the rectangle:

```
123 20    33 192 63    NEXT1:    LD HL,16320D     ;POINT TO START
123 23    62 255                 LD A,255D        ;SET END
123 25    189          BOT:      CP L             ;AT END?
123 26    202 40 123             JP Z,NEXT 2      ;IF SO, GET OUT
123 29    54 176                 LD (HL),176D     ;ELSE DRAW LINE
123 31    44                     INC L            ;SET NEXT SPOT
123 32    195 25 123             JP BOT           ;DO MORE DRAWING
123 40    201          NEXT2:    RET              ;RETURN TO BASIC
```

```
  0  REM ** BORDER-DRAWING DEMO **
 10  DATA 33,0,60,62,63,189,202,20,123,54,131,44,195,5,123
 12  DATA 33,192,63,62,255,189,202,40,123,54,176,44,195,25,123
 50  REM ** LOADER FOR TOP **
 55  FOR I=0 TO 14:READ D:POKE 31488+I,D:NEXT I
 60  REM ** LOADER FOR BOTTOM **
 65  FOR I=0 TO 14:READ D:POKE 31508+I,D:NEXT I
 67  POKE 31528,201
100  REM ** CALLING PROGRAM **
```

```
110  POKE 16526,20:POKE 16527,123
120  CLS
130  X=USR(X)
140  GOTO 140
```

The machine-language portion of the bottom-line-drawing routine isn't much different, in principle, from the TOP routine already entered and tested. The only difference here is the position of the line and, of course, the addresses of the machine-language programming.

The BASIC part of the program still contains elements of the TOP-drawing routine, but the DATA line (line 12) is added for the bottom line. Line 57 has been deleted from the program, because the end of TOP now calls the beginning of BOT—or at least it will when the two routines are merged later on.

At any rate the BOT routine begins at address 31508, as indicated by its loader in line 65. A RETurn is inserted at 31528, making it possible to get out of the routine at the point the next element of the program will begin.

Note in line 110 that the starting point of the USR-called routine is different. Instead of starting at address 31488, it begins at 31508. That means the USR function calls the new BOT routine instead of the TOP routine.

Run the program as shown here and you should see a white line across the bottom of the screen.

Merging the Two Elements of the Routine

The following BASIC program shows how it is possible to merge the TOP and BOT routines into one. The BASIC program has been cleaned up a bit, and the USR-called starting point is set back to the beginning of the machine-language program, to address 31488. So the two sections of the machine-language program automatically run in succession, responding to a single USR function in BASIC.

```
  0  REM ** BORDER-DRAWING DEMO **
 10  DATA 33,0,60,62,63,189,202,20,123,54,131,44,195,5,123
 12  DATA 33,192,63,62,255,189,202,40,123,54,176,44,195,25,123
 50  REM ** LOADER FOR TOP AND BOTTOM **
 52  FOR I=0 TO 14:READ D:POKE 31488+I,D:NEXT I
 54  FOR I=0 TO 14:READ D:POKE 31508+I,D:NEXT I
 56  POKE 31528,201
100  REM ** CALLING PROGRAM **
110  POKE 16526,0:POKE 16527,123
120  CLS
130  X=USR(X)
140  GOTO 140
```

In a sense this is not a very efficient program scheme. Leaving some unused memory space between the TOP and BOT routines, for example, makes it necessary to use two different loading operations in the BASIC program. But writing efficient or elegant programs is not the point of the present discussion. The main idea is to demonstrate how USR-called programs can be composed by sections, then worked together to make up a single program scheme.

Now it is time to add in some more programming to draw the two sides of the rectangle.

Drawing the Sides and Merging Again

Here is the programming for drawing the left side of the rectangle. The machine-language portion deals only with the left-side drawing operation, but the BASIC part of the matter includes the TOP and BOT programming already developed. You will note, however, that the USR function calls only the left-drawing part of the machine-language programming; this lets you concentrate on the new problems that might arise.

```
123 40    30 0 60       NEXT2:    LD HL,15360D      ;POINT TO TOP
123 43    54 191        LEFT:     LD (HL),191D      ;DRAW SEGMENT
123 45    125                     LD A,L            ;FETCH LSB
123 46    198 64                  ADD A,64D         ;ADD 64
123 48    218 55 123              JP C,MORE1        ;JUMP IF DONE
123 51    111                     LD L,A            ;SAVE NEW LSB
123 52    195 43 123              JP LEFT           ;DO AGAIN
123 55    124           MORE1:    LD A,H            ;FETCH MSB
123 56    254 63                  CP 63D            ;DONE?
123 58    202 70 123              JP Z NEXT3        ;IF SO, GET OUT
123 61    36                      INC H             ;SET NEW MSB
123 62    46 0                    LD L,0            ;RESTART LSB
123 64    195 43 123              JP LEFT           ;DO ALL OVER AGAIN
```

```
  0  REM ** BORDER-DRAWING DEMO **
 10  DATA 33,0,60,62,63,189,202,20,123,54,131,44,195,5,123
 12  DATA 33,192,63,62,255,189,202,40,123,54,176,44,195,25,123
 14  DATA 33,0,60,54,191,125,198,64,218,55,123,111,195,43,123,124,254,63,202,70,
     123,36,46,0,195,43,123
 50  REM ** LOADER FOR TOP AND BOTTOM **
 52  FOR I=0 TO 14:READ D:POKE 31488+I,D:NEXT I
 54  FOR I=0 TO 14:READ D:POKE 31508+I,D:NEXT I
 60  REM ** LOADER FOR LEFT **
 65  FOR I=0 TO 26:READ D:POKE 31528+I,D:NEXT I
 67  POKE 31558,201
100  REM ** CALLING PROGRAM **
110  POKE 16526,40:POKE 16527,123
120  CLS
130  X=USR(X)
140  GOTO 140
```

DATA line 14 in the BASIC programming contains the machine-code instructions, and they are loaded by the statements in line 65. Line 67 inserts a RETurn into the machine-language program, forcing the scheme to return to BASIC after drawing the left-side line on the screen. If there are any problems with the program, they will certainly show up at this point, giving you a chance to remedy the trouble without affecting the other parts of the program—the parts you have presumably tested before.

Assuming that the left-line drawing operation works, the next step is to add in the right-line drawing sequence.

123 70	33 63 60	NEXT3:	LD HL,15423D	;POINT TO TOP
123 73	54 191	RIGHT:	LD (HL),191	;DRAW SEGMENT
123 75	125		LD A,L	;FETCH LSB
123 76	198 64		ADD A,64D	;ADD 64 TO LSB
123 78	218 85 123		JP C,MORE2	;JUMP IF DONE
123 81	111		LD L,A	;SAVE NEW LSB
123 82	195 73 123		JP RIGHT	;DO AGAIN
123 85	124	MORE2:	LD A,H	;FETCH MSB
123 86	254 63		CP 63D	;DONE?
123 88	202 100 123		JP Z NEXT4	;IF SO, GET OUT
123 91	36		INC H	;SET NEW MSB
123 92	46 63		LD L,63D	;RESTART LSB
123 94	195 73 123		JP RIGHT	;DO ALL OVER AGAIN

```
0   REM ** BORDER-DRAWING DEMO **
10  DATA 33,0,60,62,63,189,202,20,123,54,131,44,195,5,123
12  DATA 33,192,63,62,255,189,202,40,123,54,176,44,195,25,123
14  DATA 33,0,60,54,191,125,198,64,218,55,123,111,195,43,123,124,254,63,202,70,
    123,36,46,0,195,43,123
16  DATA 33,63,60,54,191,125,198,64,218,85,123,111,195,73,123,124,254,63,202,100,
    123,36,46,63,195,73,123
50  REM ** LOADER FOR TOP AND BOTTOM **
52  FOR I=0 TO 14:READ D:POKE 31488+I,D:NEXT I
54  FOR I=0 TO 14:READ D:POKE 31508+I,D:NEXT I
60  REM ** LOADER FOR LEFT **
65  FOR I=0 TO 26:READ D:POKE 31528+I,D:NEXT I
70  REM ** LOADER FOR RIGHT **
75  FOR I=0 TO 26:READ D:POKE 31558+I,D:NEXT I
77  POKE 31588,201
100 REM ** CALLING PROGRAM **
110 POKE 16526,70:POKE 16527,123
120 CLS
130 X=USR(X)
140 GOTO 140
```

The BASIC part of the program is now arranged to call the new section of the machine-language program—the part that is supposed to draw the right-side line on the rectangle. Its function is quite similar to the left-side drawing operation; only the addresses are different.

Running that BASIC program should draw the right-side line for you. And if it works, you are ready to tidy up the BASIC portion of the program. The BASIC program shown next is cleaned up so that it loads the machine-language programming as efficiently as possible, given the fact that some blank spaces exist in the memory between each of the basic sections. Line 110 sets the entry point of the USR function to the very beginning of the machine-language program. So when you run the program it will draw the complete rectangle for you. As usual, you have to strike the BREAK key to get out of the loop created by the BASIC statement in line 140.

```
0    REM ** BORDER-DRAWING DEMO **
10   DATA 33,0,60,62,63,189,202,20,123,54,131,44,195,5,123
12   DATA 33,192,63,62,255,189,202,40,123,54,176,44,195,25,123
14   DATA 33,0,60,54,191,125,198,64,218,55,123,111,195,43,123,124,254,63,202,70,
     123,36,46,0,195,43,123
16   DATA 33,63,60,54,191,125,198,64,218,85,123,111,195,73,123,124,254,63,202,100,
     123,36,46,63,195,73,123
50   REM ** LOADERS **
52   FOR I=0 TO 14:READ D:POKE 31488+I,D:NEXT I
54   FOR I=0 TO 14:READ D:POKE 31508+I,D:NEXT I
56   FOR I=0 TO 26:READ D:POKE 31528+I,D:NEXT I
58   FOR I=0 TO 26:READ D:POKE 31558+I,D:NEXT I
60   POKE 31588,201
100  REM ** CALLING PROGRAM **
110  POKE 16526,0:POKE 16527,123
120  CLS
130  X=USR(X)
140  GOTO 140
```

If this whole rectangle-drawing routine is to be just one element in a larger program, you can insert a DELETE 0-65 at line 65 in the BASIC program. On running the program, then, the BASIC section will first load the machine-language programming, then delete all the DATA lines and loading statements. You can always call the rectangle-drawing routine at a later time by doing the BASIC sequence in lines 100 through 140.

Some Comments About Bottom-Up Programming

The expression *bottom-up programming* refers to a programming technique whereby the program is developed by one section at a time. Each section, or *module,* is capable of standing alone, and it is thoroughly debugged before the programmer goes on to the matter of developing another module. And when all the modules have been thus written and debugged, they are tied together to make up one big program. Chances are good the final version will work rather well, because the separate modules have been tested beforehand. This was the technique used for building up the rectangle-drawing routine.

While this bottom-up technique has the advantage of letting the programmer work with the program in a piecemeal fashion, dividing the job into a number of manageable parts, it does have its disadvantages. The most common disadvantage is that the final program is inefficient in terms of the amount of memory it uses. It is possible, for instance, to write the rectangle-drawing program using a whole lot less memory space.

An alternative to bottom-up programming is a technique known as *top-down programming*. In this case the entire program is developed from beginning to end. The procedure calls for some careful planning ahead of time and a form of thinking that is outside the scope of our present discussion. The result, though, is a program that is generally shorter than a version developed by a bottom-up procedure.

But there is something else you can do at this point to tighten up the programming. Suppose you have developed a USR-called machine-language program, using the bottom-up, module-oriented technique used in the previous example—the one that draws a rectangle on the screen. You have the program working and you are satisfied with the operation of the thing.

In the process of working out the program you have learned some things about getting the job done, perhaps learning some of those things by making some mistakes. That being the case, you are in a good position to rewrite the program in a more efficient manner.

Looking over that program, you should be able to see that the top and bottom drawing sections of the machine-language listings are quite similar. The same happens to be true for the left and right drawing parts of the program. If nothing else, you should be able to condense the program to at least two basic sections, instead of four.

That is just an example of what you can do with programs developed by the bottom-up process. Chances are good that any program developed in this fashion can be tightened up if you apply a bit of thought to the matter.

The basic idea here is that you can take advantage of what you've done while perfecting the bottom-up procedure, thus avoiding a lot of hard-to-find mistakes in a more elegant revision.

Tightening Up the Program

Here is a condensed version of the border-drawing program. The machine-language portion is shown in Table 6-3. It uses only 65 bytes of protected memory space, beginning at address 31488. The earlier version also started at that address, but it ate up 100 bytes of memory.

The revised BASIC portion of the scheme loads this new machine-language program, then executes it from lines 100 through 140.

Load the BASIC program, CSAVE it, and then give it a try. If there are any errors in the scheme, you will have a recorded copy to

Table 6-3. Machine-Language Program for BORDER-DRAWING DEMO, V.2

Address	Op Code			Label	Mnemonic	Comment
123 0	33	0	60	BORDER:	LD HL,15360D	;POINT TO TOP CORNER
123 3	62	63			LD A,63D	;SET ENDPOINT
123 5	6	131			LD B,131D	;SET CHARACTER
123 7	205	37	123		CALL DRAW1	;DRAW TOP
123 10	33	192	63		LD HL,16320D	;POINT TO BOTTOM CORNER
123 13	62	255			LD A,255D	;SET ENDPOINT
123 15	6	176			LD B,176D	;SET CHARACTER
123 17	205	37	123		CALL DRAW1	;DRAW BOTTOM
123 20	33	0	60		LD HL,15360D	;POINT TO TOP CORNER
123 23	6	0			LD B,0	;SET RESET POINT
123 25	205	44	123		CALL DRAW2	;DRAW RIGHT SIDE
123 28	33	63	60		LD HL,15423D	;POINT TO TOP RIGHT
123 31	6	63			LD B,63D	;SET RESET POINT
123 33	205	44	123		CALL DRAW2	;DRAW LEFT SIDE
123 36	201				RET	;RETURN TO BASIC
123 37	189			DRAW1:	CP L	;ENDPOINT?
123 38	200				RET Z	;RETURN IF SO
123 39	112				LD (HL),B	;ELSE DRAW SEGMENT
123 40	44				INC L	;SET NEW POINT
123 41	195	37	123		JP DRAW1	;DRAW AGAIN
123 44	54	191		DRAW2:	LD (HL),191D	;DRAW CHARACTER
123 46	125				LD A,L	;FETCH LSB OF PLACE
123 47	198	64			ADD A,64D	;SET NEW PLACE
123 49	218	56	123		JP C,MORE	;JUMP IF DONE
123 52	111				LD L,A	;ELSE SAVE NEW PLACE
123 53	195	44	123		JP DRAW2	;AND DRAW AGAIN
123 56	124			MORE:	LD A,H	;FETCH MSB OF PLACE
123 57	254	63			CP 63D	;DONE?
123 59	200				RET Z	;RETURN IF SO
123 60	36				INC H	;ELSE GET NEW PLACE
123 61	104				LD L,B	;RESET STARTING POINT
					JP DRAW2	;AND DRAW AGAIN

work with. And even if there aren't any errors, you will have a copy that is ready to go anytime you need it.

```
0   REM ** BORDER-DRAWING DEMO, V.2 **
10  DATA 33,0,60,62,63,6,131,205,37,123,33,192,63,62,255,6,176,205,37,123
12  DATA 33,0,60,6,0,205,44,123,33,63,60,6,63,205,44,123,201
14  DATA 189,200,112,44,195,37,123
16  DATA 54,191,125,198,64,218,56,123,111,195,44,123
18  DATA 124,254,63,200,36,104,195,44,123
50  REM ** LOADER **
60  FOR I=0 TO 64:READ D:POKE 31488+I,D:NEXT I
100 REM ** CALL BORDER **
110 POKE 16526,0:POKE 16527,123
120 CLS
130 X=USR(X)
140 GOTO 140
```

SUMMARY

The main point of this section is to illustrate how it is possible to use BASIC/machine-language programming to develop useful, USR-called subroutines. The discussion uses one specific example, drawing a rectangular figure, but the general procedures are applicable to any sort of routine.

So you can grasp the general ideas without thinking only in terms of a rectangle-drawing program, here are the basic points:

1. Divide the machine-language task into small elements that are each capable of doing something meaningful.
2. Compose a machine-language program for one of those elements.
3. Compose a BASIC program that both loads the machine-language program and executes it in a meaningful way.
4. Debug that portion of the scheme, getting it to work as you want it to work.
5. Repeat Steps 2 through 4 until all the smaller elements of the machine-language program have been tested.
6. Write a BASIC program that loads all the smaller elements of the machine-language program and executes them in some meaningful way.
7. Work out any bugs and, if possible, tighten up the BASIC portion of the program.
8. If you wish, insert a BASIC line that will DELETE the loader-related lines of the BASIC program, leaving just the USR-function part.
9. If you wish, use the working machine-language program to rewrite a tighter, more elegant version of it. Revise the BASIC portion accordingly.

If you save everything on cassette tape or disk as you go along, a blowup won't cost you a whole lot of time and effort. In the case of very complex machine-language programs you can divide the task into several main sections, and then divide those sections into even smaller subsections. You can build and test the subsections, one at a time, and then begin fitting them into the larger scheme.

The idea is to take advantage of the fact that BASIC-loaded, USR-called subroutines can be saved on tape, disk, or a line printer rather easily. And since the BASIC part of the program coordinates much of the machine-language programming, it is relatively easy to change things around as you go along.

Why not dream up some machine-language tasks of your own, then test your understanding of this procedure? If you have done little or no machine-language programming before, this is the most suitable approach for you. It lets you get around some of the more tedious machine-language tasks, passing them to a more familiar BASIC format.

CHAPTER 7

Hexadecimal Programming With T-BUG

All of the discussions and demonstrations in Chapters 2 through 6 deal with the TRS-80 system in a decimal format. Chapters 2, 3, and 4 consider some BASIC operations with the video memory, keyboard "memory," and user's memory—all in the decimal-oriented TRS-80 BASIC. Chapters 5 and 6 blend BASIC and some machine language, but since the machine-language programs are entered from BASIC in those two chapters, the whole business is decimal oriented.

You probably are aware, however, that the decimal number system is not the simplest system for writing machine-language programs, and that fact made the BASIC-loaded programs in Chapters 5 and 6 a bit tedious to write. All those conversions and 2-byte decimal numbers are quite troublesome. The hexadecimal number system is far more compatible with machine-language programming.

Unfortunately, the TRS-80 keyboard and display mechanisms are not set up to handle hexadecimal notation directly; they are set up for decimal-oriented BASIC programming. For this reason some other software mechanism has to be added to provide a hexadecimal i/o format. One such mechanism is Radio Shack's T-BUG monitor and debugging tool—the subject of this chapter.

T-BUG is available from Radio Shack (catalog No. 26-2001) at a reasonable price. One side of the T-BUG cassette tape loads for Level I machines, and the other loads it for Level II versions. Both work with any system of 4K or more. The T-BUG discussions in this book, however, assume that you are using a Level II system with 16K of RAM or more.

THE T-BUG ENVIRONMENT

The T-BUG monitor/debugging tool is, itself, a machine-language program. It is loaded into the TRS-80 via the SYSTEM command, and any memory space you have protected with MEMORY SIZE? is not relevant—T-BUG loads right through anything in its path.

Loading T-BUG From Its Tape

Set up the T-BUG tape for loading; then, from BASIC, type and ENTER the command SYSTEM. This will bring up the *? prompt symbols. Respond to them by typing and ENTERing the file name TBUG. The tape will load, showing the usual flashing asterisk near the upper right-hand corner of the screen.

When T-BUG is fully loaded, you will see the *? symbols again. Respond by typing and ENTERing the / (slash) symbol. This should bring up the prompt symbol for the T-BUG monitor: a pound sign.

T-BUG is thus ready to go. The useful work you can do from that point will be described shortly.

Going Between T-BUG and BASIC

T-BUG users often find it necessary to go from the T-BUG monitor to BASIC, or vice versa. Sometimes this is done on purpose; often it happens accidentally.

Going from T-BUG to BASIC can be useful at times. As you will see in Chapter 8 it is possible to write very limited BASIC programs for working the two in conjunction with one another. Other times a mistake in the machine-language program written through T-BUG will cause a "crash" that returns the system to BASIC (as indicated by the READY message and less-than prompt symbol).

There are two basic ways to get out of the resident T-BUG monitor and back to BASIC. One way is to depress the RESET push button on the back of the TRS-80 keyboard unit. Another way to accomplish the transfer is by answering the T-BUG prompt symbol by typing J0000 (it is not necessary to strike the ENTER key at the end of this entry).

In either case the system is returned to the BASIC monitor without disturbing the T-BUG programming in the least.

But once you get to BASIC from T-BUG you will probably want to get back to T-BUG again. To get from BASIC to T-BUG (assuming T-BUG is still resident from a previous tape-loading operation), simply type and ENTER the SYSTEM command, and then respond to the *? characters by typing and ENTERing /17312. That will bring up the T-BUG monitor's prompt symbol—a pound sign. Then you're back in business with T-BUG.

There are two circumstances, however, that prevent a return to T-BUG from BASIC. One is a catastrophic "blowup" of the program at the T-BUG level. Such a catastrophe generally loads the screen with a lot of meaningless characters and often ends up displaying the MEMORY SIZE? message. In such a case the T-BUG monitor, itself, is messed up, and trying to get back to it by doing a /17312 from the SYSTEM mode will not improve matters at all.

A second set of circumstances that will prevent a return from BASIC to T-BUG is one where you write some BASIC programs into the memory that is normally allocated for the T-BUG monitor. As described in Chapter 8 it is possible to write short BASIC programs of a certain nature without disturbing the T-BUG monitor, but you have to know what you are doing. Generally speaking, writing BASIC programs while the T-BUG monitor is loaded will mess up T-BUG; and doing a /17312 from SYSTEM will cause a "crash."

Naturally, turning the TRS-80 power switch off and on will kill the T-BUG monitor, too. But perhaps this should go without having to say it.

For the time being, at least, avoid going from T-BUG to BASIC and writing some BASIC programs. And if a T-BUG generated program should blow up and the system returns to BASIC, doing a /17312 from SYSTEM might get you back into T-BUG quite nicely. But if T-BUG doesn't come back or it begins doing strange things for you, you will have to load the T-BUG monitor from the tape again.

SUMMARY

To get from T-BUG to BASIC:
 a. Work the RESET push button
  or
 b. Answer the # prompt symbol with a J0000.

To get from BASIC to T-BUG:
 >SYSTEM   <do ENTER>
 *?/17312   <do ENTER>

Organization of the T-BUG Monitor

The T-BUG monitor occupies the user's memory space, between 4380H and 497FH (decimal 17280 through 18815). Comparing these figures with a Level II memory map, you will find T-BUG is resident some 50 bytes above the beginning of the space that is normally allocated for BASIC program text. Then it runs 15360

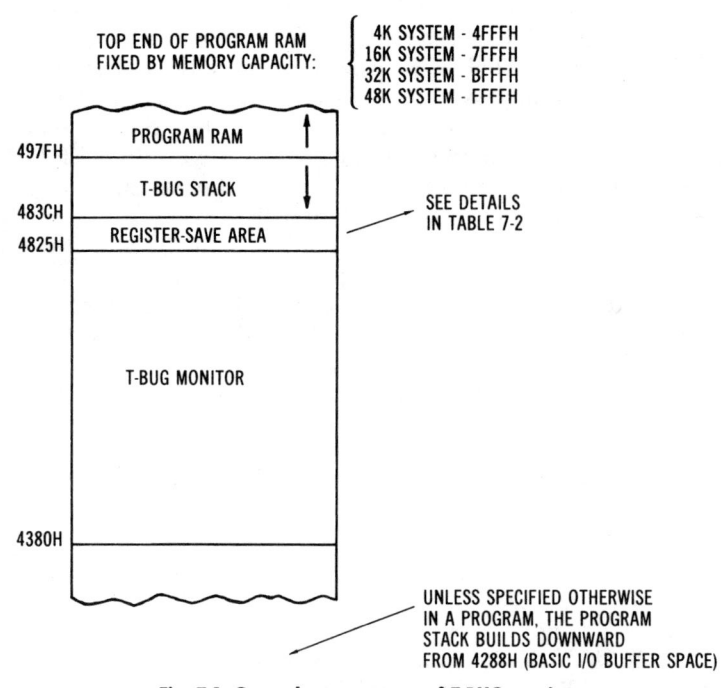

```
                TOP END OF PROGRAM RAM      ⎧ 4K SYSTEM - 4FFFH
                FIXED BY MEMORY CAPACITY:   ⎨ 16K SYSTEM - 7FFFH
                                            ⎪ 32K SYSTEM - BFFFH
                                            ⎩ 48K SYSTEM - FFFFH
         ┌──────────────────────────┐
         │     PROGRAM RAM        ↑ │
  497FH  ├──────────────────────────┤
         │     T-BUG STACK        ↓ │         SEE DETAILS
  483CH  ├──────────────────────────┤         IN TABLE 7-2
  4825H  │    REGISTER-SAVE AREA    │
         ├──────────────────────────┤
         │                          │
         │                          │
         │     T-BUG MONITOR        │
         │                          │
         │                          │
  4380H  ├──────────────────────────┤
         │                          │
         │                          │                UNLESS SPECIFIED OTHERWISE
         └──∿∿∿∿∿∿∿∿∿∿∿∿∿∿∿∿∿∿∿∿∿∿∿─┘                IN A PROGRAM, THE PROGRAM
                                                     STACK BUILDS DOWNWARD
                                                     FROM 4288H (BASIC I/O BUFFER SPACE)
```

Fig. 7-1. General memory map of T-BUG monitor.

bytes upward from there. See the T-BUG monitor's memory map in Fig. 7-1.

That entire memory space for T-BUG is not wholly occupied with the machine-language programming for it. Near the top of that space, locations 4825H through 483CH, is the so-called register-save area. These 18 addresses are used for saving the content of the Z-80's 16 working registers whenever a T-BUG operation does things calling for saving them on a temporary basis. The two additional addresses are not used, appearing at either end of the register-save area.

The memory space at the very top of the T-BUG's memory map is devoted to its own stack. When T-BUG is loaded into the TRS-80 it automatically sets the monitor's stack pointer to address 4980H. And when the stack is used during the running of the T-BUG monitor it builds downward toward the top end of the register-save area.

Incidentally, the T-BUG monitor stack and the SYSTEM stack are two entirely different things. The monitor stack, just described, is used exclusively by the monitor; you, the programmer, should not attempt to work with it directly.

The SYSTEM stack, on the other hand, is the one available to the programmer during the execution of a T-BUG generated, machine-language program. This is the one that builds downward when your program uses instructions such as nested CALLs, PUSHes, and POPs.

The T-BUG monitor automatically places the SYSTEM stack at 4288H—right smack in the TRS-80's i/o buffer for BASIC operations. This is one reason why you must be careful about trying to use BASIC and a SYSTEM-oriented machine language at the same time. Again, Chapter 8 will show how you can get out of the situation by relocating the SYSTEM stack: getting it out of the i/o-buffer space.

T-BUG OPERATIONS

Most introductory discussions of the T-BUG monitor describe the eight available commands as separate identities. Most T-BUG users, especially beginners, are far more interested in knowing how to do things than brief descriptions of the commands. So the following discussion tells how to do things with the T-BUG monitor, leaving basic command definitions to a summary on p. 140.

Examining Memory Locations

It is possible to examine the contents of all the TRS-80 memory locations from BASIC. Something such as PRINT PEEK (*address*) will do the job, where *address* is a decimal number within the system's memory map. The result is another decimal number that represents the 1-byte contents of that address.

You can do the same thing much easier, and in a hexadecimal format, from the T-BUG monitor. Just answer the # prompt symbol by striking the *M* key, followed by four hexadecimal characters representing the address location. The content of that address, in a hexadecimal format, will then appear to the right of the number you just entered. (You will not have to strike the ENTER key. The ENTER key is rarely needed for entering information in T-BUG.)

Suppose you want to examine the contents of memory location 0000H. Answer the # prompt symbol by striking keys M0000. Striking the *M* key puts the monitor into its Memory mode, and striking the zero key four times in succession specifies address 0000. Do that, and you will see this sort of display on the screen:

M 0000 F3

The machine has printed the pound sign, F3, and spaces. The main idea, however, is that the content of memory address 0000H is F3 (for whatever that might be worth to you).

Now strike the ENTER key, and the display will look like this:

```
# M 0000 F3
  0001 AF
```

The second line is showing address 0001H and its contents—AF. Strike the ENTER key several more times in succession, and the display grows in this fashion:

```
# M 0000 F3
  0001 AF
  0002 C3
  0003 74
  0004 06
  0005 C3
```

What you are doing here is examining the contents of successive memory locations, beginning with the one specified after striking the M key. The project can run indefinitely this way; if your hand holds up long enough, you can theoretically examine the entire ROM and RAM in your TRS-80.

If you want to skip to another place in memory and examine the contents from that point, you must first get out of the memory mode and back to the monitor. To get to the monitor, strike the X key, instead of the ENTER key. That will bring up the pound-sign prompt symbol again. Then strike the M key, followed by the four-digit hexadecimal address of the location you want to examine. Looking at the contents of successively higher locations is a simple matter of striking the ENTER key for each one.

Incidentally, you might notice that the backspace (left-arrow) key doesn't work as it does in BASIC. If you strike a wrong key while specifying an address for examining memory locations, striking the backspace key doesn't change anything. The only way to correct a typing error at this point is to strike the X key to return to the T-BUG's monitor mode, and then start over by striking the M key and, hopefully, the correct four-place hexadecimal address.

Here are a few notes that summarize the procedure for examining the contents of any memory location in the TRS-80:

1. Answering the # prompt symbol by striking the M key puts T-BUG into its *M*emory mode.
2. The *M*emory mode can be entered only from the monitor mode. To get to the monitor mode from any other command mode, including *M*emory, strike the X key.
3. To specify the starting address of a memory-examining sequence, strike the M key, followed by a 4-byte hexadecimal address:

    Maaaa

where the *a* terms represent the four address bytes or hexadecimal characters.
4. To view the contents of successive memory locations, strike the ENTER key for each one.
5. Escape from the Memory mode and return to the monitor mode at any time by striking the X key.
6. Correct address-entry errors by returning to the monitor mode (striking the X key) and starting over again.

Altering the Contents of RAM Locations

From BASIC it is possible to alter the contents of any RAM location by doing something such as POKE *address, data,* where *address* is the decimal-format address of the byte to be changed and *data* is the byte to be entered into that address. The *data* must also be in a decimal format.

In T-BUG the content of any RAM address can be changed from the Memory mode just described. Your thinking of this sort ought to be limited to address locations above those of the T-BUG monitor: from 4980H to the top of the RAM space for your system. Altering the contents of memory locations in the T-BUG monitor or below risks some program catastrophes.

At any rate, get the system into the T-BUG Memory mode by striking the M key and typing the address of the location to be altered. The system will respond as though you want to simply examine the contents of that location.

Instead of simply striking the ENTER key to view the contents of the next-higher address, strike two keys that specify the one byte of hexadecimal data you want to enter into that address. If you have thus typed some valid data, the system will print the new data to the right of the old data, and then automatically examine the contents of the next memory location for you.

Here is an example:

M 4A00 2E CD
4A01 FE

In this example the machine printed the pound sign to indicate the system was in the monitor mode. The user struck the M key to get into the Memory mode, then struck the 4A00 keys in succession to specify the starting address. The system then inserted the spaces and printed the current contents of address location 4A00. In this example the contents happen to be 2E, but you might see any two-character code when you try this for yourself.

At that point the display looked like this:

M 4A00 2E

But then the user struck the *CD* keys to change the contents of that address from 2E to CD. The system responded by inserting a space and the revised contents of that same memory location. After that the system automatically displayed the next-higher address and its current data. There is no need to strike the ENTER key after altering the contents of a memory location—the T-BUG does that for you.

Now, if you want to alter the contents of address 4A01, just strike the two keys representing the new contents. The system will print your new data to the right of the old (to the right of the FE in this case) and jump down to display the next address location and its current contents.

But if you want to leave the contents of address 4A01 unchanged, strike the ENTER key to get to the next address location.

This is how machine-language programs are written from T-BUG. They are written from the *M*emory mode, examining successive memory locations and altering them as necessary to build up the program you want.

The following is a short programming sequence that loads this set of Z-80 instructions:

```
        4A00  CD C9 01     CALL 01C9H    ;CALL CLS FUNCTION
        4A03  C3 03 4A     JP 4A03H      ;LOOP TO SELF

# M 4A00  01 CD
4A02 FF    C9
4A03 5E    01
4A04 88    C3
4A05 1A    03
4A06 09    4A
4A01 21
```

Answering the # prompt symbol with M4A00 put the system into the *M*emory mode, beginning at address 4A00H. The current content was 01, but I wanted it to be CD, the first instruction in the program. So I struck the *CD* keys, and the system automatically displayed the contents of address 4A01—a 21. I wanted a C9 in that location, so I struck those keys. I continued the process until the last instruction (4A) had been entered into address location 4A05. That completed the programming phase of the operation. It marked the end of my 6-byte program.

To see whether or not that program has been entered as expected, you can examine the six locations again from the *M*emory mode. But in order to get back to address 4A00 to do that sort of job, you must first exit the ongoing scheme by striking the *X* key, then answering the # prompt with an *M* and address 4A00. By doing that and striking the ENTER key several times in succession, the display will look like this:

```
# M 4A00 CD
  4A01 C9
  4A02 01
  4A03 C3
  4A04 03
  4A05 4A
```

Sure enough, this Memory-examining operation confirms that the 6-byte, machine-language program has been entered in addresses 4A00 through 4A05.

In summary, to write a machine-language program from T-BUG:

1. Get into the Memory mode by striking the M key, followed by the address (in hexadecimal) of the starting point of your program.
2. Respond to the machine's printing of the address and its contents by striking the two keys representing the data you want to enter at that address.
3. If you make a mistake in specifying the data, strike the X key to get out of the current Memory mode, then reenter the Memory mode by striking the M key and specifying the address where the mistake occurred. Alter the data accordingly.

Executing Programs From T-BUG

One of the most attractive features of T-BUG is that you can actually run the programs you write with it. The more sophisticated Editor/Assembler (described in later chapters) cannot do that. You can thus compose a machine-language program as described in the previous section and execute it on the spot, testing for any possible errors. And if you handle the execution properly, T-BUG will still be resident in your system, and you can go to the Memory mode to correct any errors you discover.

But just as a person ought to learn how to stop a car before learning how to make it go, a T-BUG user ought to know how to stop the execution of a machine-language program before trying to run one. Without knowing how to "put on the brakes," the program can zip through its end and wander into sections of memory where there is no rational programming, thus crashing the whole thing.

When running the T-BUG monitor, the least troublesome way to conclude a program is by inserting a Break at the address marking the point where you want the program to stop its execution. Suppose, for instance, you want a program to run between addresses

4A00 and 4AF6, inclusively. Before executing that program (a procedure described shortly), you should insert a T-BUG Break at the address immediately following the final instruction in the program. In this case the final instruction resides at address 4AF6; so the Break should be located at 4AF7.

How do you specify a Breakpoint? Get into the T-BUG's monitor mode, as indicated by the pound-sign prompt symbol, then strike the B key, followed immediately by the Breakpoint address. To insert the Break at address 4AF7, the presentation on the screen looks something like this:

```
#  B 4AF7
#
```

The T-BUG monitor prints the pound signs and inserts the spaces. All you have to do is answer that first pound sign with B4AF7.

Now, when you execute the program from the beginning (address 4A00 in this example), it will run until it reaches your specified Breakpoint—address 4AF7. At that time program control will break away from your machine-language program and return to the T-BUG monitor. The system will return the # symbol, waiting for your next instruction.

Here is an example to illustrate the point: get into the Memory mode, and load a program that turns out looking like this when you examine it . . .

```
#  M 4A00 CD
4A01 C9
4A02 01
4A03 21
4A04 20
4A05 3C
4A06 36
4A07 58
```

Strike the X key to get into the monitor mode, then strike B4A08 to place a Break at address 4A08—the address following the end of the program residing in locations 4A00 through 4A07.

The main point of this particular discussion is the placing of the breakpoint. But to test its effectiveness you ought to execute the program. Do that by answering the # with J4A00.

Immediately after typing that particular sequence of characters, the screen will clear, an X character will appear near the middle of the top line on the screen, and the T-BUG's prompt symbol will appear at the upper left-hand corner of the screen.

If things look this way on your screen, you know that the program has been executed to the breakpoint and that it returned to the T-BUG's monitor for you.

The program in this example is responsible for clearing the screen and printing the X character. T-BUG executed those instructions when you typed in J4A00, then the Break set at address 4A08 marked the end of the execution and returned the system to its monitor mode.

The breakpoint will remain in that same place until you either write some new instructions into location 4A08 or do a Fix operation (an operation described a bit later).

In the process of illustrating the use of T-BUG's Break function you have also initiated the execution of a program. That was the J4A00 keyboard operation.

So the simplest way to begin execution of a program from T-BUG is by answering the monitor's # symbol with a J, followed by the starting address, in a hexadecimal format, of course. To execute the previous demonstration program, for instance, you did a J4A00 —a Jump to the starting address of the program.

SUMMARY

Jssss begins execution of a program at address ssss.

Beeee specifies the end, or breakpoint, of a program at address eeee.

The breakpoint must be specified *before* the program is executed, and it must be specified at the address following the last instruction to be executed.

The system automatically returns to the T-BUG monitor on finding the breakpoint.

Actually, the Break feature of T-BUG is intended to be a debugging tool and not an endpoint marker for all machine-language programs. Machine-language programs are normally self-contained; they do not break away to some other monitor such as BASIC or T-BUG. Finished machine-language programs, in other words, have loops that keep them running indefinitely.

Machine-language programs that run as endless loops do not have to conclude with a Break function in T-BUG. A Break, under those conditions, is really irrelevant as far as marking the end of the program is concerned—the program has no end. The very nature of endlessly looping machine-language programs prevents operations from zooming into some unspecified memory space.

It is possible and, indeed, a good idea to Break machine-language loops for troubleshooting purposes; but what if you want to run the program in its normal fashion? What if you want to run the program without Breaking it? And, finally, how do you get back to the T-BUG monitor from an endlessly looping machine-language program?

Well, the only way to get out of a machine-language loop is by working the RESET push button on the back of the TRS-80 keyboard unit. When you are running a machine-language program in the SYSTEM mode, working the RESET push button immediately breaks up the program and returns control to the BASIC monitor.

Working the RESET push button while running programs in T-BUG also returns control to BASIC. As described earlier in this chapter you can then get back to the T-BUG monitor by entering SYSTEM, followed by /17312.

Here is a program that enters an endless loop:

```
#  M  4A00 CD
   4A01 C9
   4A02 01
   4A03 21
   4A04 20
   4A05 3C
   4A06 36
   4A07 58
   4A08 C3
   4A09 08
   4A0A 4A
```

You can specify a Break at the next-higher address, 4A0B, but it won't do any good. The last three bytes of the program cause it to loop around to itself, effectively creating a tight program loop that can run endlessly. There is no way the program can jump out to any unspecified memory locations. In short, the program will never see any Break that might be specified at address 4A0B.

Execute that program from its beginning by doing a J4A00. You will see the X character printed near the middle of the top line on the screen, but this time you won't see the T-BUG's pound-sign prompt character. Also notice that the keyboard is "dead." Nothing that you try at the keyboard, including striking the BREAK key, has any effect whatsoever.

The program is tied up in an endless loop. The only way out of the situation is to work the RESET push button. That will return the system to BASIC; but then you can get back to the T-BUG monitor by entering SYSTEM and answering the *? symbols by entering /17312. The appearance of the pound sign near the upper left-hand corner of the screen confirms a return to T-BUG. Now you can run the program again, modify it, write a new program, or do whatever you want from T-BUG.

Debugging Programs From T-BUG

So far in this chapter you've seen how to load the T-BUG monitor, examine the contents of memory locations, alter the contents to write a program, execute a program, and get out of a program that is being executed from T-BUG. These principles are adequate for writing just about any kind of machine-language program, but they assume any troubles are fairly easy to find and remedy. Unfortunately, machine-language bugs are not always so easy to locate; that's where the debugging power of T-BUG really pays off.

One debugging tool already described is the *Break* operation. You can insert a *Break* at the end of any complete instruction sequence in a machine-language program. Then, when you execute the program, it will run until it encounters your specified *Break* address. At that time the system returns to the T-BUG's monitor mode, and you are free to examine or alter the contents of some memory locations. More importantly in many instances, you can also examine the content of the Z-80's internal registers. More about that in a moment.

The main point is that you can stop and freeze a machine-language program at any point specified by the *Break* operation, thus giving you an opportunity to check out the program's current status.

To get rid of a *Break* you have specified at some earlier time, simply get into the T-BUG's monitor mode and strike the *F* key. This does a "Fix" on the Breakpoint, restoring any legitimate machine-language instructions that should normally appear there.

T-BUG can handle just one *Break* operation at a time. If you specify more than one Breakpoint, only the last one will work, and you will end up with meaningless instructions inserted at the memory locations for previously specified *Breaks*.

IMPORTANT

After specifying a *Break* at one point in a machine-language program, always do a *Fix* before specifying a different Breakpoint.

You don't have to keep track of the address specified for an earlier *Break* operation. Since the system is supposed to handle just one Breakpoint at a time, it keeps track of the address in the T-BUG stack. Doing a *Fix* (striking the *F* key) automatically calls up the Breakpoint address and inserts the legitimate instructions it replaced when you originally specified the *Break*.

As implied earlier in this discussion, one of the good reasons for inserting a *Break* into a machine-language program is to give you a chance to examine the contents of the Z-80's internal registers. On encountering the *Break* the system will leave the machine-language program and return to the T-BUG monitor mode, as indicated by the # prompt symbol. To view the contents of the Z-80's internal registers, simply respond to the # by striking the R (Register) key.

On striking the R key, a set of 12 hexadecimal figures pop onto the screen. Those figures represent the contents of the 12 main Z-80 registers as shown in Fig. 7-2.

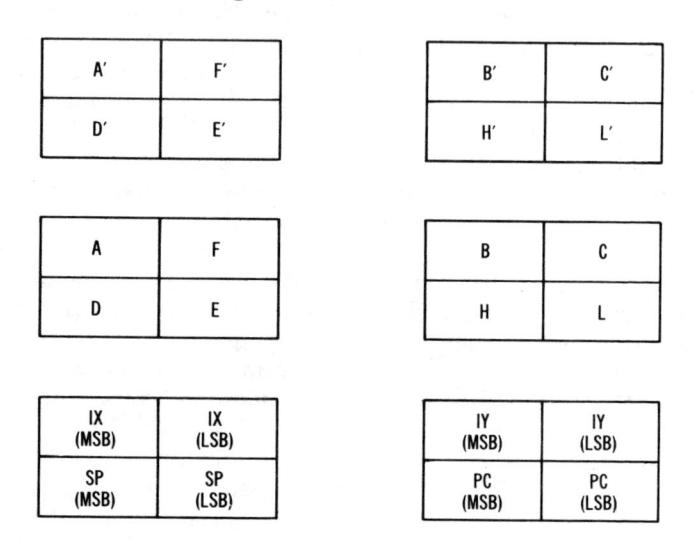

A'	F'
D'	E'

B'	C'
H'	L'

A	F
D	E

B	C
H	L

IX (MSB)	IX (LSB)
SP (MSB)	SP (LSB)

IY (MSB)	IY (LSB)
PC (MSB)	PC (LSB)

Fig. 7-2. Screen format for Register operation.

After displaying the contents of the registers in this particular fashion, the system returns to the T-BUG monitor mode, awaiting further instructions from you.

The following demonstration is a rather extensive one, but it walks you through just about all of the T-BUG principles described thus far.

The assembly-language version of the program for this demonstration appears in Table 7-1. It is basically a time-delay program. On running it you should see a white rectangle printed immediately near the upper left-hand corner of the screen. Then after a brief time delay (about ¾ of a second) a second white rectangle appears near the middle of the top line on the screen.

The first three instructions initialize the program, clearing the screen with a CALL 01C9H, loading the rectangle character code

Table 7-1. Assembly-Language Version of the Demonstration Program

Address	Contents				Mnemonics	Comment
4A00	CD	C9	01	START:	CALL 01C9H	;CLEAR THE SCREEN
4A03	3E	BF			LD A,BFH	;CHARACTER TO ACC
4A05	32	00	3C		LD (3C00H),A	;PRINT FIRST SPOT
4A08	06	FF			LD B,0FFH	;SET B TO FF
4A0A	0E	FF		SETC:	LD C,0FFH	;SET C TO FF
4A0C	0D			DECC:	DEC C	;COUNTDOWN C
4A0D	20	FD			JR NZ,DECC	;IF NOT DONE, COUNT AGAIN
4A0F	05				DEC B	;COUNTDOWN B
4A10	20	F8			JR NZ,SETC	;IF NOT DONE, START AGAIN
4A12	32	20	3C		LD (3C20H),A	;PRINT SECOND SPOT
4A15	18	FE		SELF:	JR SELF	;JUMP TO SELF

(BF) into the A register, and printing that character at video memory location 3C00H.

The next six lines, addresses 4A08 through 4A11, perform the short time delay. Those lines simply count down the BC register pair from FFFF to 0000, where the B register is the lsb for the countdown operation.

The penultimate instruction prints the second white rectangle at video memory location 3C20. And the last line simply "buzzes" to itself, thus creating an endless loop at the end of the program.

Load the program from T-BUG, beginning at address 4A00. After that, examining the program should turn up this sort of display:

```
# M 4A00 CD
4A01 C9
4A02 01
4A03 3E
4A04 BF
4A05 32
4A06 00
4A07 3C
4A08 06
4A09 FF
4A0A 0E
4A0B FF
4A0C 0D
4A0D 20
4A0E FD
4A0F 05
4A10 20
4A11 F8
4A12 32
4A13 20
4A14 3C
4A15 18
4A16 FE
```

This is the 17-byte program as it appears in T-BUG. Any data in address locations above 4A16 or below 4A00 is not relevant.

Get back into the T-BUG monitor mode by striking the X key, then run the program by doing a J4A00. This starts the program from the very beginning.

If all is going well, it should print that white rectangle near the upper left-hand corner of the screen, do a ¾-second time delay, and then print the second rectangle near the middle of the top line on the screen. The T-BUG prompt symbol should *not* appear when the program is done, for the simple reason that the program, as presented here, is never done. The looping statement at the end of the program is an endless one.

The only effective way to break out of the program (without destroying it) and return to the T-BUG monitor is by working the RESET push button and then entering SYSTEM, followed by entering /17312.

For testing purposes, the matter of RESETing to BASIC and then calling SYSTEM again is a very troublesome affair. To make things easier, specify a T-BUG Break at the beginning of the final looping instruction in the program—at address 4A15.

After inserting the Break at that point, execute the entire program with a J4A00. The program will run as before, but it automatically Breaks to the T-BUG monitor after printing the second rectangle. The first rectangle will be cleared from the screen, but only because the monitor does that clearing operation every time it is called. The fact that the first rectangle figure disappears has nothing to do with your program, itself.

To get rid of the Break at the end of the program. Strike the F key to do a Fix. Now, when you run the program with a J4A00, it will run and enter the endless loop again. Yes, you have to do a RESET, SYSTEM, /17312 to get back to T-BUG again.

Referring to the assembly-language version of the program in Table 7-1, you can see that there is nothing but register-loading operations taking place between the instructions in locations 4A03 and 4A0A. So by the time the program reaches the instruction in 4A0C, register A should have a BF in it, while registers B and C should be loaded with FF.

To test the operation of the program to that point, specify a Break at 4A0C, and then do a J4A00. The program will execute right up to address 4A0C, then return to the T-BUG monitor. Then, to see the contents of the registers, strike the R key.

Comparing the register display with the format shown in Fig. 7-2, you should see a BF in the A register and FFFF in the BC register pair. The content of the other registers shown on the screen is not relevant at this point.

If anything has been wrong with the initialization phase of the program, you would be able to spot the trouble by examining the registers at this place in the program. That being the case, you would make the necessary changes in the program and try the operation again.

Do a *F*ix to remove the *B*reak when you are ready to proceed to the next phase of this demonstration. If you wish, you can double-check the overall operation by running it from the start again—by doing a J4A00.

Now, here is something rather tricky, but meaningful: insert a *B*reak at 4A0D. This will stop the program just after the C register is decremented at 4A0C. Do a J4A00; and when the system returns to the T-BUG monitor, do an *R* to view the contents of the registers. Now the C register should show an FE, instead of an FF. Why? Because the *B*reak is located after the point in the program that calls for decrementing the C register by 1. It has counted down from FF to FE.

Here's the fun part. Do a J4A0C. That will rerun the program from the point where the C register will be decremented again. When the system returns to the monitor mode (the *B*reak is still set at 4A0D), examining the registers will show that the C register has counted down again—counted down to FD.

Run through that sequence several times: doing a J4A0C and examining the content of the C register. Each time you do that, the number in that register should get one unit smaller. In effect, you are watching the C-register down-counting operation. If you do a J4A00—start the program from the beginning—you will find the C register starting again from FE.

Do a *F*ix to get rid of the current breakpoint, and set a new *B*reak at 4A12. Run the whole program by doing a J4A00; and when the system breaks to the T-BUG monitor, strike the *R* key to look at the registers. Can you explain why the BC register pair now contains 0000?

Doing a *F*ix gets everything back to normal.

Through all of this, you should be getting at least an inkling of how T-BUG can be used for composing, debugging, and running machine-language programs.

Altering the Contents of the Registers

A more subtle debugging tool involves altering the contents of the Z-80's registers at some point during the execution of a program. You have already seen how it is possible to interrupt the execution of a program with a *B*reak function and then view the contents of the registers by doing a *R*egister function.

Before running the program again, it is sometimes useful to alter the contents of the registers first. Recall that the contents of the Z-80's registers are saved in the T-BUG's register-save area. Every time the system is returned to the monitor mode, the current contents of the Z-80's registers are saved in that area—and that's what you see displayed on the screen whenever you do the Register function.

Fig. 7-2 outlines the memory map for the register-save area in greater detail than the general memory map in Fig. 7-1 does.

Table 7-2. Register-Save Area Addresses

Register	Address	Register	Address
A	482EH	A'	4826H
B	4830H	B'	4828H
C	482FH	C'	4827H
D	4832H	D'	482AH
E	4831H	E'	4829H
H	4834H	H'	482CH
L	4833H	L'	482BH
IX (msb)	4836H	IY (msb)	4838H
IX (lsb)	4837H	IY (lsb)	3837H
SP (msb)	483AH	PC (msb)	483CH
SP (lsb)	4839H	PC (lsb)	483BH

Suppose, for some reason, you have interrupted the execution of a machine-language program and you want to set the HL register pair to BF10, where BF is the msb. That can be done as though you were writing a program at the addresses reserved for the HL pair in the register-save area. To get the BF into the H register, do an M4834 (note from Fig. 7-2 that 4834H is the address of the H register-save area). And after the system prints the current contents of 4834H, strike the BF keys. After that, the system will bring up the contents of the next address location, 4835. But you want to access 4833—the register-save location for the L register. So strike the X key to get back to the monitor, do an M4833, followed by a 10.

Now, when you do a Register function, you will see that the HL pair is set to BF10.

Of course, it would be easier to access the lower-addressed L-register location first, then let the system access the higher H-register location for you. But the main point is that you are free to alter the contents of the registers, using the ordinary T-BUG addressing and data-changing technique. The addresses of the register-save area, specified in Fig. 7-2, are your guide.

One of the most compelling reasons for tinkering around in the register-save area is to set the program counter (pc) registers to some specified point. Such an operation is indispensable when you

want to resume the execution of a program without resorting to a *Jump* function.
 The pc register in the Z-80 carries the address of the next instruction to be executed. Thus, tinkering with the pc register's contents, it is possible to specify some new starting point in the program—then use the *Go* function to begin execution.
 The *Go* function is called by striking the *G* key, but it is offered in the Radio Shack literature with some clearly stated reservations: You must know what you are doing to use it. You must know where the pc register is pointing at the time. That you can determine by examining the pc register via a *Register* function; and if you want to alter the starting point, you can use the *Memory* function for the pc register addresses to do the job. Then you can execute the operations by striking the *G* key.

Saving T-BUG-Generated Programs On Tape

 Machine-language programs generated by T-BUG functions can be saved on cassette tape by doing:

P *bbbb pppp eeee name*

where
 bbbb is the beginning address—the lowest address of the machine-language program,
 eeee is the highest-used address in the program,
 pppp is the entry point for the machine-language program—usually, but not necessarily, the same address as the beginning address,
 name is the file name, composed of one to six alphanumeric characters.

 To save the program in Table 7-1 under the file name of DELAY, for example, set the recorder to its RECORD mode and strike the following keys:

P4A004A164A00DELAY

and strike the ENTER key. The system will respond to this *Punch* operation by inserting the appropriate spaces for you. The display on the screen will thus look something like this:

\# P 4A00 4A16 4A00 DELAY

 The recorder will begin running as soon as you terminate the instruction with an ENTER. If your file name happens to have six or more characters, the recorder will start after you strike the key for the sixth character in the file name—you won't have to strike the ENTER key in that case, and any characters beyond the sixth one in the file name will be ignored.

If, during the process of entering the Punch sequence, you decide something is wrong with it, you can abort it by striking the X key. But if you've got as far as the file name, you can abort the Punch operation only by striking the BREAK key. (The system would otherwise think the X is part of the file name.)

To load a machine-language program previously saved from the T-BUG monitor, set the recorder to the beginning of the program, set it for the PLAY mode, and strike the L (Load) key. The usual flashing asterisk indicates the loading operation is taking place.

It is also possible to work with machine-language programs not specifically generated via T-BUG, but such programs must fit into memory spaces that aren't occupied by any portion of the T-BUG monitor (between 4380H and 497FH). Any SYSTEM-oriented tape can be resident with the T-BUG monitor as long as it loads above 497FH.

SUMMARY OF T-BUG OPERATIONS

Memory (M key)—M *aaaa* displays address *aaaa* and its contents in a hexadecimal format. The data at that address can be altered by striking the two appropriate keys.

Jump (J key)—J *aaaa* begins the execution of a machine-language program at address *aaaa*.

Break (B key)—B *aaaa* sets the breakpoint at address *aaaa*.

Fix (F key)—Striking the J key restores the instructions that were set aside by the last-specified Break function.

Register (R key)—Striking the R key displays the contents of the Z-80's internal registers as shown in Fig. 7-1.

Go (G key)—Striking the G key begins execution of a program at the address contained in the Z-80's pc registers.

Punch (P key)—P *aaaa pppp eeee name* saves a machine-language program on cassette tape. The program begins at *aaaa*, ends at *pppp*, has an entry point specified by *eeee*, and goes by the file name *name*.

Load (L key)—Striking the L key loads a tape version of a machine-language program that was previously saved by a Punch operation.

CHAPTER 8

Exploring the TRS-80 With T-BUG

Using the T-BUG monitor brings up the possibility of working with the TRS-80/Z-80 system in a hexadecimal format—a scheme that is much easier to use than BASIC and its decimal numbers for machine-language programming. This chapter considers the TRS-80 video, keyboard, and user memory from a hexadecimal point of view.

It is assumed that you already understand some of the fundamentals of these topics from a decimal viewpoint, as presented in Chapters 2, 3, and 4. Here, then, it is possible to concentrate on T-BUG and hexadecimal notation without having to cover a lot of material about the structure of the video, keyboard, and user memory.

THE HEXADECIMAL VIDEO ENVIRONMENT

The TRS-80's video memory occupies RAM addresses 3C00H through 3FFFH. Each of those addresses contains a byte of data that represents an alphanumeric or TRS-80 graphics code, and each address "points" to a well-defined position on the crt screen.

Fig. 8-1 shows the addresses in the video memory line up with endpoint positions on the screen. Address 3C00H, for example, corresponds to the first character position on the top line; 3C3FH corresponds to the last character position on that top line; and 3FFFH represents the last character position on the last line.

There are 40H character positions on each line; so if you want to position a character near the middle of a given line, you can figure it is about 20H positions to the right of the first character position. What, then, is the address in video memory for a character

141

ADDRESS	LINE	ADDRESS
3C00H	⊣ ⊢	3C3FH
3C40H	⊣ ⊢	3C7FH
3C80H	⊣ ⊢	3CBFH
3CC0H	⊣ ⊢	3CFFH
3D00H	⊣ ⊢	3D3FH
3D40H	⊣ ⊢	3D7FH
3D80H	⊣ ⊢	3DBFH
3DC0H	⊣ ⊢	3DFFH
3E00H	⊣ ⊢	3E3FH
3E40H	⊣ ⊢	3E7FH
3E80H	⊣ ⊢	3EBFH
3EC0H	⊣ ⊢	3EFFH
3F00H	⊣ ⊢	3F3FH
3F40H	⊣ ⊢	3F7FH
3F80H	⊣ ⊢	3FBFH
3FC0H	⊣ ⊢	3FFFH

Fig. 8-1. Hexadecimal video memory/screen format.

to be positioned near the middle of the screen? Well, a line near the middle of the screen begins with address 3E00H, and moving 20H positions to the right of 3E00H gives us 3E20H. Try it yourself with Program 8-1.

Program 8-1. Assembly language for placing a rectangle of light near the middle of the video screen/memory.

```
4A00  CD C9 01   START:   CALL 01C9H     ;CLEAR THE SCREEN
4A03  21 20 3E            LD HL,3E20H    ;SET THE VIDEO POINTER
4A06  36 BF               LD(HL),191D    ;PRINT A CHARACTER
4A08  18 FE      DONE:    JR DONE        ;LOOP TO SELF
```

Since Program 8-1 concludes with a "loop-to-self" operation, you will have to work the RESET push button to get out of it.

If you want to explore the video memory on your own, comparing the positions indicated in Fig. 8-1 with your own plots, just change the VIDEO POINTER address for the HL pair in the second line of Program 8-1. Use any valid video address between 3C00H and 3FFFH.

Program 8-2 demonstrates the addressing makeup of the video memory/display in a more dynamic fashion. The first line sets the starting point of the video memory/display, and the second line marks the end of it. Load and run the program from T-BUG and you will see the first group of four lines filled with 0s, the second group of four filled with 1s, the third group with 2s, and the bottom group of four lines filled with 3s.

Besides showing that the video memory starts at 3C00H and ends at 3FFFH, Program 8-2 shows how the lsb of the 2-byte memory address cycles between 00H and FFH four different times through the video memory/display.

142

Program 8-2. Assembly listing for video memory demonstration.

```
4A00  21 00 3C              LD HL,3C00H       ;POINT TO START OF VIDEO
4A03  01 FF 3F              LD BC,3FFFH       ;POINT TO END OF VIDEO
4A06  16 30                 LD D,48D          ;SET FIRST CHARACTER
4A08  72        AGN:        LD(HL),D          ;PRINT CHARACTER
4A09  79                    LD A,C            ;FETCH LSB OF VIDEO
4A0A  BD                    CP L              ;END OF QUADRANT?
4A0B  28 03                 JR Z,MSB          ;IF SO,DO MSB TEST
4A0D  23        NXT:        INC HL            ;SET NEXT VIDEO POS.
4A0E  18 F8                 JR AGN            ;AND JUMP TO AGN
4A10  78        MSB:        LD A,B            ;FETCH MSB OF VIDEO
4A11  BC                    CP H              ;END OF VIDEO?
4A12  28 03                 JR Z,DUN          ;IF SO,JUMP TO DUN
4A14  14                    INC D             ;ELSE SET NEW CHAR.
4A15  18 F6                 JR NXT            ;AND DO AGAIN
4A17  18 FE     DUN:        JR DUN            ;LOOP TO SELF
```

Then try the program specified here as Program 8-3. This one is an example of some machine-language animation graphics. It generates a small white rectangle that bounces back and forth across the middle of the screen.

The first line of Program 8-3 clears the screen. The second line sets the initial position of the rectangle at 3E01H—to a position

Program 8-3. Assembly listing for a bouncing rectangle of light.

```
4A00  CD C9 01    START:    CALL 01C9H        ;CLEAR THE SCREEN
4A03  21 01 3E              LD HL,3E01H       ;SET INITIAL POINT
4A06  11 00 3E              LD DE,3E00H       ;SET 'OLD' POSITION
4A09  06 FF .               LD B,0FFH         ;SET RIGHT PHASE
4A0B  3E 20       PLOT:     LD A,32D          ;SET ERASE CHARACTER
4A0D  12                    LD(DE),A          ;ERASE OLD POINT
4A0E  5D                    LD E,L            ;SAVE NEW POINT
4A0F  36 BF                 LD(HL),191D       ;PLOT NEW POINT
4A11  D5          TIME:     PUSH DE           ;SAVE 'OLD' POSITION
4A12  16 08                 LD D,08H          ;SET MSB OF DELAY
4A14  1E FF       SETE:     LD E,0FFH         ;SET LSB OF DELAY
4A16  1D          DECE:     DEC E             ;COUNTDOWN LSB
4A17  20 FD                 JR NZ,DECE        ;IF NOT DONE,COUNT AGAIN
4A19  15                    DEC D             ;ELSE COUNTDOWN MSB
4A1A  20 F8                 JR NZ,SETE        ;IF NOT DONE,COUNT MORE
4A1C  D1                    POP DE            ;ELSE FETCH 'OLD' POS.
4A1D  CB 40       RUN:      BIT 0,B           ;RIGHT PHASE?
4A1F  28 0E                 JR Z,LTLIM        ;IF NOT,CHECK LEFT LIMIT
4A21  3E 2F                 LD A,3FH          ;GET RIGHT LIMIT
4A23  BD                    CP L              ;AT RIGHT LIMIT?
4A24  20 06                 JR NZ,INC         ;IF NOT,THEN INCREMENT
4A26  06 00                 LD B,0            ;ELSE SET FOR LEFT PHASE
4A28  2D          DEC:      DEC L             ;DECREMENT TO LEFT
4A29  C3 0B 4A              JP PLOT           ;PLOT NEW POINT
4A2C  2C          INC:      INC L             ;INCREMENT TO RIGHT
4A2D  18 FA                 JR PLOT           ;PLOT NEW POINT
4A2F  AF          LTLIM:    XOR A             ;SET LEFT LIMIT
4A30  BD                    CP L              ;AT LEFT LIMIT?
4A31  20 F5                 JR NZ,DEC         ;IF NOT,DECREMENT
4A33  06 FF                 LD B,0FFH         ;ELSE SET RIGHT PHASE
4A35  18 F5                 JR INC            ;AND JUMP TO INCREMENT
```

near the beginning of the middle line on the screen. The HL register pair is the video pointer, where H is always at 3E, but L is incremented and decremented between 00H and FFH to make the figure move back and forth across the screen.

The ASCII character set, already described in Chapter 2 in a decimal format, applies equally well to machine-language and T-BUG operations; but, of course, the characters have to be specified in a hexadecimal form. (See Appendix C.)

The same idea applies to the special TRS-80 graphics characters. These, too, can be applied to machine-language and T-BUG programs, in a hexadecimal version, of course. (See Appendix D.)

The main difference between BASIC decimal-oriented video operations and the T-BUG hexadecimal-oriented video is the fact that the latter cannot deal with cursor-control operations in a meaningful way. Much of the material in Chapter 2 deals with cursor-control operations, including those specified with decimal numbers 0 through 31, and 192 through 255. None of those are relevant in machine-language programming. You have to write in your own cursor controls now.

If, for instance, you print a character at one position on the screen, and you want to print another character at the next position to the right, you must insert a machine-language instruction that moves the character pointer—increments it. And if you want to do a line-feed/carriage-return operation, you have to write machine-language instructions that set the character pointer (whatever register pair you are using to indicate video addressing) to the beginning of the next line.

This does not necessarily mean that every video printing or graphic operation has to be written as a tedious, step-by-step, machine-language program. The TRS-80 contains a number of ROM functions that can help you with the programming task. It is, in other words, possible to do some CALLs from machine language that will cause interesting and highly useful things to happen in the video environment. Those CALLs, however, mean a lot more when they are used in conjunction with some keyboard operations.

So the next section in this chapter takes up the subject of the keyboard environment, as viewed in a hexadecimal format. And in the process of demonstrating some of the keyboard principles, you will also uncover some useful video "tricks."

THE HEXADECIMAL KEYBOARD ENVIRONMENT

Whether working in BASIC or machine language, the TRS-80 keyboard is the system's primary input control device. The following material expands on the basic keyboard principles outlined in Chapter 3, putting things into a machine-language–oriented, hexadecimal format.

The Keyboard Matrix

Anytime a single key is depressed, at least one address in the "keyboard memory" takes on a well-defined, predictable hexadecimal number. Table 8-1 illustrates this particular keyboard principle.

Table 8-1. The Hexadecimal Keyboard Matrix Format

Data	Keyboard Addresses							
	3801H	3802H	3804H	3808H	3810H	3820H	3840H	3880H
01H	@	H	P	X	0	(8	ENTER	SHIFT
02H	A	I	Q	Y	! 1	) 9	CLEAR	
04H	B	J	R	Z	" 2	* :	BREAK	
08H	C	K	S		# 3	+ ;	↑	
10H	D	L	T		$ 4	< ,	↓	
20H	E	M	U		% 5	= −	←	
40H	F	N	V		& 6	> .	→	
80H	F	O	W		' 7	? /	SPACE	

The keyboard addresses, shown along the top of the table, indicate the primary keyboard "memory" locations. The corresponding data to appear at those addresses is shown running down along the left side of the table.

So if you happen to be depressing the *H* key, you will find that address 3802H contains data 01H. Depressing the *V* key, however, turns up data 40H at address 3804H. Each key thus has a specific address/data combination assigned to it.

You can check out the table for yourself, using the program listed as Program 8-4A. That program fetches the content of address 3801H, tests for any key depression at that address, and if there is a key depression involving any of the keys under address 3801H, the program returns to the T-BUG monitor. At that time you can do a *R*egister function to view the contents of the A register—the one carrying the data byte from 3801H.

Keyboard Demonstrations

Program 8-4A. Checking for key depression in row 3801H.

```
4A00  3A 01 38    FETCH:   LD  A,(3801H)     ;FETCH BYTE FROM KB
4A03  B7                   OR  A             ;CHECK FOR KEY DEPRESSION
4A04  28 FA                JR  Z,FETCH       ;IF NOT, FETCH AGAIN
4A06  C3 A0 43             JP  43A0H         ;ELSE RETURN TO T-BUG
```

Program 8-4B. Checking for key depression anywhere on the keyboard.

```
4A00  21 7F 38             LD  HL,387FH     ;POINT TO WHOLE KB
4A03  7E          WAIT:    LD  A,(HL)       ;FETCH KB BYTE
4A04  B7                   OR  A            ;CHECK FOR CLEAR
4A05  20 FC                JR  NZ,WAIT      ;IF NOT, WAIT AGAIN
4A07  7E          FETCH:   LD  A,(HL)       ;ELSE FETCH KB BYTE
4A08  B7                   OR  A            ;CHECK FOR ANY KEY
4A09  28 FC                JR  Z,FETCH      ;IF NOT,FETCH AGAIN
4A0B  C3 A0 43             JP  43A0H        ;ELSE RETURN TO T-BUG
```

Program 8-4C. Checking for depression of the A key.

```
                  WAIT:    LD  A,(387FH)    ;FETCH BYTE FROM WHOLE KB
4A00  3A 7F 38             OR  A            ;CHECK FOR ANY KEY DEPR.
4A03  B7                   JR  NZ,WAIT      ;IF SO,WAIT AGAIN
4A04  20 FA       FETCH:   LD  A,(3801H)    ;GET BYTE FROM A ROW
4A06  3A 01 38             CP  2H           ;IS IT 'A'?
4A09  FE 02                JR  NZ,FETCH     ;IF NOT,FETCH AGAIN
4A0B  20 F9                JP  43A0H        ;ELSE RETURN TO T-BUG
4A0D  C3 A0 43
```

You can use Program 8-4A to check the operation of any of the addresses on the basic keyboard matrix table. Simply change the memory address in the first line to the one you want to inspect.

Perhaps you are getting an inkling of what can be done here with respect to controlling the operation of machine-language programs from the keyboard. This is one kind of "wait for keyboard response" operation. The only problem is that the program is sensitive to any one of a number of keys within the specified "keyboard memory" address. Usually a wait-for-key-response function works with two extremes: do something when *any* key is depressed, or do something when one specific key is depressed. Programs 8-4B and 8-4C illustrate these two extremes of keyboard controls.

Program 8-4B is sensitive to any key depression. The point in the "keyboard memory" to search for any key depression is 387FH. That address isn't shown on the matrix chart in Table 8-1, but it simply represents a logical ORing of all the addresses that are there. So if a key depression occurs at any of the prime "keyboard memory" addresses, address 387FH will take on a hexadecimal value other than zero.

Now, there is a small problem inherent in the idea of writing a program that senses any key depression: depressing some key in order to initiate the program can be sensed and considered a key depression for the operation of the program itself. Because of that effect Programs 8-4B and 8-4C begin with a WAIT operation—one that does not begin looking for new key depressions until a key (the key that initiates the program) is released.

Load the program in Program 8-4B and you will see it does nothing until you depress any *key* on the keyboard. The last line in the program then brings up the T-BUG monitor, making it convenient for you to do a *R*egister function and inspect the content of the A register.

Going to the opposite extreme, it is often important to make the scheme sensitive to the depression of just one particular key. You must determine which key in advance and then write the program accordingly.

The listing for Program 8-4C is sensitive only to the A key. It appears to do nothing at all until you strike that particular key; then the program returns to the T-BUG monitor.

The WAIT phase of Program 8-4C "buzzes" the keyboard until it is completely free of any key depressions, then the FETCH phase begins looking for the depression of the A key. According to the matrix table, the A key is characterized by data 02H at address 3801H. Thus the FETCH portion of the program is written to inspect the content of address 3801H, compare it with 02H, and come to an end if the comparison is true.

Three Classes of Keyboard Entries

In-line, keyboard-entry situations generally fall into one of three categories:

- Interrupt the program and wait for a certain keystroke (similar to BASIC's INPUT statement).
- Interact with the program via a keystroke but do not interrupt ongoing activity (similar to BASIC's INKEY$ operations).
- Interact with, but do not interrupt, an ongoing program only as long as a key is depressed (similar to the PEEK(1446) operations in Chapter 3).

Program 8-5, flowcharted in Fig. 8-2, is an example of interrupting the execution of a program until a keystroke is made. In this case, striking the ENTER key resumes program operation, causing a rectangle of light to flash in the upper left-hand corner of the screen.

The program continuously looks for an ENTER keystroke (01H at address 3840H) until that condition is satisfied. This amounts to an interruption of the overall program. Once the operator strikes the ENTER key, the program breaks out of the FETCH loop and begins flashing the light on the screen.

Program 8-5. A keyboard-entry operation that interrupts the program until the ENTER key is depressed.

```
4A00  3A 7F 38    WAIT:    LD  A,(387FH)    ;FETCH BYTE FROM WHOLE KB
4A03  B7                   OR  A            ;CHECK FOR KEY DEPRESSION
4A04  20 FA                JR  NZ,WAIT      ;IF SO,WAIT AGAIN
4A06  3A 40 38    FETCH:   LD  A,(3840H)    ;GET BYTE FROM 'ENTER' ROW
4A09  FE 01                CP  1            ;IS IT 'ENTER'?
4A0B  20 F9                JR  NZ,FETCH     ;IF NOT, FETCH AGAIN
4A0D  CD C9 01             CALL 01C9H       ;ELSE CLEAR THE SCREEN
4A10  CD 20 4A             CALL FLASH       ;AND CALL FLASH
4A20  21 00 3C    FLASH:   LD  HL,3C00H     ;POINT TO VIDEO
4A23  1D          DECE:    DEC E            ;COUNT DOWN
4A24  20 FD                JR  NZ,DECE      ;IF NOT DONE,COUNT AGAIN
4A26  15                   DEC D            ;ELSE COUNT DOWN D
4A27  CB 6A                BIT 5,D          ;CHECK IF 'OFF' CYCLE
4A29  28 04                JR  Z,OFF        ;IF NOT,DO 'OFF' CYCLE
4A2B  36 BF                LD  (HL),191D    ;ELSE TURN ON THE SPOT
4A2D  18 4F                JR  DECE         ;AND TIME AGAIN
4A2F  36 20       OFF:     LD  (HL),32D     ;TURN OFF THE SPOT
4A31  18 FA                JR  DECE         ;AND TIME AGAIN
```

Since FLASH THE LIGHT is an endless-loop operation in this example, you must operate the RESET key to get out of it. The important point, however, is that the program holds that FETCH

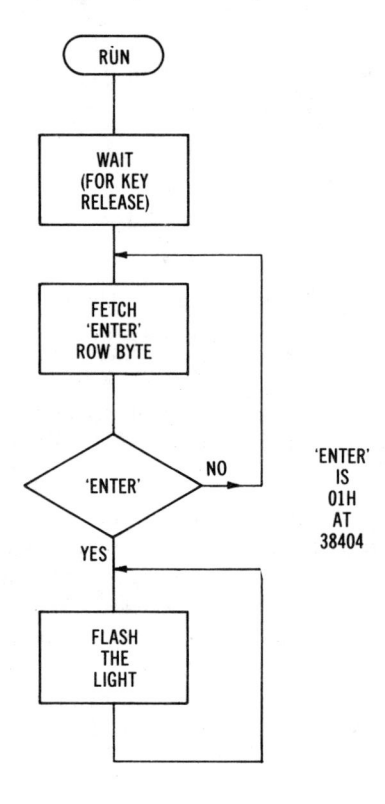

Fig. 8-2. Flowchart for Program 8-5.

loop—interrupting progress—until a certain keystroke occurs. The program flowcharted in Fig. 8-3 is an entirely different sort of key-entry situation. The listing in Program 8-6 allows the light to flash continuously, whether the operator is striking a key or not. But every FLASH ONE CYCLE operation ends by polling the keyboard—polling specifically for an *L* or *R* keystroke.

If an *L* keystroke occurs during that keyboard-polling interval, the spot of light flashes at the upper left-hand corner of the screen. But if an *R* keystroke occurs, the position of the flashing light changes to the upper right-hand corner of the screen.

Program 8-6. A keyboard-entry operation that accepts keyboard controls without interrupting the ongoing program.

4A00	3A 7F 38	WAIT:	LD A,(387FH)	;POINT TO KB
4A03	B7		OR A	;ANY KEY DEPRESSED?
4A04	20 FA		JR NZ,WAIT	;IF SO, WAIT AGAIN
4A06	CD C9 01		CALL 01C9H	;ELSE CLEAR THE SCREEN
4A09	21 00 3C		LD HL,3C00H	;AND INITIALIZE VIDEO
4A0C	3A 06 38	FETCH:	LD A,(3806H)	;CHECK ROWS FOR 'L','R'
4A0F	B7		OR A	;EITHER KEY DEPRESSED?
4A10	20 05		JR NZ,CODE	;IF SO, DO CODE
4A12	CD 30 4A	DOIT:	CALL FLASH	;ELSE FLASH AS IS
4A15	18 F5		JR FETCH	;AND FETCH AGAIN
4A17	FE 10	CODE:	CP A,10H	;IS IT 'L'?
4A19	20 04		JR NZ,RGHT	;IF NOT,SET RIGHT
4A1B	2E 00		LD L,0	;ELSE SET LEFT
4A1D	18 F3		JR DOIT	;AND FLASH
4A1F	FE 04	RGHT:	CP A,4	;IS IT 'R'?
4A21	20 FA		JR NZ,DOIT	;IF NOT, FLASH AS IS
4A23	2E 3F		LD L,3FH	;ELSE SET RIGHT
4A25	18 F6		JR DOIT	;AND FLASH
4A30	1D	FLASH:	DEC E	;COUNT DOWN E
4A31	20 FD		JR NZ,FLASH	;IF NOT DONE,DO AGAIN
4A33	15		DEC D	;ELSE COUNT DOWN D
4A34	CB 6A		BIT 5,D	;CHECK IF 'OFF' CYCLE
4A36	28 04		JR Z,OFF	;IF NOT,THEN DO 'OFF'
4A38	36 BF		LD (HL),191D	;ELSE TURN ON THE SPOT
4A3A	18 F4		JR FLASH	;AND DO TIMING AGAIN
4A3C	36 20	OFF:	LD (HL),32D	;TURN OFF THE SPOT
4A3E	C9		RET	;CHECK KEYBOARD AGAIN

So keyboard operations do not interrupt the flashing light. Striking the *L* or *R* keys influences the program, however.

Finally, Program 8-7 and Fig. 8-4 illustrate a situation where depressing and holding down a certain key influences, but does not interrupt, the behavior of a program. In this case the flashing rectangle of light appears on the screen as long as the ENTER key is depressed. Otherwise, the light is turned off.

The program polls the keyboard after each light-flashing cycle or after finding that the ENTER key is not depressed. When the ENTER key is depressed, the program does a light-flashing cycle.

149

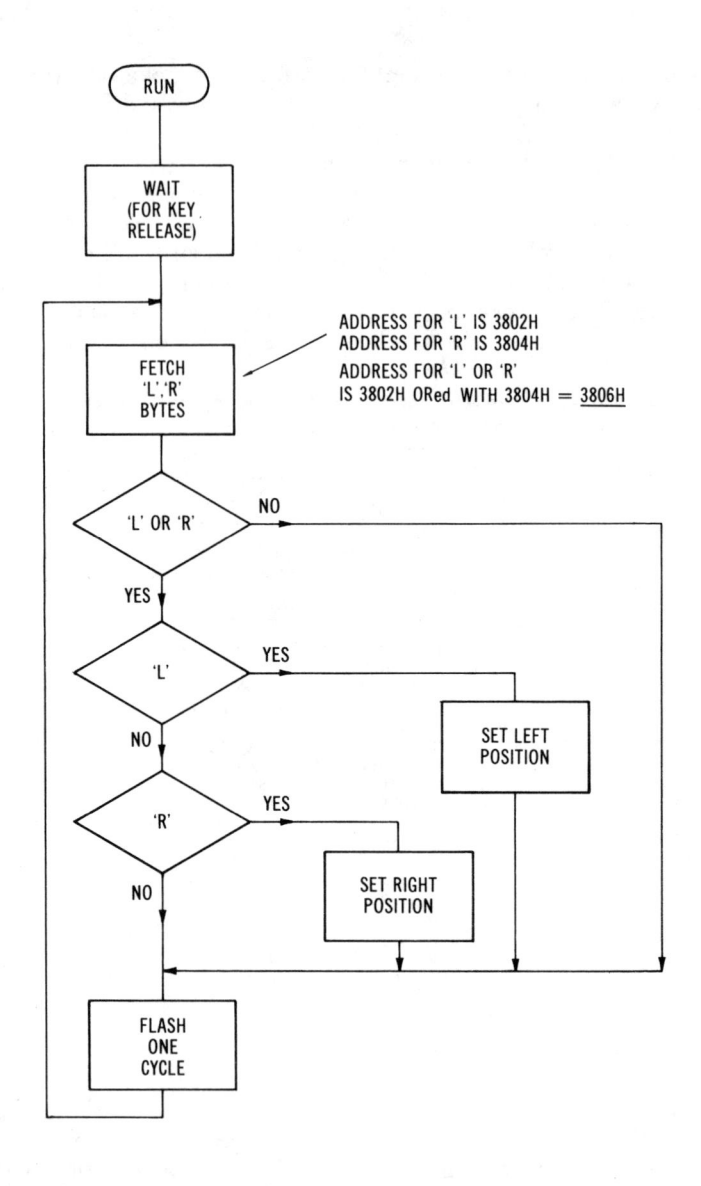

Fig. 8-3. Flowchart for Program 8-6.

SOME SPECIAL VIDEO/KEYBOARD FUNCTIONS

Your TRS-80 is provided with a number of useful functions that are stored in the ROM space. Such functions can be CALLed from a machine-language program, thus performing important video/key-

Program 8-7. A keyboard-entry operation that is sensitive to holding down a key.

```
4A00   21 00 3C    TOGL:     LD  HL,3C00H      ;POINT TO VIDEO
4A03   CD C9 01              CALL 01C9         ;CLEAR THE SCREEN
4A06   3A 40 38    FETCH:    LD  AA,(3840H)    ;GET BYTE FROM 'ENTER' ROW
4A09   FE 01                 CP  1             ;IS IT 'ENTER'?
4A0B   20 F9                 JR  NZ,FETCH      ;IF NOT,FETCH AGAIN
4A0D   AF                    XOR A             ;ZERO THE ACCUMULATOR
4A0E   CD 30 4A              CALL FLASH        ;AND CALL FLASH
4A11   C3 06 4A              JP  FETCH         ;JUMP TO FETCH
```

Also add FLASH subroutine, addresses 4A30 through
4A3E, from Program 8-6

board operations without your having to do a great deal of tedious programming—it has been done for you.

Table 8-2 lists some of the most useful kinds of ROM CALLs. A simple CALL 01C9H, for example, does all the work necessary

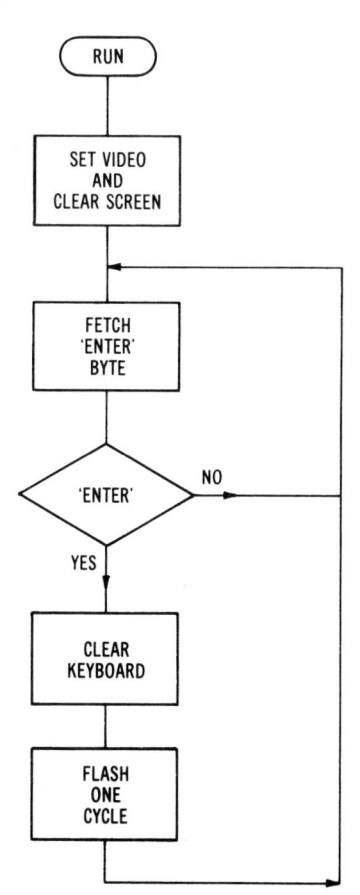

Fig. 8-4. Flowchart for Program 8-7.

for clearing the screen and sending the cursor to home. That CALL does not turn on the cursor, however; as shown in Table 8-2, turning on the cursor is a two-step operation: LD A,14D, followed by CALL 033AH.

Table 8-2. Some Useful ROM-Based Cursor-Control Routines

Contents	Mnemonic	Comment
CD C9 01	CALL 01C9H	;CLEAR THE SCREEN AND HOME THE CURSOR
CD 49 00	CALL 0049H	;FULLY DECODED (ASCII) KB CHARACTER ;TO THE ACCUMULATOR
CD 3A 03	CALL 033AH	;PRINT ASCII CHARACTER FROM ACCUMULATOR, ;ADVANCE THE CURSOR POSITION, AND ;SCROLL THE DISPLAY IF NECESSARY
3E 0E CD 3A 03	LD A,14D CALL 033AH	;SET CURSOR 'TURN ON' TO ACCUMULATOR ;PRINT CURSOR 'ON'
3E 0F CD 3A 03	LD A,15D CALL 033AH	;SET CURSOR 'TURN OFF' TO ACCUMULATOR ;PRINT CURSOR 'OFF'
3E 0D CD 3A 03	LD A,13D CALL 033AH	;SET 'LINE FEED/CARRIAGE RETURN' TO ACC. ;'PRINT' IT
3E 1C CD 3A 03	LD A,28D CALL 033AH	;SET 'HOME CURSOR' TO ACCUMULATOR ;'PRINT' IT
3E 1D CD 3A 03	LD A,29D CALL 033AH	SET 'CURSOR TO BEGINNING OF CURRENT LINE' ;TO ACCUMULATOR ;'PRINT' IT
3E 1E CD 3A 03	LD A,30D CALL 033AH	;SET 'ERASE TO END OF CURRENT LINE' TO ;ACCUMULATOR ;'PRINT' IT
3E 1F CD 3A 03	LD A,31D CALL 033AH	;SET 'CLEAR TO END OF FRAME' TO ACC. ;'PRINT' IT

Notice that a CALL 0049H places a fully decoded (hexadecimal ASCII) keyboard character into the accumulator. There is no need to write lengthy keyboard-decoding programs—this one does it for you.

A CALL 033AH prints an ASCII character from the accumulator to the screen. It mimics a single-character PRINT operation from BASIC. Like the PRINT command in BASIC, this CALL executes all the cursor functions. The procedure is to load the character or function into the accumulator, then do the CALL 033AH. See more examples in Table 8-2 and some working demonstrations in Program 8-8.

Program 8-8A uses the CALL 0049H and CALL 033AH combination to get a keyboard character and print it on the screen. Those two operations, included in the KB sequence, are part of a loop that allows you to fill the screen with characters if you choose to do so.

A Simple Text-Writing Program

Program 8-8A. Printing and editing screen text without a cursor.

```
4A00   3A 7F 38    WAIT:   LD A,(387FH)    ;LOOK AT KB
4A03   B7                  OR A            ;ANY KEY DEPRESSED?
4A04   20 FA               JR Z,WAIT       ;IF SO,WAIT AGAIN
4A06   CD C9 01    CLS:    CALL 01C9H      ;ELSE CLEAR AND HOME
4A09   CD 49 00    KB:     CALL 0049H      ;KB CHAR TO A
4A0C   FE 2A               CP 42D          ;IS IT '*'?
4A0E   28 F6               JR Z,CLS        ;IF SO,CLEAR AND HOME
4A10   CD 3A 03            CALL 033AH      ;ELSE PRINT CHAR
4A13   18 F4               JR KB           ;AND GET THE NEXT ONE
```

Program 8-8B. Printing and editing screen text with the help of a cursor.

```
4A00   3A 7F 38    WAIT:   LD A,(387FH)    ;LOOK AT KB
4A03   B7                  OR A            ;ANY KEY DEPRESSED?
4A04   20 FA               JR Z,WAIT       ;IF SO,WAIT AGAIN
4A06   CD C9 01    CLS:    CALL 01C9H      ;ELSE CLEAR AND HOME
4A09   3E 0E               LD A,14D        ;SET 'CURSOR ON' CODE
4A0B   CD 3A 03            CALL 033AH      ;PRINT THE CURSOR
4A0E   CD 49 00    KB:     CALL 0049H      ;KB CHAR TO A
4A11   FE 2A               CP 42D          ;IS IT '*'?
4A13   28 F1               JR Z,CLS        ;IF SO, CLEAR AND HOME
4A15   CD 3A 03            CALL 033AH      ;ELSE PRINT CHARACTER
4A18   18 F4               JR KB           ;AND GET THE NEXT ONE
```

Program 8-8C. Text writing and editing with a cursor/no-cursor control option.

```
4A00   3A 7F 38    WAIT:   LD A,(387FH)    ;LOOK AT WHOLE KB
4A03   B7                  OR A            ;ANY KEY DEPRESSED?
4A04   20 FA               JR Z,WAIT       ;IF SO,WAIT AGAIN
4A06   CD C9 01            CALL 01C9H      ;ELSE CLEAR AND HOME
4A09   3E 3F       SET:    LD A,63D        ;'?' TO A
4A0B   CD 3A 03            CALL 033AH      ;PRINT IT
4A0E   CD 49 00    KB1:    CALL 0049H      ;FETCH KB CHARACTER
4A11   FE 43               CP 67D          ;IS IT 'C'?
4A13   28 0B               JR Z,CURON      ;IF SO,TURN ON CURSOR
4A15   FE 4E               CP 78D          ;IS IT 'N'?
4A17   20 F5               JR NZ,KB1       ;IF NOT,GET CHAR AGAIN
4A19   3E 0F               LD A,0FH        ;ELSE TURN OFF CURSOR
4A1B   CD 3A 03            CALL 033AH      ;PRINT
4A1E   18 05               JR CLS2         ;AND START TYPING
4A20   3E 0E       CURON:  LD A,0EH        ;SET CURSOR ON CODE
4A22   CD 3A 03            CALL 033AH      ;PRINT IT
4A25   CD C9 01    CLS2:   CALL 01C9H      ;CLS AND HOME THE CURSOR
4A28   3A 40 38    KB2:    LD A,(3840H)    ;GET 'CLEAR' ROW FROM KB
4A2B   FE 02               CP 2            ;IS IT 'CLEAR'?
4A2D   28 DC               JR Z,SET        ;IF SO,DO SET AGAIN
4A2F   CD 49 00            CALL 0049H      ;FETCH KB CHAR TO A
4A32   CD 3A 03            CALL 003AH      ;PRINT IT
4A35   18 F1               JR KB2          ;AND GET NEXT CHARACTER
```

153

But the KB sequence is also sensitive to a striking of the asterisk key. Whenever that happens, operations are sent to CLS—a CALL 01C9H that clears the screen and homes the cursor. So you can type a lot of characters, then strike the * key to clear the screen, and start all over again. It is possible to edit the text by taking advantage of the SHIFT *arrow key* functions.

The WAIT sequence at the beginning of all three programs is necessary only for these demonstrations. It makes certain nothing is printed on the screen until you release the key that starts the programs in the first place.

When running Program 8-8A you will find things a bit awkward because the cursor symbol isn't there to let you know where the next character will be printed—a feature that is especially troublesome when one is attempting to move the cursor to a position in a blank portion of the screen. So Program 8-8B fixes that.

Program 8-8B runs the same way as the first one in the series, but it includes the LD A,14D and CALL 033AH sequence to turn on the cursor symbol. Those two instructions, included in the CLS operations, perform the same task as BASIC's PRINT CHR$(14) as described in Chapter 2.

The notions are further refined in Program 8-8C. The WAIT sequence ends with a CALL 01C9H to clear the screen and home the cursor. But then the SET sequence loads the hexadecimal code for a question mark into the accumulator and uses a CALL 033AH to print it. You thus see a clear screen with a question mark appearing in the upper left-hand corner.

The KB1 sequence gives you an opportunity to see or not see the cursor symbol. Using a CALL 0049H to pick up a keyboard character, this sequence is sensitive to both the C and N keys (CP 67D and CP 78D, respectively). If you choose to see the cursor and respond to the question mark by striking the C key, operations jump down to CURON—a set of two instructions that turn on the cursor symbol. But if you answer the question mark with a N, the last three lines in the KB1 sequence turn off the cursor and jump operations to CLS2.

CLS2 clears the screen and homes the cursor, and then the sequence in KB2 allows you to print characters at your heart's content. That particular video/keyboard sequence, incidentally, improves on the first two programs by doing away with the idea of clearing the screen by striking the asterisk key. Instead, the LD A,(3840) and CP 02H sequence makes the system sensitive to the CLEAR key.

So when you strike the CLEAR key while the system is running the screen-printing KB2 sequence, the system returns to SET. You then have a chance to select seeing or not-seeing the cursor, and on making your selection the screen clears and you are back in the typing business again.

The main point of Program 8-8C is to illustrate the operation of the cursor-on/cursor-off operations—examples of cursor controls CALLed from a machine-language program. In the process of illustrating the point, however, you will find a review of much of the material already described in this chapter.

T-BUG AND THE MEMORY ENVIRONMENT

The memory environment for T-BUG isn't nearly as complicated as that of BASIC. T-BUG, itself, is loaded as a SYSTEM-oriented, machine-language program between 4380H and 497FH (see Fig. 7-1). Obviously, any program written from T-BUG ought not alter the content of any address in that area—otherwise T-BUG will be destroyed.

All addresses from 4980H through the top of your RAM space are thus free for programming applications. Note, for instance, that most of the previous demonstrations begin at address 4A00H. This leaves plenty of space between the top of T-BUG and the beginning of those programs.

There is, however, some additional RAM space below the T-BUG monitor area: everything from 41E6H (the beginning of BASIC's i/o buffer) to 437FH (the address just below T-BUG). T-BUG users generally avoid this RAM space for a couple of reasons. First, it is a relatively small amount of space compared to that available above T-BUG. Second, any SYSTEM program, unless instructed otherwise, will set the program stack at 4288H—in the BASIC i/o space.

Nevertheless, the RAM space below T-BUG can prove quite useful, as shown later in this chapter. The fact that it is a fairly small amount of memory space isn't relevant to the applications that will be cited at that time, and the stack can always be pointed elsewhere, say to the top of your available memory space.

Now, let us take a look at some memory operations that take advantage of the wealth of RAM above T-BUG.

Working With User's RAM Above T-BUG

Program 8-9 allows you to compose text on the video screen and then transfer it to some user's RAM space where it can be saved for an indefinite period. In the meantime, you can tinker around in video memory, recalling the original text whenever you choose.

One of the most impressive features of this program is the speed at which saved text can be restored to the screen. BASIC users are accustomed to a fairly slow printing rate, even when using direct

Program 8-9. Assembly listing for a program that allows you to transfer video memory/screen information to a block of higher memory space.

```
4A00  CD C9 01    NEXT:   CALL 01C9H      ;CLS AND HOME THE CURSOR
4A03  3E 3F       QUERY:  LD A,63D        ;'?' TO ACCUMULATOR
4A05  CD 3A 03            CALL 033AH      ;PRINT IT
4A08  CD 49 00            CALL 0049H      ;KB CHAR TO ACCUMULATOR
4A0B  FE 52               CP 82D          ;IS IT 'R'?
4A0D  CA 60 4A            JP Z,DISP       ;IF SO,RECALL DISPLAY
4A10  FE 43               CP 67D          ;IS IT 'C'?
4A12  CA 20 4A            JP Z,COMP       ;IF SO, COMPOSE
4A15  C3 03 4A            JP QUERY        ;ELSE QUERY AGAIN
                                          ;
4A20  CD C9 01    COMP:   CALL 01C9H      ;CLS AND HOME THE CURSOR
4A23  3E 0E               LD A,14D        ;SET 'CURSOR ON' CODE
4A25  CD 3A 03            CALL 033AH      ;PRINT IT
4A28  CD 49 00    KB:     CALL 0049H      ;GET KB CHARACTER
4A2B  FE 2A               CP 42D          ;IS IT '*'?
4A2D  CA 40 4A            JP Z,SAVE       ;IF SO,SAVE DISP IN MEM
4A30  CD 3A 03            CALL 033AH      ;ELSE PRINT THE CHAR.
4A33  18 F3               JR KB           ;AND GET THE NEXT ONE
                                          ;
4A40  3E 0F       SAVE:   LD A,15D        ;SET 'CURSOR OFF' CODE
4A42  CD 3A 03            CALL 033AH      ;PRINT IT
4A45  21 00 3C            LD HL,3C00H     ;POINT TO VIDEO
4A48  11 00 4B            LD DE,4B00H     ;POINT TO MEMORY
4A4B  01 00 04            LD BC,1024D     ;SET NUMBER OF BYTES
4A4E  ED B0               LDIR            ;XFER SCREEN TO MEMORY
4A50  C3 00 4A            JP NEXT         ;AND BACK TO BEGINNING
                                          ;
4A60  CD C9 01    DISP:   CALL 01C9H      ;CLS AND HOME THE CURSOR
4A63  21 00 4B            LD HL,4B00H     ;POINT TO MEMORY
4A66  11 00 3C            LD DE,3C00H     ;POINT TO VIDEO
4A69  01 00 04            LD BC,1024D     ;SET NUMBER OF BYTES
4A6C  ED B0               LDIR            ;XFER MEMORY TO SCREEN
4A6E  CD 49 00    HOLD:   CALL 0049H      ;KB CHAR TO ACCUMULATOR
4A71  FE 2A               CP 42D          ;IS IT '*'?
4A73  20 F9               JR NZ,HOLD      ;IF NOT, HOLD AGAIN
4A75  C3 00 4A            JP NEXT         ;ELSE BACK TO BEGINNING
```

POKE and PEEK operations. But this machine-language program flashes a full screen of text into place in a very short time—certainly too short a time to see the characters being printed individually.

Load the program and run it from 4A00H. The screen will clear and a question mark will appear in the upper left-hand corner of the screen. Reply by striking the C (Compose) key. That will replace the question mark with the typing cursor.

Now type in any sort of text you want, using any editing keys as you wish. When done, strike the * key. As soon as you do that the screen will clear and the question mark will appear again.

This time, respond by striking the R (Recall) key. Presto! there is your original text returned to the screen.

The general idea is to compose new text (and save it by striking the * key) or recall old text from memory.

Note the use of special video/keyboard CALLs in the listing, as well as the Z-80's block-transfer instruction, LDIR. In view of past demonstrations you should be able to figure out the operating details yourself. Hint: All 1024 video bytes, beginning at 3C00H are saved in RAM, beginning at 4B00H.

Program 8-10 is a somewhat more sophisticated version of the one just described. This program allows you to generate the effect of doubling the video screen capacity; it allows you to work with two different "pages" of text.

You can, for instance, compose or edit some text appearing on the screen, and then exchange it with a full screen of text previously saved in memory. That text can also be deleted or edited and exchanged again with the original. The effect is that of working with two separate crt screens (although you can really work with just one at a time).

Program 8-10. Listing for a memory exchange program gives the user two "pages" of text to work with.

```
4A00  CD 49 00    NEXT:   CALL 0049H       ;FETCH KB CHARACTER
4A03  FE 58               CP   88D         ;IS IT 'X'?
4A05  28 14               JR   Z,CEX       ;IF SO, DO EXCHANGE
4A07  FE 4E               CP   78D         ;IS IT 'N'?
4A09  28 0B               JR   Z,CLR       ;IF SO,CLEAR THE SCREEN
4A0B  FE 45               CP   69D         ;IS IT 'E'?
4A0D  28 02               JR   Z,CED       ;IF SO, DO EDITING
4A0F  18 DF               JR   NEXT        ;ELSE LOOK AT KB AGAIN
4A11  CD 30 4A    CED:    CALL COMP        ;CALL COMPOSE MODE
4A14  18 F9               JR   NEXT        ;THEN START AGAIN
4A16  CD C9 01    CLR:    CALL 01C9H       ;CLS AND HOME THE CURSOR
4A19  18 F9               JR   NEXT        ;THEN START AGAIN
4A1B  CD 50 4A    CEX:    CALL EXCH        ;CALL EXCHANGE OPS
4A1E  18 F9               JR   NEXT        ;THEN START AGAIN
                                           ;
4A30  3E 0E       COMP:   LD   A,14D       ;SET 'CURSOR ON' CODE
4A32  CD 3A 03            CALL 033AH       ;PRINT IT
4A35  CD 49 00    KB:     CALL 0049H       ;FETCH KB CHARACTER
4A38  FE 2A               CP   42D         ;IS IT '*'?
4A3A  28 05               JR   Z,CROFF     ;IF SO, WRAP IT UP
4A3C  CD 33 00            CALL 033AH       ;ELSE PRINT THE CHAR.
4A3F  18 F4               JR   KB          ;AND GET THE NEXT ONE
4A41  3E 0F               LD   A,15D       ;SET 'CURSOR OFF' CODE
4A43  CD 3A 03            CALL 033AH       ;PRINT IT
4A36  C9                  RET              ;RETURN TO NEXT

4A50  21 00 4B    EXCH:   LD   HL,4B00H    ;POINT TO MEMORY
4A53  11 00 3C            LD   DE,3C00H    ;POINT TO VIDEO
4A56  01 00 04            LD   BC,1024D    ;SET NUMBER OF BYTES
4A59  1A          SWAP:   LD   A,(DE)      ;VIDEO BYTE TO ACC.
4A5A  ED A0               LDI              ;MEMORY BYTE TO VIDEO
4A5C  2B                  DEC  HL          ;POINT BACK MEMORY ADDR.
4A5D  77                  LD   (HL),A      ;ACC. TO MEMORY
4A5E  23                  INC  HL          ;POINT AHEAD MEMORY ADDR.
4A5F  AF                  XOR  A           ;CLEAR ACCUMULATOR
4A60  B9                  CP   C           ;LSB OF COUNTER DONE?
4A61  20 F6               JR   NZ,SWAP     ;IF NOT,SWAP ANOTHER BYTE
4A63  B8                  CP   B           ;MSB OF COUNT DONE?
4A64  C8                  RET  Z           ;IF SO, RETURN TO NEXT
4A65  18 F2               JR   SWAP        ;ELSE SWAP ANOTHER BYTE
```

The program uses three control characters from its monitor mode: N clears the screen and the "page" residing there, E sets up the Edit mode that allows you to type new information or alter some old text on the displayed page, and X exchanges the two pages—transfers the one currently on the screen to memory, and displays the page previously saved in memory.

Striking the * key gets the system out of the Edit or exchange mode and returns it to the monitor. The only way out of the program is to work the RESET push button.

So load Program 8-10 and give it a try. Play with the program for a bit and then you will be in a better position to appreciate the internal workings.

With the program loaded, run it by doing a J4A00. Then delete the text on the screen by striking the N key. After that, get into the Edit mode by striking the E key. At that time the cursor symbol should appear in the upper left-hand corner of the screen.

Now type in some text—anything will do. Notice you can move around the cursor, without disturbing the text, by working the arrow keys when the SHIFT key is depressed.

When you are satisfied with the text on this first page, strike the * key to return to the monitor. To save that page and call up its alternate, strike the X key.

There's no telling what the alternate page will look like at this time, but you can always clear it up by striking the N key and then the E key to type some new stuff. And when you are done with that page, strike the * key.

To bring back the original page, strike the X key. Everything should appear as it did earlier in the demonstration. If you want to see your second page again, simply strike the X key again.

The main point of the demonstration is that exchange operation—swapping the contents of the video memory with some user's memory of equal size elsewhere in the system. That "hidden-page" memory, incidentally, begins at 4B00H, and occupies 1024 (decimal) bytes from there. In a manner of speaking, this program creates an alternate video memory.

Referring to the listing for Program 8-10, labels NEXT, CED, CLR, and CEX make up the "monitor." This group of instructions uses a CALL 0049H to pick up a keystroke and put its ASCII character code into the accumulator. After that, a series of compare instructions look for the control characters and call the appropriate routines.

The COMP routine, for instance, is called whenever you want to Edit, or compose, some new text on the screen. It begins by turning on the cursor (so you will know where the screen printing will begin) and CALLing 0049H to pick up an ASCII character code from the keyboard. The routine uses a CALL 033AH to print the characters and advance the cursor.

If, while running the COMP routine, the system sees an asterisk character, it turns off the cursor (so that it will not be saved in memory with the other text) and returns operations to the monitor.

Striking the N key from the NEXT routine does a CALL 01C9H to clear the screen and home the cursor.

The EXCH routine is the one responsible for exchanging the contents of the video memory with the alternate video memory space. It simply runs through both memory blocks, passing a byte at a time through the accumulator. When the exchange is completed, operations automatically return to the monitor.

You can change the address of the alternate video memory by changing the hexadecimal address loaded into the HL register pair at the beginning of the EXCH routine.

Using the I/O Buffer Space

The i/o buffer is located between 41E6 and 42E7H on the TRS-80 memory map. That isn't very much RAM space, compared to that above the T-BUG's space, but it can be useful. The i/o buffer space is especially useful when one is attempting to control machine-language programs, using keyboard entries having more than one character in them. Thus far all keyboard controls have used just one character.

A CALL 0361H connects the keyboard to the i/o buffer. That CALL does a lot of routine housekeeping for you. For instance, it automatically begins loading keyboard characters from the first character location in the buffer; there is no need to initialize it yourself. That CALL also turns on the cursor symbol for you, and, after each keyboard entry, it advances the cursor position and i/o pointer.

What's more, the system remains in that i/o loop until you strike the ENTER key. There is no need for dreaming up a special control character for breaking out of the routine.

What's the price to pay for all of these nice features? It turns out to be rather small. Remember that any SYSTEM tape will set its program stack into the i/o memory space, unless instructed to do otherwise. So if you fail to relocate the program stack before doing a CALL 0361H, you run the risk of losing the program.

Before doing a CALL 0361H, then, you should relocate the stack with a LD SP,NN type of instruction. LD SP,7FFF for example. (That particular address represents the top of RAM space for a 16K machine.) You can put the stack anywhere in the user's RAM space, remembering that the stack will always build downward.

To get a feeling for how this keyboard i/o scheme works, try this:

```
4A00  31 FF 4F      LD SP,4FFFH    ;GET STACK OUT OF I/O
4A03  CD C9 01      CALL 01C9H     ;CLEAR THE SCREEN
4A06  CD 61 03      CALL 0361H     ;KB TO I/O
```

and insert a Break at 4A09.

Running from 4A00 then lets you type in all sorts of characters—much like typing a new program line in BASIC or answering an INPUT instruction. When you are through entering some characters, strike the ENTER key. If you have inserted the Break as suggested, the system will return safely to the T-BUG monitor.

After leaving a CALL 0361H routine, your text will be saved in the i/o buffer space. Adding the following instructions to the previous ones will show you the contents of the entire i/o buffer. That, of course, should confirm that your information was indeed entered there from the keyboard.

```
4A09  21 E7 41      LD HL,41E7H    ;POINT TO START OF I/O
4A0C  11 00 3C      LD DE,3C00H    ;POINT TO START OF VIDEO
4A0F  01 FF 00      LD BC,00FFH    ;SET BYTE COUNT
4A12  ED 80         LDIR           ;SHOW I/O BUFFER
```

and insert a Break at 4A14.

Now you can run from 4A00, load some characters into the i/o buffer and strike the ENTER key to end the loading operation and display the contents of the i/o buffer.

There will most likely be a lot of garbage in the display, but your keyboard input will always appear at the beginning. Also note that your characters are bracketed by @ symbols. Those represent the nulls that are automatically inserted into a buffer string for BASIC interpretation purposes. (See "The I/O Buffer" in Chapter 4.)

Program 8-11 represents an application of this i/o buffer routine. The point of the demonstration is to show how the buffer can be used as an entry point for control expressions having more than one character in them. The control expressions in this case are *BL*, *EX*, and *EN*. Doing a *BL* makes a small rectangle of light blink on and off. Entering an *EX* makes that rectangle exchange positions —from the left to right or from the right to left corners of the screen. Entering expression *EN* ends the program and returns operations to the T-BUG monitor.

The program begins by setting the stack of the i/o buffer and to address 4FFFH. Then it clears the screen and prints a question-mark prompt symbol. The idea is to let you know it is time to designate one of the three basic functions: BLink, EXchange, or ENd.

Instruction CALL 0361H calls the i/o routine, and it remains in that loop until you strike the ENTER key. The system's sensitivity to the ENTER key is built into the routine—you don't have to write it into the program itself.

Program 8-11. Using the i/o buffer as an entry point for multiple-character keyboard commands.

```
4A00  31 FF 4F    STAK:   LD   SP,4FFFH      ;SET STACK OUT OF I/O
4A03  CD C9 01    START:  CALL 01C9H         ;CLEAR THE SCREEN
4A06  3E 3F               LD   A,3FH         ;SET UP '?'
4A08  CD 3A 03            CALL 033AH         ;PRINT IT
4A0B  CD 61 03            CALL 0361H         ;KB INPUT TO I/O BUFFER
4A0E  21 00 3C            LD   HL,3C00H      ;SET LEFT VIDEO POINTER
4A11  11 3F 3C            LD   DE,3C3FH      ;SET RIGHT VIDEO POINTER
4A14  01 E7 41            LD   BC,41E7H      ;SET I/O POINTER
4A17  0A          GETC:   LD   A,(BC)        ;GET CHAR FROM I/O
4A18  FE 20               CP   20H           ;IS IT ALPHABETICAL?
4A1A  30 08               JR   NC,TRY        ;IF SO,GIVE IT A TRY
4A1C  FE EF               CP   0EFH          ;END OF USEFUL I/O SPACE?
4A1E  CA 03 4A            JP   Z,START       ;IF SO, START AGAIN
4A21  03                  INC  BC            ;ELSE LOOK AT NEXT I/O
4A22  18 F3               JR   GETC          ;AND GET IT
4A24  FE 42       TRY:    CP   42H           ;IS 1ST CHAR 'B'?
4A26  20 0D               JR   NZ,NEXT       ;IF NOT,CHECK FOR 'E'
4A28  03                  INC  BC            ;ELSE LOOK AT 2ND CHAR
4A29  0A                  LD   A,(BC)        ;2ND CHAR TO A
4A2A  FE 4C               CP   4CH           ;IS IT 'L'?
4A2C  C2 03 4A            JP   NZ,START      ;IF NOT,START ALL OVER
4A2F  CD 00 4C            CALL BLINK         ;ELSE BLINK THE SPOT
4A32  C3 03 4A            JP   START         ;AND START ALL OVER
4A35  FE 45       NEXT:   CP   45H           ;IS 1ST CHAR 'E'?
4A37  C2 00 4A            JP   NZ,START      ;IF NOT,START ALL OVER
4A3A  03                  INC  BC            ;ELSE POINT TO NEXT I/O
4A3B  0A                  LD   A,(BC)        ;AND PUT IT INTO A
4A3C  FE 58               CP   58H           ;IS 2ND CHAR 'X'?
4A3E  20 06               JR   NZ,NEXT2      ;IF NOT, TRY FOR 'N'
4A40  CD 20 4C            CALL EXCH          ;ELSE CALL EXCHANGE
4A43  C3 03 4A            JP   START         ;AND START ALL OVER
4A46  FE 4E       NEXT2:  CP   4Eh           ;IS 2ND CHAR 'N'?
4A48  C2 03 4A            JP   NZ,START      ;IF NOT,START ALL OVER
4A4B  CD 80 43            CALL 4380H         ;CALL T-BUG TO GET AWAY
                                             ;
4C00  CD C9 01    BLINK:  CALL 01C9H         ;CLEAR THE SCREEN
4C03  36 20       RBLNK:  LD(HL),20H         ;CLEAR SPOT
4C05  CD 15 4C            CALL DELAY         ;DO TIME DELAY
4C08  36 BF               LD (HL),191D       ;PRINT SPOT
4C0A  CD 15 4C            CALL DELAY         ;DO TIME DELAY AGAIN
4C0D  3A 40 38            LD   A,(3840H)     ;GET 'BREAK' KB ROW
4C10  FE 04               CP   4H            ;IS IT 'BREAK' KEY?
4C12  20 EF               JR   NZ,RBLINK     ;IF NOT,BLINK AGAIN
4C14  C9                  RET                ;ELSE RETURN
4C15  06 1F       DELAY:  LD   B,1FH         ;SET MSB OF DELAY
4C17  0E FF       SETC:   LD   C,0FFH        ;SET LSB OF DELAY
4C19  0D          DECC:   DEC  C             ;COUNT DOWN LSB
4C1A  20 FD               JR   NZ,DECC       ;IF NOT DONE,DO MORE
4C1C  05                  DEC  B             ;ESLE COUNT DOWN MSB
4C1D  20 F8               JR   NZ,SETC       ;IF NOT DONE,DO LSB AGAIN
4C1F  C9                  RET                ;ELSE RETURN TO BLINK
4C20  EB          EXCH:   EX   DE,HL         ;SWAP VIDEO LOCATIONS
4C21  C3 00 4C            JP   BLINK         ;AND MAKE IT BLINK
```

Thus, the instruction following CALL 0361H begins a decoding operation. That decoding operation runs through the i/o buffer, looking for character patterns BL, EX, and EN. On finding one of those sequences the program takes appropriate action, using one of the subroutines beginning at address 4C00H.

If the program does not find a BL, EX, or EN combination in the i/o buffer, it defaults to START, giving you a chance to enter the characters again. Incidentally, the program works equally well if you enter the full words, BLINK, EXCHANGE, or END. The i/o decoding scheme just looks for the first two characters in each case—if other characters follow, that's of no consequence.

SUMMARY

CALL 0361H connects the keyboard to the i/o buffer.
It also:
- Turns on the cursor symbol.
- Enters keyboard characters from the beginning of the buffer space.
- Automatically advances the cursor position.
- Remains in effect until the user strikes the ENTER key.

A CALL 0361H must be preceded by an LD SP,NN operation to get the SYSTEM program stack out of the i/o space.

CHAPTER 9

Introducing the TRS-80 Editor/Assembler

At first thought, Radio Shack's Editor/Assembler software (Catalog No. 26-2002) might seem to be little more than a convenient language translator—a cassette-based system that translates standard Z-80 mnemonics into machine code. Certainly Editor/Assembler (or EDTASM) does that, and that is a nice feature. But there is a lot more to it.

In fact, if you have never used an assembler system before, you can be easily confused by all the special features that carry it far beyond being a simple language translator. This assembler is a system that is best understood by working into it gradually, starting with some familiar ideas and letting first-hand experience lead you to a real appreciation of the power of EDTASM.

This is the approach used in this chapter and the one that follows.

A FEW PRELIMINARY NOTES

The main purpose of EDTASM is to let you type in assembly or source-code instructions from the keyboard. You still have to design the overall program yourself, but EDTASM does all the legwork involved in translating the mnemonics into machine-language, or object-code, instructions. EDTASM also saves a lot of time by letting you specify variables in terms of decimal numbers and specify jumps and calls in terms of labels, and by generally letting you avoid a lot of routine and often tedious figuring and table searching.

In short, EDTASM takes advantage of the computing power of your machine, doing a lot of clerical work for you. And you will find that using EDTASM makes hand assembling seem primitive.

So EDTASM lets you type in machine-language programs in an assembly-language format. When you are done with that phase of the task, you enter a command that tells the system to assemble the program into machine code. It is possible to view your assembly or source code listing right along with the assembled machine-code listing.

If you make any errors in the assembly listing, EDTASM will let you know about it. Of course, EDTASM cannot be held responsible for mistakes in the overall program, but it does seek out syntax errors—improperly specified or misspelled source instructions.

Programs generated with EDTASM can be saved on cassette tape and written out to a line printer.

The only drawback is that you cannot actually test your program while the EDTASM program is residing in the user's memory space. In order to check the operation of an EDTASM-generated, machine-language program, you must first save the program on cassette tape. Then the program has to be entered as an ordinary machine-language program under the SYSTEM command. EDTASM is thus lost in the process, but you can check the operation of the program.

If you don't like the way the program runs, you have the option of debugging it with T-BUG or by reloading EDTASM and fixing the problem in assembly language.

There is a very practical reason for this shortcoming of EDTASM —not being able to test a machine-language program without destroying EDTASM. The reason is that most TRS-80 users do not have enough RAM to support both EDTASM and a machine-language program of any reasonable size.

The EDTASM program occupies some 6300 bytes of RAM. The entry point is 18058 (decimal), but there are special registers located at lower memory addresses and, indeed, in the i/o buffer space as well.

A program of this sort that occupies only about 6K of RAM would seem to leave a lot of RAM for machine-language programs you develop with EDTASM—about 7K of memory for a 16K system. But there's a snag at this point.

As you type in the assembly codes they are stored in RAM, beginning at the point where the assembler program, itself, leaves off. So as you type in the assembly program it grows upward in the user's RAM space, taking up one byte of memory for every character you enter. And you will find that even a modest assembly listing will use up at least a couple of thousand bytes of memory. But that isn't all.

When you tell EDTASM to assemble the program the object codes start filling up more RAM space, beginning where the source codes left off. So there goes another big chunk of RAM space.

This all adds up to the fact that EDTASM eats up a whole lot of RAM, leaving little space for entering the machine-language program you are trying to develop. What's more, EDTASM uses up the prime memory space that you normally want for the program you are writing.

No, we cannot test a program developed by EDTASM without losing or writing over EDTASM. And that is why we have to live with the awkward process of first saving the program on tape and then entering it again under the SYSTEM command.

There is another trouble with EDTASM. It is a minor, but sometimes annoying, problem. Recall that it is possible to bomb out of T-BUG and end up in the BASIC monitor. Whenever that happens you can return to T-BUG by calling SYSTEM and entering /17312. But that cannot be done as effectively with EDTASM.

Once you return to BASIC from EDTASM, some valuable registers are disrupted. It is possible to call SYSTEM and return to EDTASM by entering /18058; and it will seem that EDTASM is working again. But it won't take long to find that things don't work out very well—you will sooner or later notice some strange effects, such as seeing the video display suddenly change to a 32-character line format.

So if, for any reason, you find the system going from EDTASM to BASIC, prepare yourself to lose everything you've done so far and load the EDTASM system again from scratch.

It is not the purpose of this discussion to cast a bad light on EDTASM. Rather, the idea is to point out a couple of problems that must be clearly understood from the start. Difficulties aside, EDTASM is a powerful programming tool.

BRINGING UP EDTASM

Obviously, the first step in using EDTASM is to acquire a copy of the cassette tape and load it into your system. Since it is a machine-language program, it is loaded from the SYSTEM command.

So enter SYSTEM, set up the cassette player for playing the EDTASM tape, and then enter the file name EDTASM. The program is long, so it takes a few minutes to load. The familiar flashing asterisk in the upper left-hand corner of the screen confirms a good loading operation.

When the EDTASM tape is fully loaded into your system, you will see the machine-language prompt symbol (an asterisk), followed by a question mark and cursor symbol. Respond by entering a slash (/).

The screen will then clear and you will see a title message and an asterisk, indicating that EDTASM is up and ready to go.

You can respond at this point by typing anything you choose from the keyboard. But if the assembler is to be of any use, the things you type and enter ought to make sense in the context of a few rules.

LINE NUMBERS, ORG, AND END

One important rule is that every assembly-language program must begin by specifying the origin of that program. The origin actually spells out the address at which the machine-language program you develop should begin loading—when, indeed, you load it from cassette tape later on in the process.

A good many T-BUG programs cited in earlier chapters began at address 4A00H. That is the idea here. You can set the origin of your machine-language program anywhere you choose within the system's available memory space.

Before learning how to specify the origin of the program, it is important to understand that assembly listings you enter from the keyboard must have line numbers assigned to them. These line numbers serve as convenient identifiers for each line of assembly text you enter from the keyboard. The numbers are not saved on tape with the finished machine-language program.

When you are ready to begin entering an assembly program under EDTASM, the first task is to specify a line number and an interval between line numbers. It works something like BASIC's AUTO command.

Suppose you have just brought up EDTASM as described in the previous section. To specify the starting line number and interval, respond to the asterisk by entering something such as I100,10. This is telling the assembler to begin numbering the text lines at 100 and to use increments of 10. After that, the assembler takes care of numbering the lines for you.

As another example, entering I10,5 tells the numbering scheme to begin at line 10 and increment in steps of 5.

Here is how the first couple of steps in an assembly programming operation could appear on the screen:

```
*I100,10
00100        ORG      4A00H
00110_
```

In this case the user responded to the asterisk by entering I100,10. That set up the line-numbering scheme to begin at line 100 and increment in steps of 10.

The assembler printed the 00100 following that particular entry. The 00100 is a five-digit version of the starting line number, 100.

You need not specify line numbers with the leading zeros, but the assembler will always insert them as it goes along.

As mentioned earlier, an assembly program should begin by specifying the origin of the machine-language program you will ultimately develop. That is the purpose of the text in line 00100. Here, the user responded by striking the right-arrow key (→), typing ORG, striking the right-arrow key again, typing 4A00H, and, finally, striking the ENTER key. This sequence of operations completes the necessary process of specifying the program's origin. In this case the origin is set at address 4A00H, and when the finished program is loaded into the system at some later time the machine codes will begin loading at address 4A00H.

Once the user completes that ORG line and strikes the ENTER key, the assembler accepts the information and responds by printing out the next line number.

NOTES

The ultimate origin of a machine-language program generated under EDTASM must be specified by ORG, followed by the origin address.

The ORG code must be written at the beginning of the second vertical field on the screen—an effect accomplished easily by striking the right-arrow key just one time.

If the ORG address is specified as a hexadecimal number, it must be followed by an H. Otherwise, the assembler will attempt to interpret the number as a decimal version of the address.

Every assembly program must conclude with an END operation. Specifically, it must conclude with END, followed by an address. The END line specifies the entry point of the machine-language program that you have prepared.

Often the ORG address and END are the same, thus indicating that the execution of the machine-language program begins at the lowest address it occupies in RAM. But it is often desirable to enter a program at an address that is somewhat higher than the origin. This being the case, the END address will be different from the one specified in the ORG line.

So here is the simplest possible assembly program as it appears on the screen:

```
*100,10
00100        ORG      4A00H
00110        END      4A00H
00120_
```

The program specifies an origin and an entry point. Note that the END operation, like ORG, must be written at the beginning of the second vertical field.

This program won't do anything, because there are no real machine instructions appearing between ORG and END. The example merely illustrates how an assembly program is started and concluded.

NOTES

   The END, followed by an address, at the conclusion of an assembly listing accomplishes two things:
   1. The END marks the end of the assembly text.
   2. The END address marks the entry point of the machine-language program being generated under EDTASM.

   EDTASM will accept initial line numbers and generate line numbers automatically thereafter in the range of 00000 through 65529.

DELETING AND WRITING PROGRAM TEXT

Every assembly program must begin with an ORG and address and conclude with an END and address. The actual program text is fit in between.

If you have actually entered the simple, do-nothing assembly text illustrated in the previous section, it is necessary to delete it before beginning the next example. (Program text could be *inserted* between those two ORG and END operations, but that sort of editing function is reserved for a later discussion.)

To delete an entire assembly listing, first strike the BREAK key to return to EDTASM's monitor mode. This will break up the automatic line-numbering operation and return an asterisk. The asterisk is the prompt symbol for the monitor mode.

Once you are back into the monitor mode you can delete the entire text by answering the asterisk with D#:* and entering it. This particular set of characters literally means delete (the D) from the beginning of the text (#) to (:) the end of the text (*). This is much the same thing as doing the NEW command in BASIC.

After entering D#:* the system returns an asterisk prompt symbol, signaling the fact that the system is ready for the next command. So do the following to get another program-writing operation underway:

```
*1100,10
00100          ORG      4A00H
00110_
```

168

With the origin of the program thus specified, you can begin writing some program text. To keep things simple, suppose you are working with a one-instruction program that loads 3C00H to the HL register pair.

So strike the right-arrow key to set the beginning of the instruction at the start of the second vertical field, then type in the appropriate instruction, and strike the ENTER key to signal the end of the line of text. By doing that, the display should look something like this:

```
*1100,10
00100        ORG   4A00H
00110        LD    HL,3C00H
00120_
```

Next, signal the end of the listing by entering END 4A00H:

```
*1100,10
00100        ORG   4A00H
00110        LD    HL,3C00H
00120        END   4A00H
00130_
```

This example represents a complete assembly program. It certainly isn't a very sophisticated program, but it illustrates the general procedures described thus far.

Notice that the Z-80 instruction is typed as it appears on the instruction-set listings. The H appearing at the end of the 3C00 address indicates that the number is in hexadecimal. If you omit the H, the assembler will attempt to interpret it as a decimal number.

Obviously you can enter more than one instruction line. The upper limit on the number of instructions in the assembly listing depends on the memory capacity of your TRS-80 system: the larger the memory capacity, the greater the number of instructions the assembler can handle.

ASSEMBLING THE SOURCE PROGRAM

After entering the assembly program text—the source program—it is time to let EDTASM assemble it for you. The assembly operation automatically translates the instructions into machine code and assigns those codes to the proper address locations.

Assuming you have entered the simple one-line program cited in the previous section, first return to EDTASM's monitor mode by striking the BREAK key. The appearance of the asterisk prompt character confirms that the system has returned to the monitor.

To assemble the program, answer the asterisk by entering an A from the keyboard. After that, the screen should show this sort of display:

```
*1100,10
00100            ORG   4A00H
00110            LD    HL,3C00H
00120            END   4A00H
00130
*A
4A00             00100      ORG   4A00H
4A00  21003C     00110      LD    HL,3C00H
4A00             00120      END   4A00H
```

The first phase of the display—the portion showing line numbers at the left-hand end—is the part you entered as assembly program text. After doing the BREAK and answering the asterisk with an A, the listing shows the assembled version of the program.

The assembled portion shows addresses in the first vertical field, followed by hexadecimal versions of the machine code. The second field shows the original line numbers for convenient reference, and the third vertical field shows the original assembly text.

The important feature is the next-to-the-last line that reads: 4A00 21003C. This shows the address location of the beginning of a 3-byte, machine-language instruction, 21003C. And what does 21003C mean? It means load 3C00H to the HL register pair—an operation originally specified with the mnemonics LD HL,3C00H. Yes, indeed, EDTASM assembled LD HL,3C00H into machine code and assigned it to the ORG address 4A00H. This is the same result you would get by hand assembling that particular instruction.

Incidentally, if you are actually trying this experiment on your machine, you will see some additional material, namely:

```
00000 TOTAL ERRORS
READY CASSETTE
—
```

Those messages inform you that you have made no errors in the assembly listing and that the program has been successfully assembled into machine code. It is then time to save the machine code, or object code, on cassette tape. If you want to save that one-instruction, machine-language program on tape, all you have to do is set up the cassette player for recording a program and then answer the cursor symbol by striking the ENTER key.

When the assembled program is thus recorded, EDTASM will return an asterisk, indicating it is back to its monitor mode and awaiting the next command. But if you don't want to record the assembled program, simply strike the BREAK key to return to the monitor mode.

Now the system is ready to do something else. Perhaps you want to delete the old program. In that case answer the asterisk by entering D#:*. Then you are ready to start all over again, doing something such as I100,10 to begin writing a new assembly, source-code program.

> ### SUMMARY
>
> - Striking the BREAK key interrupts the current activity and returns EDTASM to its monitor mode.
> - I*nn,i* sets up the Insert mode, beginning reference line numbers at *nn* and incrementing each of them at intervals of *i* line numbers.
> - ORG   *addr* specifies the address, *addr*, where the machine-language program is to begin loading. Every assembly program must begin with that pseudo-operation.
> - END   *addr* specifies the address, *addr*, where the machine-language program is to begin execution. It is often the same as the ORG address, but not necessarily. As demonstrated later, the *addr* in this pseudo-op can be replaced by a line label.
> - Entering an *A* from the monitor mode causes EDTASM to assemble your source-code listing, to convert the mnemonic-oriented source code into machine addresses and instructions.

This time, write a program that will actually do something. Begin by answering the asterisk with D#:* and entering it. This ensures that the old program is wiped out. Then answer the asterisk with an I100,10 to begin at line number 100 and set up line increments of 10. Type in the assembly listing as shown in Program 9-1.

Chances are quite good you won't be able to type in the entire listing without making at least one typing error. If that happens, there are several procedures for correcting it. The following error-correcting procedure is not the simplest one available, but it is the

Program 9-1. A typical source code listing for EDTASM.

```
00100              ORG   4A00H
00110  TON         CALL  01C9H       ;CLEAR THE SCREEN
00120  PON         LD    HL,3C00H    ;SET VIDEO POINTER
00130              LD    (HL),42D    ;PRINT ASTERISK
00140              LD    A,H         ;MSB OF POINTER TO A
00150              CP    3DH         ;END OF QUADRANT?
00160              JR    Z,CTD       ;IF SO,DO DELAY
00170              INC   HL          ;ELSE INCREMENT POINTER
00180              JR    PON         ;AND PRINT MORE
00190  CTD         CALL  TD          ;CALL TIME DELAY
00200              CALL  01C9H       ;CLEAR THE SCREEN
00210              CALL  TD          ;CALL TIME DELAY
00220              JR    TON         ;AND DRAW AGAIN
00230  TD          LD    B,0CH       ;SET MSB OF TD
00240  SETC        LD    C,0FFH      ;SET LSB OF TD
00250  DECC        DEC   C           ;COUNT LSB
00260              JR    NZ,DECC     ;IF NOT DONE, DO MORE
00270              DEC   B           ;ELSE COUNT MSB
00280              JR    NZ,SETC     ;IF NOT DONE,DO LSB AGAIN
00290              RET               ;ELSE RETURN
00300              END   4A00H
```

most straightforward in the context of what has been discussed. To correct an error in the assembly listing:
1. Strike the BREAK key to return to EDTASM's monitor mode.
2. Delete the defective line by answering the asterisk with a *D*, followed by the appropriate line number. If the problem is in line 00180, for example, enter D180 (leading zeros need not be typed in).
3. Insert a corrected version of the line after answering the asterisk with an *I*, followed by the appropriate line number, for example, I180. The system is now in the Insert mode and at the line number you just entered. Type in the corrected version of the entire line. Inserting a corrected line will usually turn up a NO ROOM BETWEEN LINES message. Don't worry about that now; it is simply telling you that the next line in the sequence has some information in it.
4. With the system back in the monitor mode, as signaled by the asterisk prompt symbol, you can resume programming by entering I*nn*, where *nn* is the next line number you want to work with.

The error is corrected, and you are back on the right track for completing the job.

The program in Program 9-1 ultimately causes the system to draw four lines of asterisks across the top of the screen, making them flash on and off. But it is far too soon to check its operation.

Line 100 specifies the origin of the machine-language program at address 4A00H. Line 300, the last line, specifies the entry point at that same address. In other words, the first address for the program is the place where execution is to begin.

Line 110 calls the ROM-based operation for clearing the screen. Notice that the address concludes with the letter H. An H must follow any data or address that is specified in a hexadecimal format.

NOTE

Following a data or address number with an H specifies a hexadecimal number.

Following a data or address number with a D, or no letter at all, specifies a decimal format.

Following a data or address number with an O specifies an octal number.

Hexadecimal numbers must begin with a number, and not a letter. EDTASM, for example, will not accept data FFH; but it will understand its equivalent 0FFH.

So line 110 specifies a screen-clearing operation. It concludes with a comment. In assembly listings, comments serve the same purpose as REMs in BASIC; they are a convenient way to make some notes concerning the operations at hand. *Comments must be preceded by a semicolon.*

Line 120 sets the video pointer to the first video memory location, 3C00H. Now that line begins with a label. You can make up your own labels, following a few simple rules that are spelled out in the next NOTE. Their true purpose and assembly power won't be apparent, however, until we get further into this analysis.

NOTE

Labels are used to mark critical points in an assembly program.

A label must follow the reference line number.

A label can be any combination of alphanumeric characters, up to six and always beginning with an alphabetical character. A $ must not be used anywhere in a label.

There are some reserved labels that must not be used. See Chart 9-1. This list of reserved labels corresponds to BASIC's list of reserved words that cannot be used as variable names.

Chart 9-1. Reserved Labels for EDTASM*

A	IX
B	IY
C	SP
D	PC
E	AF
H	BC
L	DE
I	HL
R	

*These letters may be used within a label, but they must not stand alone as a label.

Line 130 prints the asterisk at the point indicated by the HL pair on the screen. Note that the ASCII character is specified in a decimal format in this case. A 2AH would work out equally well.

Skipping down to line 160, you find the instruction JR Z,CTD. That is saying: jump relative if zero to the line labeled CTD. You don't have to count the number of bytes to be jumped—just specify the label. This is at least an introductory note concerning the power of labels in EDTASM. The computer is going to figure out how many program bytes to be jumped.

See the same sort of things taking place in lines 180, 190, 210, 220, 260, and 280. Knowing how to use the labels, you should be able to work your way through the entire program to see how it works. Hopefully, the comments will be of great help, too.

In the process of discussing the assembly listing in Program 9-1, you should be getting some idea about how to use labels and comments. Both serve to simplify the programming operation and clarify what is going on.

Once the listing is in place as illustrated in Program 9-1, the next job is to let EDTASM assemble it for you. First, get back to the monitor by striking the BREAK key; then assemble the program by entering an *A*.

The assembled version of the program will be dumped onto the screen—far too quickly for you to study it. The important thing now, however, is the number of TOTAL ERRORS. If there are none, you've done a good job. But if that counter shows some errors, you have some editing work to do.

Program 9-2 is a hardcopy version of the assembled program. The program is too long to be seen in its entirety on the screen, so you will have to use Program 9-2 as a guide for the time being.

Program 9-2. Assembled version of Program 9-1.

```
4A00              00100        ORG     4A00H
4A00   CDC901     00110        CALL    01C9H       ;CLEAR THE SCREEN
4A03   21003C     00120 TON    LD      HL,3C00H    ;SET VIDEO POINTER
4A06   362A       00130 PON    LD      (HL),42D    ;PRINT ASTERISK
4A08   7C         00140        LD      A,H         ;MSB OF POINTER TO A
4A09   FE3D       00150        CP      3DH         ;END OF QUADRANT?
4A0B   2803       00160        JR      Z,CTD       ;IF SO, DO DELAY
4A0D   23         00170        INC     HL          ;ELSE INCREMENT POINTER
4A0E   18F6       00180        JR      PON         ;AND PRINT MORE
4A10   CD1B4A     00190 CTD    CALL    TD          ;CALL TIME DELAY
4A13   CDC901     00200        CALL    01C9H       ;CLEAR THE SCREEN
4A16   CD1B4A     00210        CALL    TD          ;CALL TIME DELAY
4A19   18E8       00220        JR      TON         ;AND DRAW AGAIN
4A1B   060C       00230 TD     LD      B,0CH       ;SET MSB OF TD
4A1D   0EFF       00240 SETC   LD      C,0FFH      ;SET LSB OF TD
4A1F   0D         00250 DECC   DEC     C           ;COUNT LSB
4A20   20FD       00260        JR      NZ,DECC     ;IF NOT DONE,DO MORE
4A22   05         00270        DEC     B           ;ELSE COUNT MSB
4A23   20F8       00280        JR      NZ,SETC     ;IF NOT DONE, DO LSB AGAIN
4A25   C9         00290        RET                 ;ELSE RETURN
4A00              00300        END     4A00H
00000  TOTAL ERRORS

DECC       4A1F
SETC       4A1D
TD         4A1B
CTD        4A10
PON        4A06
TON        4A03
```

Let's suppose that it turns out that you have made a syntactical error somewhere in the program; the TOTAL ERRORS message shows something other than 00000. This means you have to do some editing. But first you have to find the error.

If you don't know what the error is, the following procedure helps you locate it:

1. Get to the monitor by striking the BREAK key.
2. Answer the asterisk by entering A/WE.

Doing this, the system will begin assembling the program again. This time, however, the /WE part of the command tells the system to stop assembling when it encounters an error and write a message describing its nature. You can then figure out what the error is and correct the error by referring to the appropriate line number.

One method for correcting errors was described earlier. Basically it amounted to deleting the entire line of text containing the error and then going to the Insert mode to reenter the entire line from scratch. There is, however, a simpler way to do the same thing.

EDTASM has a Replace command. Answer the asterisk with an R*nn*, where *nn* specifies the line number of the line to be replaced. The system automatically deletes the line for you and waits for you to type in the corrected version of the line. The R command takes the place of the Delete/Insert sequence.

The best way to edit a line having just one or two minor errors, however, is to take advantage of EDTASM's Edit mode of operation. This Edit feature works almost exactly the same way as BASIC's EDIT mode.

To get into the Edit mode, answer the asterisk with E*nn*, where *nn* is the line number of the text to be edited. Then use the BASIC-like EDIT commands to fix the trouble. The Edit instructions in your *Editor/Assembler Instruction Manual* adequately describe all the Edit commands you will ever need.

Continue doing the A/WE process until there are no longer any errors in the text. At that time the listing on the screen will resemble that in Program 9-2.

Notice, incidentally, that the assembled listing ends by specifying the absolute addresses of all the labeled instructions. Label DECC, for example, refers to the machine instruction beginning at address 4A1F. Such a listing can be invaluable when it comes to debugging a very long program.

WORKING WITH THE OBJECT CODE VERSION

After going through the processes described in the previous section, the program is still not ready to be tested on line. It must be transferred to cassette tape first and then loaded back into the machine under the SYSTEM command.

Assembled programs should be saved on tape under a file name. If you do not specify a file name, EDTASM will automatically assign NONAME as a file name. But as long as you have control over matters, it is a good idea to assign a name that means something significant to you. The following NOTES show a few rules for composing file names for machine programs written under EDTASM.

NOTES

A file name can be composed of combinations of alphanumeric characters, not exceeding six characters in length.

The first character must be an alphabetical character.

To assign a file name to a program, get into the monitor mode and then answer the asterisk by typing an A, followed by one space and your chosen file name.

The A instructs the system to assemble the program again, but under the specified *file name*. A space between the A and *file name* is mandatory.

After assembling the program under the designated file name, the system brings up the message READY CASSETTE. Set up your tape machine for recording, then strike the ENTER key. Within just a few moments the system will load the machine-language portion of the program to the tape. *None of the assembly text is loaded this way.*

Now, if you are perfectly confident that the program will run as you expect, and if you are sure you will never want to edit it from EDTASM at any time in the future, you are done with the assembly operations.

But you might want to save the assembly text for future reference. To save the source-code part of the program—the stuff you typed into the machine originally—do this:

1. Set up the tape machine for recording a program.
2. From the monitor mode, enter W *file name*, where *file name* is a name composed according to the rules outlined earlier.
3. Answer READY CASSETTE by striking the ENTER key.

When the recording is done, you have the assembly text saved on tape.

The object code listing—the actual machine-language program—is always recorded immediately after doing an assembly operation.

The source code listing can be saved on tape only by going to the Write mode—entering W *file name*.

Suppose, for instance, you want to save the object code from Program 9-2 under the file name OBLINK. To do that, enter A OBLINK; and when you see the READY CASSETTE, record the program by striking the ENTER key.

If you want to save the source listing under the file name SBLINK, enter W SBLINK, and record it by striking the ENTER key in response to READY CASSETTE.

By this time you have composed and assembled a program with EDTASM. The machine-language version is saved on cassette tape as OBLINK, and the source version is saved as SBLINK. Now it is time to test the program's actual operation—finally.

Unfortunately, EDTASM has to be destroyed. To get out of EDTASM, answer the asterisk by entering a B. Entering a B from EDTASM returns things to the power-up sequence for BASIC. You will thus see MEMORY SIZE?

Then set up the cassette player for entering the machine-language version of the program—the one saved as OBLINK. Enter SYSTEM, and respond to the asterisk by typing OBLINK. The tape will load the program into the machine and signal the end of the loading process by showing the usual SYSTEM symbols *?_. Respond by entering the slash (/)—and, presto, there are the flashing lines of asterisks.

But wait! There are a couple of problems. EDTASM checked for syntactical error in the assembly listing, but it did not (and cannot) check the validity of the program, itself. One problem is that the asterisks appear to be flashing too rapidly; maybe you would like to see them flashing at a somewhat lower rate. Then, too, there is a programming problem that causes an extra asterisk to appear at the beginning of the fifth line on the screen—it's a "small" problem, but one of a type that could cause some real trouble under different circumstances.

So there is a need to debug the program; the original version isn't quite good enough.

Exactly how to go about fixing those problems is often a matter of opinion. One approach is to load T-BUG and fix the troubles, using the original EDTASM as a guide to the relevant address locations. This approach is a good one if the "fixes" aren't very extensive (as is the case here). Another nice thing about fixing things with T-BUG is that you can test the program on the spot. The only disadvantage is that your original EDTASM listings are no longer valid.

The second approach is to reload EDTASM, load the source version of the program into it, and fix it at the assembly level. That way, you end up with fresh listings; but then you have to do a lot of recording and reloading to see whether or not the "fixes" really do the job.

In this particular case it seems better to load T-BUG. Load T-BUG and refer to the listing in Program 9-2 to see what has to be done to fix the troubles.

To make the time delay longer, and hence get a lower flashing rate, register B in line 230 can be loaded with CFH, instead of 0CH. So change address 4A1C from 0C to CF. Do a J 4A00, and you will see that did, indeed, lower the flashing rate.

The fact that an extra asterisk appears at the beginning of the fifth line comes about as the result of a common sort of programming error. Referring to Program 9-2, incrementing the HL register pair should take place *before* the H register is tested for a value of 3D. Thus the operations beginning at line 130 should read:

4A06	362A	00130 PON	LD (HL),42D	;PRINT ASTERISK
4A08	23	00140	INC HL	;INCREMENT POINTER
4A09	7C	00150	LD A,H	;MSB OF POINTER TO A
4A0A	FE 3D	00160	CP 3DH	;END OF QUADRANT?
4A0C	28 02	00170	JR Z,CTD	;IF SO, DO DELAY
4A0E	18 F6	00180	JR PON	;ELSE PRINT MORE

Everything else is the same before and after this sequence.

In this case we were lucky enough to have the "fix" fit exactly within the memory space already allocated for the drawing sequence. Had there not been enough room, it would be necessary to do the fix from EDTASM.

So enter the "fix" from T-BUG, changing the data content of addresses 4A06 through 4A0F as necessary. Doing a J 4A00 will show that the program works better this time.

The machine-code version can be saved on cassette tape from T-BUG by using the Punch command. In many instances this marks the end of the programming job. But, for the sake of illustration, suppose you want to make the changes from EDTASM instead of T-BUG. You might use T-BUG to confirm the validity of your changes, but you want to make corrected versions of the source listings. Here is how that is done.

First, reload EDTASM from scratch, as described in the opening part of this chapter. Then, to save some time, load the defective source code listing.

To load a source listing under EDTASM, answer the asterisk with L *file name*. If you specify no *file name*, the system will accept the first program loaded from cassette tape. You could, in this instance, load under the file name, SBLINK—that was the name attached to the original source listing.

When the loading is done, as signaled by a new asterisk prompt symbol, you can confirm entry of the right program by entering P#:*. That will display the entire source listing on the screen.

> NOTE
>
> Under the EDTASM monitor, a *P* command causes a printing of the source listing. See the *Editor/Assembler Instruction Manual* for some useful variations of the Print command.

The system is now set up so that you can make the necessary changes in the source listing, using Deletes, Inserts, Replaces, and Edit commands. A corrected and assembled version of the program appears as Program 9-3.

OTHER EDTASM COMMANDS AND VARIATIONS

With this sort of experience behind you, you should be able to learn a lot more from the *Editor/Assembler Instruction Manual*.

Program 9-3. Assembled and corrected version of Program 9-2.

```
4A00              00100         ORG     4A00H
4A00   CDC901     00110         CALL    01C9H       ;CLEAR THE SCREEN
4A03   21003C     00120 TON     LD      HL,3C00H    ;SET VIDEO POINTER
4A06   362A       00130 PON     LD      (HL),42D    ;PRINT ASTERISK
4A08   23         00140         INC     HL          ;INCREMENT POINTER
4A09   7C         00150         LD      A,H         ;MSB OF POINTER TO A
4A0A   FE3D       00160         CP      3DH         ;END OF QUADRANT?
4A0C   2802       00170         JR      Z,CTD       ;IF SO,DO DELAY
4A0E   18F6       00180         JR      PON         ;AND PRINT MORE
4A10   CD1B4A     00190 CTD     CALL    TD          ;CALL TIME DELAY
4A13   CDC901     00200         CALL    01C9H       ;CLEAR THE SCREEN
4A16   CD1B4A     00210         CALL    TD          ;CALL TIME DELAY
4A19   18E8       00220         JR      TON         ;AND DRAW AGAIN
4A1B   060C       00230 TD      LD      B,0CH       ;SET MSB OF TD
4A1D   0EFF       00240 SETC    LD      C,0FFH      ;SET LSB OF TD
4A1F   0D         00250 DECC    DEC     C           ;COUNT LSB
4A20   20FD       00260         JR      NZ,DECC     ;IF NOT DONE,DO MORE
4A22   05         00270         DEC     B           ;ELSE COUNT MSB
4A23   20F8       00280         JR      NZ,SETC     ;IF NOT DONE, DO LSB AGAIN
4A25   C9         00290         RET                 ;ELSE RETURN
4A00              00300         END     4A00H
00000  TOTAL ERRORS

DECC    4A1F
SETC    4A1D
TD      4A1B
CTD     4A10
PON     4A06
TON     4A03
```

See what you can learn on your own from the following sections of that manual:

Assemble (A)
BASIC (B)
Delete (D)
Edit (E)
Find (F)
Hardcopy (H)—line-printer applications only
Insert (I)
Load (L)
Number (N)
Print (P)
Replace (R)
Type (T)—line-printer applications only
Scroll up (↑)
Scroll down (↓)
Tab (→)
Delete character (←)
Delete line (shift ←)
Pause (shift @)
Write (W)

The best way to get familiar with EDTASM is by actually working with it, composing interesting programs of your own design. But if you think EDTASM is a powerful machine-language programming tool at this point, wait until you have a chance to get into the discussions in the next chapter.

CHAPTER 10

Real Assembly Power With Pseudo-Ops

In the context of writing assembly programs, pseudo-ops are operations that affect the assembly operation but do not appear as legitimate machine-language instructions. Chapter 9 specified two pseudo-ops: ORG and END.

ORG and END are operations used by the assembler, but they do not appear in the assembled, object-code version of the listing. In a sense they are housekeeping operations for the assembler; they are important, to be sure, but they are not part of the finished product—the fully assembled, ready-to-run, machine program.

EDTASM supports a number of other pseudo-ops. They are not mandatory, as are the ORG and END operations; rather, they save the programmer a great deal of time and effort.

SIMPLE EQU PSEUDO-OPS

One of the simplest, yet most used, optional pseudo-ops is EQU. It is used to assign a specific data or address value to a label of your own invention. Consider the following line of assembly text:

```
00100    CLS    EQU    01C9H    ;DEFINE CLS
```

In this example, label CLS is assigned the 2-byte, hexadecimal address 01C9. That particular address, you may recall, is the entry point for a ROM-based TRS-80 operation that clears the screen and homes the cursor.

Without taking advantage of the EQU pseudo-op, setting up an instruction for clearing the screen meant doing a CALL 01C9H in the assembly program. And each time you wanted to use that instruction, you would have to type it in full.

But by doing a CLS   EQU   01C9H at some early point in the assembly listing, writing an instruction for clearing the screen is a simple matter of doing CALL CLS. Once a number is assigned to a label via an EQU pseudo-op, any subsequent references to that label automatically bring up the value originally assigned to it. One advantage is that a label such as CLS is certainly easier to remember than 01C9H when you are in the middle of writing an assembly program.

Program 10-1. Source and assembled versions of a program that uses simple EQU operations to define labels.

```
00100                   ORG        4A00H
00110   CLS             EQU        01C9H
00120   KBIN            EQU        0049H
00130   PCHR            EQU        033AH
00140   ;BEGINNING OF THE PROGRAM
00150                   CALL CLS       ;CLEAR THE SCREEN
00160   GET             CALL KBIN      ;GET A KEYBOARD CHARACTER
00170                   CALL PCHR      ;AND PRINT IT
00180                   JR GET         ;GET NEXT CHARACTER
00190                   END    4A00H


4A00                00100           ORG        4A00H
01C9                00110   CLS     EQU        01C9H
0049                00120   KBIN    EQU        0049H
033A                00130   PCHR    EQU        033AH
                    00140   ;BEGINNING OF THE PROGRAM
4A00 CDC901         00150           CALL CLS       ;CLEAR THE SCREEN
4A03 CD4900         00160   GET     CALL KBIN      ;GET A KEYBOARD CHARACTER
4A06 CD3A03         00170           CALL PCHR      ;AND PRINT IT
4A09 18F8           00180           JR GET         ;GET NEXT CHARACTER
4A00                00190           END    4A00H
00000   TOTAL  ERRORS

GET     4A03
PCHR    033A
KBIN    0049
CLS     01C9
```

By way of a convincing demonstration, type in the assembly listing in the first part of Program 10-1. That listing begins with the mandatory ORG pseudo-op, but then there are three optional EQU pseudo-ops.

The EQU operation in line 110 defines label CLS as 01C9H, the KBIN label in line 120 is defined as 0049H (entry point for a keyboard character to the accumulator), and PCHR in line 130 is a label assigned to 033AH (entry point for printing a character from the accumulator and advancing the cursor).

With the critical entry addresses thus defined as labels, the working part of the program, lines 150 through 180, uses the labels to work out a simple assembly program: one that clears the video screen and then allows you to type and print characters from the keyboard.

The exciting part of the job doesn't become apparent, however, until the listing is assembled. See the second part of Program 10-1.

In line 150, for example, CALL CLS is assembled into machine code CDC901. Sure enough, there is the actual address that was assigned to label CLS in an earlier EQU operation (in line 110). And in lines 160 and 170 you can see that the assembler kept track of the other addresses as well.

Now there is no longer any need to cite particular addresses or data values over and over again in an assembly listing. Just assign the values to a label with an EQU pseudo-op and then cite that label whenever the number is needed at any later time.

Incidentally, EDTASM allows you to assign decimal numbers to labels via the EQU operation. This is a handy feature in instances where you happen to know a value in decimal terms but don't want to make the effort to translate it into hexadecimal notation. See Program 10-2.

Program 10-2. Assembled listing for a program that illustrates the fact that EQU can define labels in hexadecimal or decimal terms.

```
7000            00100           ORG     7000H
01C9            00110 CLS       EQU     01C9H
00BF            00120 CHAR      EQU     191
                00130 ;BEGINNING OF PROGRAM
7000   CDC901   00140           CALL    CLS             ;CLEAR THE SCREEN
7003   060A     00150           LD      B,10            ;SET COUNTER
7005   21003C   00160           LD      HL,3C00H        ;INITIALIZE VIDEO POINTER
7008   36BF     00170 PLOT      LD      (HL),CHAR       ;PLOT A RECTANGLE
700A   05       00180           DEC     B               ;COUNTDOWN
700B   20FB     00190           JR      NZ,PLOT         ;IF NOT DONE, PLOT MORE
700D   18FE     00200 LOOP      JR      LOOP            ;ELSE LOOP TO SELF
7000            00210           END     7000H
00000   TOTAL ERRORS

LOOP   700D
PLOT   7008
CHAR   00BF
CLS    01C9
```

In line 120, label CHAR is assigned, by an EQU operation, the decimal value 191. Radio Shack lists the graphics codes in decimal, and this sort of assignment operation avoids the task of determining

183

the hexadecimal version. But notice how the assembler does that job for you in the machine code in line 170.

EQU OPERATIONS WITH MATH EXPRESSIONS

Simple EQU pseudo-ops let you define a label as some specific numerical value, but there is more to it. EQU also allows assignments of values that are expressed in a mathematical form. In BASIC, for example, you can do something such as PRINT A, but if A has some preassigned value, you can also do PRINT A+2. That same sort of thing is possible with the EQU pseudo-op.

Suppose you are writing an assembly program that calls for plotting a character at the beginning and end of the top line on the video screen. You probably know the beginning address, perhaps because you've used it so many times in the past. Thus a line such as

```
TSTART    EQU    3C00H
```

doesn't put much of strain on your brain. But then you must also specify the ending address of that line—and you cannot remember it. Of course, you can figure it out on paper or look it up in a table of video addresses; it is easier, however, to do something such as this:

```
TSTART    EQU    3C00H
TEND      EQU    TSTART+63
```

Recalling that the end of a horizontal line on the screen is displaced 63 (decimal) character spaces above the starting address of that line, you can define TEND—the end of the first line—as TSTART plus 63. And after defining TEND in that fashion, citing it later in the program will call up the proper address, 3C3F.

Yes, indeed, the EQU pseudo-op can attach the result of a math expression to a label name, and, what's more, part of that expression can be another label defined elsewhere in the program.

The EQU pseudo-op can handle both addition and subtraction expressions. It is possible to use any number and combinations of + and − operators. The assembler always executes the operators in a strictly left-to-right fashion, but it cannot handle a grouping of operations by parentheses.

See an application in Program 10-3.

The purpose of Program 10-3 is to plot a rectangle of light in the corners of the screen. The programmer happened to know the address of the start of video memory (3C00H) and the end (3FFFH) but not the addresses for the points at the upper-right and lower-left corners. Rather than taking the time and effort to work it out on paper, the programmer defined those points with EQU math expressions. See lines 120 and 140.

Program 10-3. Source and assembled versions of a program that shows how labels can be defined with EQU and math expressions.

```
00100                ORG      4A00H
00110  TSTART        EQU      3C00H       ;DEFINE START OF TOP LINE
00120  TEND          EQU      TSTART+63   ;DEFINE END OF TOP LINE
00130  BEND          EQU      3FFFH       ;DEFINE END OF BOTTOM LINE
00140  BSTART        EQU      BEND-63     ;DEFINE START OF BOTTOM LINE
00150  CHAR          EQU      191         ;DEFINE CHARACTER
00160  ;BEGINNING OF PROGRAM
00170                CALL     01C9H       ;CLEAR THE SCREEN
00180                LD       HL,TSTART   ;POINT TO UPPER LEFT
00190                LD       (HL),CHAR   ;PLOT CHAR
00200                LD       HL,TEND     ;POINT TO UPPER RIGHT
00210                LD       (HL),CHAR   ;PLOT CHAR
00220                LD       HL,BSTART   ;POINT TO LOWER LEFT
00230                LD       (HL),CHAR   ;PLOT CHAR
00240                LD       HL,BEND     ;POINT TO LOWER RIGHT
00250                LD       (HL),CHAR   ;PLOT CHAR
00260  LOOP          JR       LOOP        ;LOOP TO SELF
00270                END      4A00H
```

```
4A00              00100                ORG      4A00H
3C00              00110  TSTART        EQU      3C00H       ;DEFINE START OF TOP LINE
3C3F              00120  TEND          EQU      TSTART+63   ;DEFINE END OF TOP LINE
3FFF              00130  BEND          EQU      3FFFH       ;DEFINE END OF BOTTOM LINE
3FC0              00140  BSTART        EQU      BEND-63     ;DEFINE START OF BOTTOM LINE
00BF              00150  CHAR          EQU      191         ;DEFINE CHARACTER
                  00160  ;BEGINNING OF PROGRAM
4A00  CDC901      00170                CALL     01C9H       ;CLEAR THE SCREEN
4A03  21003C      00180                LD       HL,TSTART   ;POINT TO UPPER LEFT
4A06  36BF        00190                LD       (HL),CHAR   ;PLOT CHAR
4A08  213F3C      00200                LD       HL,TEND     ;POINT TO UPPER RIGHT
4A0B  36BF        00210                LD       (HL),CHAR   ;PLOT CHAR
4A0D  21C03F      00220                LD       HL,BSTART   ;POINT TO LOWER LEFT
4A10  36BF        00230                LD       (HL),CHAR   ;PLOT CHAR
4A12  21FF3F      00240                LD       HL,BEND     ;POINT TO LOWER RIGHT
4A15  36BF        00250                LD       (HL),CHAR   ;PLOT CHAR
4A17  18FE        00260  LOOP          JR       LOOP        ;LOOP TO SELF
4A00              00270                END      4A00H
00000  TOTAL ERRORS

LOOP     4A17
CHAR     00BF
BSTART   3FC0
BEND     3FFF
TEND     3C3F
TSTART   3C00
```

The second part of the listing is the assembled version of the same program. Note the object codes in lines 200 and 220—those lines calling for the math-generated TEND and BSTART labels. You can see that the assembler did the figuring for the programmer, coming up with a hexadecimal value of 3C3F for the upper-right corner and 3FC0 for the lower-left corner.

REDEFINING A LABEL WITH DEFL

A label that is defined by an EQU pseudo-op is committed to the designated value through the entire program listing. Any attempt to change the value assigned to a label will result in a multiple-definition assembly error message.

There are occasions, however, when it is desirable to change the definition of a label during the course of the assembly process. Assigning values to labels, using the DEFL pseudo-op instead of EQU, allows this sort of redefinition to take place.

The example in Program 10-4 plots a character at the four corners of the screen, just as Program 10-3 does. In this example, however, the character is changed each time.

Program 10-4. Assembled program showing an application of the DEFL pseudo-op.

```
4A00            00100         ORG     4A00H
3C00            00110 TSTART  EQU     3C00H       ;DEFINE START OF TOP LINE
3C3F            00120 TEND    EQU     TSTART+63   ;DEFINE END OF TOP LINE
3FFF            00130 BEND    EQU     3FFFH       ;DEFINE END OF BOTTOM LINES
3FC0            00140 BSTART  EQU     BEND-63     ;DEFINE START OF BOTTOM LINE
                00150 ;BEGINNING OF THE PROGRAM
4A00  CDC901    00160         CALL    01CH9       ;CLEAR THE SCREEN
4A03  21003C    00170         LD      HL,TSTART   ;POINT TO UPPER LEFT
0041            00180 CHAR    DEFL    65          ;DEFINE 'A'
4A06  3641      00190         LD(HL),CHAR         ;PLOT FIRST CHARACTER
4A08  213F3C    00200         LD      HL,TEND     ;POINT TO UPPER RIGHT
0042            00210 CHAR    DEFL    66          ;DEFINE 'B'
4A0B  3642      00220         LD      (HL),CHAR   ;PLOT SECOND CHARACTER
4A0D  21C03F    00230         LD      HL,BSTART   ;POINT TO LOWER LEFT
0043            00240 CHAR    DEFL    67          ;DEFINE 'C'
4A10  3643      00250         LD      (HL),CHAR   ;PLOT THIRD CHARACTER
4A12  21FF3F    00260         LD      HL,BEND     ;POINT TO LOWER RIGHT
0044            00270 CHAR    DEFL    68          ;DEFINE 'D'
4A15  3644      00280         LD      (HL),CHAR   ;PLOT FOURTH CHARACTER
4A17  18FE      00290 LOOP    JR      LOOP        ;LOOP TO SELF
4A00            00300         END     4A00H
00000  TOTAL ERRORS

LOOP    4A17
CHAR    0044
BSTART  3FC0
BEND    3FFF
TEND    3C3F
TSTART  3C00
```

In line 180, the DEFL pseudo-op defines CHAR as decimal 65, the letter A. Line 210 changes the definition to decimal 66, line 240 uses another DEFL to change CHAR to 67, and finally line 270 sets up the final value of 68.

Of course, it would be easier in this case to omit the CHAR definitions altogether, loading the desired value in an immediate fashion—LD (HL),65, for example. But this is merely an illustrative example. And, indeed, the assembler accepts the redefinition of CHAR in each case.

The DEFL pseudo-op also accepts simple math expressions as shown in Program 10-5. It accepts the same expressions as the EQU pseudo-op, and the rules and limitations are the same as well.

Program 10-5. Assembled listing of a program that demonstrates the use of math expressions with DEFL pseudo-ops.

```
4A00                00100             ORG     4A00H
3C00                00110  TSTART     EQU     3C00H           ;DEFINE START OF TOP LINE
3C3F                00120  TEND       EQU     TSTART+63       ;DEFINE END OF TOP LINE
3FFF                00130  BEND       EQU     3FFFH           ;DEFINE END OF BOTTOM LINE
3FC0                00140  BSTART     EQU     BEND-63         ;DEFINE START OF BOTTOM LINE
                    00150  ;BEGINNING OF THE PROGRAM
4A00   CDC901       00160             CALL    01C9H           ;CLEAR THE SCREEN
4A03   21003C       00170             LD      HL,TSTART       ;POINT TO UPPER LEFT
0041                00180  CHAR       DEFL    65              ;DEFINE 'A' CHARACTER
4A06   3641         00190             LD      (HL),CHAR       ;PLOT FIRST CHARACTER
4A08   213F3C       00200             LD      HL,TEND         ;POINT TO UPPER RIGHT
0042                00210  CHAR       DEFL    CHAR+1          ;REDEFINE CHAR
4A0B   3642         00220             LD      (HL),CHAR       ;PLOT SECOND CHARACTER
4A0D   21FF3F       00230             LD      HL,BSTART       ;POINT TO LOWER LEFT
0043                00240  CHAR       DEFL    CHAR+1          ;REDEFINE CHAR
4A10   3643         00250             LD      (HL),CHAR       ;PLOT THIRD CHARACTER
4A12   21FF3F       00260             LD      HL,BEND         ;POINT TO LOWER RIGHT
0044                00270  CHAR       DEFL    CHAR+1          ;REDEFINE CHAR
4A15   3644         00280             LD      (HL),CHAR       ;PLOT FOURTH CHARACTER
4A17   18FE         00290  LOOP       JR      LOOP            ;LOOP TO SELF
4A00                00300             END     4A00H
00000   TOTAL ERRORS

LOOP    4A17
CHAR    0044
BSTART  3FC0
BEND    3FFF
TEND    3C3F
TSTART  3C00
```

It is important to bear in mind that the DEFL pseudo-op alters the assembly process and not the execution of the machine-language program being generated. A label that is defined by a DEFL will carry the assigned value through every line of the assembly listing, at least until the label is redefined by another DEFL. Note in Programs 10-4 and 10-5 that CHAR in the label lists carries a value of 0044. Values assigned by DEFL earlier in the program are not listed.

LEAVING MEMORY SPACE WITH DEFS

In earlier chapters dealing with T-BUG programming, it was explained why it is desirable to leave small blocks of unused memory at strategic places in a machine-language program. The general idea was to leave some room for making revisions that might call for fitting in a few extra instructions. As described thus far, EDTASM does not leave any room between instructions. But that can be done with the DEFS pseudo-op.

Suppose you are writing a program under EDTASM and you want to leave eight successive memory locations blank. One part of the program is to end with eight address locations that are uncommitted and pick up with another part of the program after that. A line such as SPACE   DEFL 8 will do the job. See the illustration of this effect in Program 10-6.

Program 10-6. Assembled listing demonstrating the use of DEFS to allocate some uncommitted memory bytes.

```
4A00            00100         ORG     4A00H
4A00   21003C   00110         LD      HL,3C00H        ;SET VIDEO POINTER
4A03   CDC901   00120 TON     CALL    01C9H           ;CLEAR THE SCREEN
4A06   CD1A4A   00130         CALL    TIME            ;DO TIME DELAY
4A09   36BF     00140         LD      (HL),191        ;TURN ON THE LIGHT
4A0B   CD1A4A   00150         CALL    TIME            ;DO TIME DELAY
4A0E   18F3     00160         JR      TON             ;AND START ALL OVER
000A            00170 SPACE   DEFS    10              ;LEAVE SOME MEMORY SPACE
                00180 ;TIME   DELAY SUBROUTINE
4A1A   06CF     00190 TIME    LD      B,0CFH          ;SET MSB OF TIME DELAY
4A1C   0EFF     00200 SETC    LD      C,0FFH          ;SET LSB OF TIME DELAY
4A1E   0D       00210 DECC    DEC     C               ;COUNT LSB
4A1F   20FD     00220         JR      NZ,DECC         ;IF NOT DONE, COUNT AGAIN
4A21   05       00230         DEC     B               ;ELSE COUNT MSB
4A22   20F8     00240         JR      NZ,SETC         ;IF NOT DONE,COUNT MORE
4A24   C9       00250         RET                     ;ELSE RETURN
4A00            00260         END     4A00H
00000    TOTAL ERRORS

DECC    4A1E
SETC    4A1C
SPACE   4A10
TIME    4A1A
TON     4A03
```

This program causes a small rectangle of light to flash on and off in the upper left-hand corner of the screen. A TIME subroutine, occupying assembler lines 190 through 250, sets the flashing rate.

Line 120 effectively turns off the rectangle of light by clearing the entire screen, and then line 130 calls the TIME delay subroutine. After that, line 140 turns on the light, and then line 150 calls the TIME delay again. The instruction in line 160 returns operations back to line 120, thus keeping the program running in an endless loop.

The whole point of the program, however, is to demonstrate the application of DEFS. See the assembly instruction in line 170— SPACE   DEFS 10. That assembly instruction tells the system to leave 10 consecutive memory locations uncommitted. The subsequent TIME subroutine thus begins at address 4A1AH, instead of

4A10H—an address that would immediately follow the 2-byte instruction in line 160.

A DEFS pseudo-op must be preceded by a label in the first vertical field. In the example cited here, the label happens to be SPACE. It can be any valid label name that isn't used elsewhere in the program.

DEFS also supports simple math expressions as described for EQU and DEFL. This provides a means for leaving some uncommitted memory and picking up the next part of the program at some well-defined address. Suppose, for example, a section of the program leaves off at address 4A0FH. You don't care how many successive memory locations are left unused after that, just so the next part of the program picks up at address 4A20H. Letting the assembler figure the number of blank memory locations for you, you can enter SPACE   DEFL   4A20H-4A0FH-1. That will do it.

NOTE

To leave some uncommitted memory space and pick up the program again at a well-defined address, use a DEFL with the expression:

new starting address - old ending address - 1.

You can use DEFL to leave any number of gaps in the machine-language addressing. The labels preceding the DEFL pseudo-op must be different in each case, however.

DEFINING MEMORY CONTENTS WITH DEFB AND DEFW

Certain classes of machine-language programs require fetching data from a table of some sort. Each item in the table has a specific address, and it is fetched from the table by loading from its address. EDTASM's DEFB and DEFW pseudo-ops allow you to build tables of 1- and 2-byte data, respectively.

Program 10-7 is another program that really doesn't do anything useful, but it does illustrate the building of a small data table.

The data table in this instance consists of the ASCII codes for letters A, B, and C. The table is built by means of the DEFB pseudo-ops in lines 110, 120, and 130. For purposes of further demonstration the three characters are defined in three different ways: as a decimal version of *A* (DEFB 65), a hexadecimal version of character *B* (DEFB 42H), and as a single-character string enclosed in apostrophes (DEFB 'C').

Program 10-7. Assembled listing that shows the use of the DEFB pseudo-op.

```
4A00              00100        ORG      4A00H
4A00    41        00110        DEFB     65         ;'A' CHARACTER
4A01    42        00120        DEFB     42H        ;'B' CHARACTER
4A02    43        00130        DEFB     'C'        ;'C' CHARACTER
000D              00140 BLAND  DEFS     4A10H-4A02H-1   ;LEAVE SOME SPACE
                  00150 ;BEGINNING OF 'PROGRAM'
4A10    3A004A    00160 PROG   LD  A,(4A00H)       ;'A' TO ACCUMULATOR
4A13    3A014A    00170        LD  A,(4A01H)       ;'B' TO ACCUMULATOR
4A16    3A024A    00180        LD  A,(4A02H)       ;'C' TO ACCUMULATOR
4A19    18FE      00190 LOOP   JR  LOOP            ;LOOP TO SELF
4A10              00200        END      PROG
00000   TOTAL ERRORS

LOOP    4A19
PROG    4A10
BLAND   4A03
```

What is more important, however, is the fact that the assembler assigns the ASCII codes to address locations 4A00H through 4A02H. *A DEFB operation inserts the data byte at the current address.* In this particular instance the ORG sets the beginning of the program at 4A00H, and since the following operation is a DEFB the data byte thus defined is automatically assigned to address 4A00H. The second byte then goes to 4A01H, and the third to 4A02H.

This simple, three-character table concludes with some uncommitted memory space that is generated by the DEFS operation in line 140.

The actual operating program picks up at line 160—at the PROG label. It then proceeds to cite the addresses of the data in the table, calling the content of those three addresses to the accumulator. So once the data table is built, the contents can be called by merely citing the appropriate addresses. The only trick, as far as the programmer is concerned, is to keep track of where the desired data byte is located in the table.

The data table does not have to be located at the beginning of the machine-language listing. It can be inserted anywhere you choose. But since it is located at the beginning of the listing in Program 10-7, it is absolutely necessary to use the type of END statement specified in line 200.

When the TRS-80 is executing a program generated under EDTASM, it must not attempt to execute the contents of a data table. The table of data must not be treated as instructions—doing that ensures a total blowup of the program. So to avoid this situation the END statement specifies the entry point of the actual, executable part of the program at label PROG, which happens to be at address 4A10H in this case. This procedure is based on the notion that the END statement specifies the entry point of the program; and this happens to be the first example in the current series of discussions where it is necessary to start the machine-language listing and execution of the program at two distinctly different places.

The DEFW pseudo-op works just like the DEFB operation, except that the former allocates two successive byte locations in the data table. DEFW is especially useful for building a table of 2-byte address locations.

Program 10-8 uses DEFW pseudo-ops to build a table of 2-byte addresses. The table begins at address 4A00H and runs through 4A07H. See lines 120 through 150.

The four addresses entered into that table point to the corners of the video screen. The first 2 bytes point to the upper left-hand corner, the next 2 point to the upper right-hand corner, then 2 point to the lower left corner, and the last one points to the lower right. Note that it is possible to define a "word" with a simple math expression (line 140).

After building this sort of address table the program can call the 2-byte contents as illustrated in lines 210 through 240. In this particular example the program plots small rectangles (TRS-80 graphic 191) in the four corners.

BUILDING MESSAGE TABLES WITH DEFM

DEFB allocates a byte of memory for a data byte, DEFW allocates two successive bytes of memory for 2-byte data or address "words," and DEFM sets aside an indefinitely large section of

Program 10-8. Assembled listing demonstrating the use of DEFW.

```
4A00                00100          ORG    4A00H              ;SET ORIGIN
                    00110   ;VIDEO POINT ADDRESS TABLE
4A00   003C         00120          DEFW   3C00H              ;UPPER LEFT
4A02   3F3C         00130          DEFW   3C3FH              ;UPPER RIGHT
4A04   C03F         00140          DEFW   3FFFH-63           ;LOWER LEFT
4A06   FF3F         00150          DEFW   3FFFH              ;LOWER RIGHT
00BF                00160   CHAR   EQU    191                ;DEFINE CHAR
0008                00170   BLANK  DEFS   4A10H-4A07H-1      ;LEAVE SOME MEMORY
                    00180   ;START OF PROGRAM
4A10   CDC901       00190   DRAW   CALL   01C9H              ;CLEAR THE SCREEN
4A13   3EBF         00200          LD     A,CHAR             ;SET CHARACTER
4A15   32004A       00210          LD     (4A00H),A          ;PRINT UPPER LEFT
4A18   32024A       00220          LD     (4A02h),A          ;PRINT UPPER RIGHT
4A1B   32044A       00230          LD     (4A04H),A          ;PRINT LOWER LEFT
4A1E   32064A       00240          LD     (4A06H),A          ;PRINT LOWER RIGHT
4A21   18FE         00250   LOOP   JR     LOOP               ;LOOP TO SELF
4A10                00260          END    DRAW
00000  TOTAL ERRORS

LOOP   4A21
DRAW   4A10
BLANK  4A08
CHAR   00BF
```

191

memory for string messages. It would be possible to build a message table using DEFB pseudo-ops, but using a single DEFM line is much simpler. Consider the following comparison:

```
DEFB 'H'
DEFB 'E'
DEFB 'L'
DEFB 'L'
DEFB 'O'
```

Now, if you write some programming that calls the 5 bytes of data memory generated by that sequence of DEFB operations and prints them in sequence on the screen, you will end up printing HELLO. But using a single DEFW operation allows exactly the same thing to happen in a simpler fashion:

```
DEFW 'HELLO'
```

This will set up the message, HELLO, in some data memory locations, and the characters can be called to the video screen in sequence.

Programs 10-9 and 10-10 illustrate an application of the DEFM pseudo-op. Program 10-9 is the assembly listing as it appears after entering it, and Program 10-10 is the assembled version.

The program prints three messages: HELLO, NOW YOU SEE IT, and NOW YOU DON'T. You can find the HELLO designated with a DEFM pseudo-op in line 110 of Program 10-9, and NOW YOU SEE IT is defined in a similar fashion in line 130. Note that those messages are enclosed in apostrophes (as opposed to string-defining quotes as used in BASIC).

The fact that the NOW YOU DON'T message contains an apostrophe thus brings up a minor problem: The assembler will interpret the apostrophe between the N and T in that message as a closing apostrophe for the message, and it thinks you want to spell out NOW YOU DON.

Lines 150 through 170 show how to get around that particular difficulty. Line 150 uses a DEFM operation to spell out the message up to the point where the apostrophe is to occur. Line 160 then uses a DEFB pseudo-op to designate the ASCII code for an apostrophe. Finally, line 170 uses a DEFB to attach the character T to the end of the message.

Also notice that each of the three messages concludes with a DEFB 0 operation. The idea is to mark the end of each message with some sort of unique character or character code. The zero, or null character, is used here because it is the same one used to mark the end of text statements in BASIC. (Recall the discussion of BASIC text in Chapter 4.)

Program 10-9. Source listing for a program that uses a message table built by means of the DEFM operations.

```
00100               ORG    4A00H            ;SET THE ORIGIN
00110               DEFM   'HELLO'          ;DEFINE MESS1
00120               DEFB   0                ;SET END MARKER
00130               DEFM   'NOW YOU SEE IT  ;DEFINE MESS2
00140               DEFB   0                ;SET END MARKER
00150               DEFM   'NOW YOU DON'    ;DEF PART OF MESS3
00160               DEFB   39               ;DEF APOSTROPHE
00170               DEFB   'T'              ;DEF 'T'
00180               DEFB   0                ;SET END MARKER
00190 SKIP1         DEFS   8                ;LEAVE SOME MEMORY
00200 CLS           EQU    01C9H            ;DEFINE CLS
00210 TOP           EQU    3C00H            ;DEF START OF VIDEO
00220 ;TIME DELAY SUBROUTINE
00230 TIME          LD     C,0FFH           ;SET LSB OF TIME
00240 DECC          DEC    C                ;COUNT LSB OF TIME
00250               JR     NZ,DECC          ;IF NOT DONE,COUNT MORE
00260               DEC    B                ;COUNT MSB OF TIME
00270               JR     NZ,TIME          ;IF NOT DONE,COUNT MORE
00280               RET                     ;ELSE RETURN
00290 ;MESSAGE SUBROUTINE
00300 CMESS         LD     A,(DE)           ;FETCH CHARACTER
00310               CP     0                ;IS IT NULL?
00320               RET    Z                ;IF SO,RETURN
00330               LD     (HL),A           ;ELSE PRINT CHARACTER
00340               INC    DE               ;GO TO NEXT CHARACTER
00350               INC    HL               ;NEXT VIDEO LOCATION
00360               JR     CMESS            ;AND GET NEXT CHARACTER
00370               DEFS   8                ;SKIP SOME MEMORY
00380 ;BEGINNING OF MAINLINE PROGRAM
00390 BLINK         CALL   CLS              ;CLEAR THE SCREEN
00400               LD     HL,TOP           ;SET VIDEO POINTER
00410               LD     DE,4A00H         ;POINT TO MESS1
00420               CALL   CMESS            ;PRINT IT
00430               LD     A,0FH            ;SET UP LONG DELAY
00440 TAGN          LD     B,0FFH
00450               CALL   TIME             ;DO DELAY
00460               DEC    A                ;COUNT A
00470               JR     NZ,TAGN          ;IF NOT DONE,DO AGAIN
00480 TON           CALL   CLS              ;CLEAR THE SCREEN
00490               LD     HL,TOP           ;SET VIDEO POINTER
00500               LD     (HL),191         ;TURN ON LIGHT
00510               INC    HL               ;SPACE
00520               INC    HL               ;SPACE
00530               LD     DE,4A06H         ;POINT TO MESS2
00540               CALL   CMESS            ;PRINT IT
00550               LD     B,0DFH           ;SET SHORT DELAY
00560               CALL   TIME             ;DO DELAY
00570               CALL   CLS              ;CLEAR THE SCREEN
00580               LD     HL,TOP           ;SET VIDEO POINTER
00590               INC    HL               ;SPACE
00600               INC    HL               ;SPACE
00610               LD     DE,4A15H         ;POINT TO MESS3
00620               CALL   CMESS            ;PRINT IT
00630               LD     B,0DFH           ;SET SHORT DELAY
00640               CALL   TIME             ;DO DELAY
00650               JR     TON              ;AND REPEAT
00660               END    BLINK
```

Program 10-10. Assembled version of the message-printing program listing in Program 10-9.

```
4A00            00100           ORG     4A00H           ;SET ORIGIN
4A00    48      00110           DEFM    'HELLO'         ;DEFINE MESS1
4A01    45
4A02    4C
4A03    4C
4A04    4F
4A05    00      00120           DEFB    0               ;SET END MARKER
4A06    4E      00130           DEFM    'NOW YOU SEE IT'    ;DEFINE MESS2
4A07    4F
4A08    57
4A09    20
4A0A    59
4A0B    4F
4A0C    55
4A0D    20
4A0E    53
4A0F    45
4A10    45
4A11    20
4A12    49
4A13    54
4A14    00      00140           DEFB    0               ;SET END MARKER
4A15    4E      00150           DEFM    'NOW YOU DON'   ;DEF PART OF MESS3
4A16    4F
4A17    57
4A18    20
4A19    59
4A1A    4F
4A1B    55
4A1C    20
4A1D    44
4A1E    4F
4A1F    4E
4A20    27      00160           DEFB    39              ;DEF APOSTROPHE
4A21    54      00170           DEFB    'T'             ;DEF 'T'
4A22    00      00180           DEFB    0               ;SET END MARKER
0008            00190   SKIP1   DEFS    8               ;LEAVE SOME MEMORY
01C9            00200   CLS     EQU     01C9H           ;DEFINE CLS
3C00            00210   TOP     EQU     3C00H           ;DEF START OF VIDEO
                00220   ;TIME DELAY SUBROUTINE
4A2B    0EFF    00230   TIME    LD  C,0FFH              ;SET LSB OF TIME
4A2D    0D      00240   DECC    DEC C                   ;COUNT LSB OF TIME
4A2E    20FD    00250           JR  NZ,DEC              ;IF NOT DONE,COUNT MORE
4A30    05      00260           DEC B                   ;COUNT MSB OF TIME
4A31    20F8    00270           JR  NZ,TIME             ;IF NOT DONE,COUNT MORE
4A33    C9      00280           RET                     ;ELSE RETURN
                00290   ;MESSAGE SUBROUTINE
4A34    1A      00300   CMESS   LD  A,(DE)              ;FETCH CHARACTER
4A35    FE00    00310           CP  0                   ;IS IT NULL?
4A37    C8      00320           RET Z                   ;IF SO,RETURN
4A38    77      00330           LD  (HL),A              ;ELSE PRINT CHARACTER
4A39    13      00340           INC DE                  ;GOT TO NEXT CHARACTER
4A3A    23      00350           INC HL                  ;NEXT VIDEO LOCATION
4A3B    18F7    00360           JR  CMESS               ;AND GET NEXT CHARACTER
0008            00370           DEFS    8               ;SKIP SOME MEMORY
                00380   BEGINNING OF MAINLINE PROGRAM
4A45    CDC901  00390   BLINK   CALL CLS                ;CLEAR THE SCREEN
4A48    21003C  00400           LD  HL,TOP              ;SET VIDEO POINTER
4A4B    11004A  00410           LD  DE,4A00H            ;POINT TO MESS1
4A4E    CD344A  00420           CALL CMESS              ;PRINT IT
4A51    3E0F    00430           LD  A,0FH               ;SET UP LONG DELAY
4A53    06FF    00440   TAGN    LD  B,0FFH
4A55    CD2B4A  00450           CALL TIME               ;DO DELAY
4A58    3D      00460           DEC A                   ;COUNT A
4A59    20FB    00470           JR  NZ,TAGN             ;IF NOT DONE,DO AGAIN
4A5B    CDC901  00480   TON     CALL CLS                ;CLEAR THE SCREEN
4A5E    21003C  00490           LD  HL,TOP              ;SET VIDEO POINTER
4A61    36BF    00500           LD  (HL),191            ;TURN ON LIGHT
4A63    23      00510           INC HL                  ;SPACE
```

```
4A64   23         00520    INC HL              ;SPACE
4A65   11064A     00530    LD DE,4A06H         ;POINT TO MESS2
4A68   CD344A     00540    CALL CMESS          ;PRINT IT
4A6B   06DF       00550    LD B,0DFH           ;SET SHORT DELAY
4A6D   CD2B4A     00560    CALL TIME           ;DO DELAY
4A70   CDC901     00570    CALL CLS            ;CLEAR THE SCREEN
4A73   21003C     00580    LD HL,TOP           ;SET VIDEO POINTER
4A76   23         00590    INC HL              ;SPACE
4A77   23         00600    INC HL              ;SPACE
4A78   11154A     00610    LD DE,4A15H         ;POINT TO MESS3
4A7B   CD344A     00620    CALL CMESS          ;PRINT IT
4A7E   06DF       00630    LD B,0DFH           ;SET SHORT DELAY
4A80   CD2B4A     00640    CALL TIME           ;DO DELAY
4A83   18D6       00650    JR TON              ;AND REPEAT
4A45              00660    END     BLINK
00000  TOTAL ERRORS

TON      4A5B
TAGN     4A53
BLINK    4A45
CMESS    4A34
DECC     4A2D
TIME     4A2B
TOP      3C00
CLS      01C9
SKIP1    4A23
```

The "message table" concludes at line 190 by leaving 8 bytes of unused memory—perhaps for future expansion of that table.

The remainder of the program runs a routine that calls these string messages. Upon executing it, the screen clears (line 390) and HELLO appears in the upper left-hand corner of the screen. That message remains on the screen for about 30 seconds.

When this HELLO phase is done, the program shows a rectangle of light and the NOW YOU SEE IT message. That one remains in place for about 1 second. Then the rectangle of light disappears and the message changes to NOW YOU DON'T. And that message remains on the screen for about 1 second.

After that, the program alternates between the two latter messages—at 1-second intervals—until you interrupt it by working the RESET push button.

The program uses two subroutines: TIME (beginning at line 230) does the time-delay operations, and CMESS (beginning at line 300) calls the messages from the message table and prints them onto the screen. The main program—the one that controls the overall operations and calls the subroutines—begins at BLINK (line 390) and runs through the end of the listing.

The program thus begins with the message table, followed by the two subroutines and, finally, the mainline program. The entry point is at BLINK in line 390. How does the computer know it is to begin running operations from that point? The END BLINK operation in line 660 defines that entry point.

So when this program is loaded under the SYSTEM command, it begins actual operation from the BLINK label. That first line clears the screen, then the following lines set the video pointer—the HL register pair—to the TOP, video address 3C00H. Line 410 sets the DE register pair to the beginning address of the first message, HELLO, and line 420 calls the CMESS subroutine to print the message onto the screen.

CMESS, beginning at line 300, fetches the first character in the message, checks to see whether or not it is the end-marking null character, and returns to the mainline program if, indeed, it sees that zero character. But if there is more to the message, line 330 prints the character, and the next two lines increment both the message pointer (the DE pair) and the video pointer (the HL pair). Line 360 then calls for repeating the message-printing operation.

In short, subroutine CMESS continues printing characters onto the screen until it finds the end marker—the null character. On returning to the mainline program the next few lines set up and call the time delay routine, TIME.

The same general procedure applies to printing the NOW YOU SEE IT and NOW YOU DON'T messages. The trick, as far as the programmer is concerned, is figuring out where the messages begin in the message table.

The HELLO message certainly begins at 4A00H, because that is where the ORG operation begins loading. But where does NOW YOU SEE IT begin? You can count the characters in the message, add an extra count for the end marker, and figure the address of the next message. This is tedious and offers a fine opportunity to make a serious mistake.

A better way to determine the starting addresses of messages in a message table is to do an assembly operation immediately after the table has been entered into the assembler. After typing in lines 100 through 180, for example, do an A/WE. You will get a NO END STATEMENT message, but that isn't important. What is important is the way the message table is assembled. See the assembled table in lines 100 through 180 in Program 10-10.

In this assembled listing, you can see that HELLO is assembled as hexadecimal ASCII codes in addresses 4A00H through 4A04H. The null character then appears in address 4A50H, and NOW YOU SEE IT begins at 4A06H. The latter address is the starting point for printing out that particular message.

Then at address 4A15H, you find the beginning of the NOW YOU DON'T message.

So the entry points for printing the messages are thus identified for you. It is therefore a good idea to enter such a table first and assemble it before writing the portions of the program that must call the message strings. This way, you know the exact starting addresses for all the messages.

CHAPTER 11

Putting It All Together

Only the simplest BASIC and machine-language programs are developed as a one-shot operation. All but the most modest programs ought to be built in a piecemeal fashion, with the loading and testing of critical sections before integrating them into an increasingly complex and useful master program.

This chapter demonstrates some approaches to composing relatively complicated programs. Although the examples, themselves, hardly reach staggering proportions, they illustrate the overall spirit of devising programs of any size.

The whole TRS-80 ROM system is built around a lot of general-purpose routines. A number of examples cited earlier in this book take advantage of some of those routines.

In many instances, however, a TRS-80 ROM routine cannot be run until some important parameters are loaded into specified RAM locations. As the ROM routine is executed, it calls those parameters as they are needed to transform a general set of operations into a very specific one. That is the approach featured in this chapter.

The examples in this chapter are all oriented toward video graphics, but the general ideas apply equally well to any sort of i/o medium.

BUILDING A GENERAL-PURPOSE FILL ROUTINE

One of the most useful graphics routines is one that draws blocks of characters on the screen. It should allow the programmer to specify the position and dimensions of the graphic as well as the character type it is built from. Once those parameters are entered

197

into some well-defined RAM locations, the general-purpose FILL routine uses them to draw the graphic. The routine can draw any graphic—the RAM parameters determine its nature.

So when you want to draw some figures on the screen, first build a RAM table of all the parameters and then call the FILL routine.

Program 11-1 is an assembled version of a FILL routine. It includes the essential elements of a general-purpose routine, including some goofproofing operations that prevent the system from going crazy in the event of a programming error.

The program allocates a 5-byte RAM table for the critical parameters:

4A00	CHARACTER TYPE
4A01	LSB OF STARTING ADDRESS
4A02	MSB OF STARTING ADDRESS
4A03	NUMBER OF CHARACTERS PER LINE
4A04	NUMBER OF LINES

CHARACTER TYPE determines the alphanumeric or graphic character to be used for drawing the figure on the screen. It can be any hexadecimal number between 20H and FFH. If no specific CHARACTER TYPE is designated by the programmer, the routine automatically sets up 191 (decimal). See line 120 in the listing.

The FILL routine builds the graphic by scanning one character space at a time, from left to right, across the screen. When one line is done, it begins the next line directly below the starting point of the previous one. This scheme means it is necessary to designate a starting point, a line length, and the number of lines.

The START ADDRESS is loaded into the parameter table at addresses 4A01 and 4A02. It can be any 2-byte hexadecimal number but, of course, it ought to be within the video memory space—3C00H through 3FFFH. Since any attempt to "draw" a figure outside the video memory space can cause some serious blowups of existing programs, you will find that the FILL routine includes a goofproofing feature to prevent such a disaster. But more about that later.

As shown in line 130, the START ADDRESS defaults to 3C00H. Unless the programmer designates a different one, the routine begins drawing the graphic in the upper left-hand corner of the screen.

With the CHARACTER TYPE and START ADDRESS thus specified, all that remains in the parameter table is NO. OF LINES and CHAR PER LINE. These are both 1-byte hexadecimal numbers located at addresses 4A03H and 4A04H, respectively. If no parameters are entered by the programmer, lines 140 and 150 in the listing show that the default NO. OF LINES is 2, and CHAR PER LINE is 4.

Program 11-1. Assembled listing for FILL2.

```
                00100 ;FILL ROUTINE -- VER 2: FILENAME FILL2
4A00            00110       ORG     4A00H
4A00    BF      00120       DEFB    191             ;CHARACTER TYPE
4A01    003C    00130       DEFW    3C00H           ;START ADDRESS
4A02    02      00140       DEFB    2               ;NO. OF LINES
4A03    04      00150       DEFB    4               ;CHAR PER LINE
4A05    46      00160       DEFM    'FILL OFLOW'    ;OVERFLOW MESSAGE
4A06    49
4A07    4C
4A08    4C
4A09    20
4A0A    4F
4A0B    46
4A0C    4C
4A0D    4F
4A0E    57
4A0F    00      00170       DEFB    0               ;ALWAYS '0'
4A10    2A014A  00180 FILL  LD      HL,(4A01H)      ;FETCH START ADDR
4A13    CD3B4A  00190       CALL    OFLO            ;VALID POINTER?
4A16    3A034A  00200       LD      A,(4A03H)       ;FETCH NO. OF LINES
4A19    47      00210       LD      B,A             ;NO. OF LINES TO B
4A1A    3A044A  00220 LINE  LD      A,(4A04H)       ;FETCH CHAR/LINE
4A1D    4F      00230       LD      C,A             ;CHAR/LINE TO C
4A1E    3A004A  00240       LD      A,(4A00H)       ;FETCH CHAR TYPE
4A21    54      00250       LD      D,H             ;SET LINE START
4A22    5D      00260       LD      E,L
4A23    77      00270 PLOT  LD      (HL),A          ;PLOT CHARACTER
4A24    0D      00280       DEC     C               ;DECREMENT CHAR COUNT
4A25    CA2F4A  00290       JP      Z,NLINE         ;IF DONE, DO NEXT LINE
4A28    23      00300       INC     HL              ;ELSE INCREMENT POINTER
4A29    CD3B4A  00310       CALL    OFLO            ;CHECK FOR OVERFLOW
4A2C    18F5    00320       JR      PLOT            ;AND PLOT AGAIN
0001            00330       DEFS    1
4A2F    05      00340 NLINE DEC     B               ;DECREMENT LINE COUNT
4A30    C8      00350       RET     Z               ;RETURN IF DONE
4A31    214000  00360       LD      HL,64           ;SET LINEFEED
4A34    19      00370       ADD     HL,DE           ;START OF NEW LINE
4A35    CD3B4A  00380       CALL    OFLO            ;CHECK FOR OVERFLOW
4A38    18E0    00390       JR      LINE            ;PLOT NEW LINE
0001            00400       DEFS    1
4A3B    3E3F    00410 OFLO  LD      A,3FH           ;SET MAX MSB OF VIDEO
4A3D    BC      00420       CP      H               ;LESS THAN MSB OF VIDEO?
4A3E    380B    00430       JR      C,FLOMES        ;IF SO,PRINT MESSAGE
4A40    7C      00440       LD      A,H             ;GET MSB OF VIDEO
4A41    FE3C    00450       CP      3CH             ;UNDERFLOW?
4A43    3806    00460       JR      C,FLOMES        ;IF SO,PRINT OFLO
4A45    3A004A  00470       LD      A,(4A00H)       ;ELSE RESTORE CHAR TYPE
4A48    C9      00480       RET                     ;AND RETURN
0002            00490       DEFS    2
4A4B    21003C  00500 FLOMES LD     HL,3C00H        ;ELSE SET VIDEO POINTER
4A4E    11054A  00510       LD      DE,4A05H        ;POINT TO MESSAGE
4A51    1A      00520 MESCHR LD     A,(DE)          ;GET MESSAGE CHAR
4A52    FE00    00530       CP      0               ;DONE?
4A54    2805    00540       JR      Z,LOOP          ;IF SO,LOOP TO SELF
4A56    77      00550       LD      (HL),A          ;PRINT CHAR
4A57    23      00560       INC     HL              ;ELSE NEXT MESS CHAR
4A58    13      00570       INC     DE
4A59    18F6    00580       JR      MESCHR
4A5B    18FE    00590 LOOP  JR      LOOP            ;LOOP TO SELF
4A10            00600       END     FILL
00000   TOTAL ERRORS
```

```
LOOP     4A5B
MESCHR   4A51
FLOMES   4A4B
NLINE    4A2F
PLOT     4A23
LINE     4A1A
OFLO     4A3B
FILL     4A10
```

The point of this part of the discussion is to show the following principles in action:

1. Most general-purpose routines require a table of working parameters that can be called as the routine is executed.
2. The items in the parameter table must have well-defined and documented addresses (a programmer must know the address and purpose of each item in order to preset them).
3. The program should be written so that the items in the parameter table have valid values from the outset. These determine the default parameters, and leaving them undefined can cause serious problems.
4. Each item in the parameter table should be documented in terms of allowable values. Either that, or the routine should be written so that invalid parameters will not cause a total blowup of the program.

Before running the FILL routine, then, the programmer should preset the items in the parameter table. They can, for instance, be preset by means of POKE statements under BASIC, or they can be set directly under T-BUG. When the FILL routine is finally used as part of a larger graphics program, however, the parameters will be set by means of some LD instructions to the appropriate addresses.

Line 160 sets up a FILL OFLOW message that is called whenever the FILL routine attempts to plot a character outside the video memory range. As described later, that message appears in the upper left corner of the screen whenever such an overflow (or underflow) occurs.

The entry point of the FILL routine is at line 180, address 4A01H. That address must be part of the routine's documentation; any programmer must know where the routine begins its execution.

That first working instruction loads the START ADDRESS into the HL register pair. It does that by fetching the 2-byte address beginning at 4A01H. The next instruction checks that parameter to see whether or not it is a valid one—somewhere within the video memory space. This is done by calling a subroutine labeled OFLO (see line 410).

Assuming the START ADDRESS is valid, the program resumes operation at line 200. The instruction in that line fetches the NO. OF LINES parameter from the parameter table, and the next instruction loads it to register B. Register B then keeps track of the number of lines yet to be drawn.

Line 220 marks the beginning of the line-drawing part of the routine. It begins by fetching the CHAR PER LINE parameter from the parameter table, and then loading it into register C. Then line 240 fetches the CHAR TYPE to register A.

The current-line starting address is saved in the DE register pair by the instructions in lines 250 and 260. The routine must "remember" the starting address of each line so that it can set the start address of the next one later on.

Finally, the plotting operation begins at line 270. The CHAR TYPE is loaded to the screen at an address determined by the content of the HL register pair. Then CHAR/LINE is decremented and checked for its end. If it so happens that register C is not decremented to zero, operations pick up at line 300.

The INC HL in line 300 sets the video pointer to the next character space. CALL OFLO checks to see whether or not the operation will run the pointer out of video memory; if not, operations loop back to PLOT, and another character is loaded to the screen.

Operations continue looping in the PLOT sequence until one of two things happen: either register C decrements to zero, indicating a line is done, or the HL pointer increments out of video memory space. In the latter case the system prints FILL OFLOW and goes into a harmless loop. In the former case—the more desirable one—line 290 jumps operations to NLINE.

NLINE begins a series of instructions that reset the drawing operation to the beginning of the next line to be drawn. The NO. OF LINES register, register B, is first decremented (line 340 in the listing). If B is not yet zero, 64 (decimal) is added to the starting address of the previous line. CALL OFLO in line 380 checks for a possible overflow out of video memory, and then line 390 returns operations to the LINE routine.

Assuming that no overflows occur, the routine runs until all lines have been drawn: until register B is decremented to zero and the RET Z in line 350 is satisfied. At that time, control returns to the program that called FILL in the first place.

The OFLO routine, beginning at line 410, checks the current value of the video pointer (the HL register pair) for an address that is outside the video memory space. If that fault condition occurs, operations pick up at FLOMES in line 500.

FLOMES and MESCHR print the FILL OFLOW message stored in 4A05H through 4A0FH, using methods already described in some earlier examples. (See Chapter 10.) And once the overflow message is printed, LOOP in line 590 causes the program to "buzz" on that one instruction until the programmer operates the RESET push button. Having the program latch up in this safe fashion is far better than letting it wander off into undefined portions of memory, thus running the risk of losing a lot of programming.

If you want to work through the examples in this chapter on a first-hand basis, load the listing in Program 11-1 under EDTASM, check for errors, and then save the object code with the file name FILL2. The source version can then be saved on tape as SFILL2.

Chart 11-1 illustrates the sort of documentation required for general-purpose routines and FILL2 specifically. Such information is just as valuable as the recorded program, itself.

Chart 11-1. Overall Documentation for the FILL2 Routine

Memory Location:	4A00H–4A5BH (86 bytes)
Entry Point:	4A10H
Parameter Table:	
4A00H	CHARACTER TYPE (1 byte)
4A01H	START ADDRESS (2 bytes)
4A03H	NUMBER OF LINES (1 byte)
4A04H	NUMBER OF CHARACTERS PER LINE (1 byte)

Aside from the use of a parameter table, there is little involved in the construction of this FILL routine that hasn't been discussed to some extent in earlier chapters.

The only "problem" with FILL, as it is shown in Program 11-1, is that it cannot be executed alone. The RET Z instruction in line 350 marks the end of the routine, and it spells out a return to a calling program. But what calling program? There is none. You have to write a calling program in order to use a general-purpose routine of this sort.

A calling routine for FILL is shown in Program 11-2. The program is so short that you might be ahead of the game by loading it under T-BUG—it is intended to work in conjunction with T-BUG anyway. So you could do this:

1. Load FILL2 under system.
2. Respond to *? at the end of the loading of FILL2 by operating the RESET push button.
3. Load T-BUG under system.
4. Respond to *? by entering a slash (/). That will bring up T-BUG.

202

Program 11-2. A test routine for FILL2.

```
                00100  ;FILL TEST ROUTINE -- VER 1 -- FILENAME FLTST1
7000            00110         ORG     7000H
7000   CDC901   00120  FLTST1 CALL 01C9H     ;CLEAR THE SCREEN
7003   CD104A   00130         CALL 4A10H     ;CALL FILL2
7006   3A4038   00140  KB     LD A,(3840H)   ;LOOK AT KEYBOARD
7009   FE01     00150         CP 1           ;IS IT ENTER?
700B   C20670   00160         JP NZ,KB       ;IF NOT,LOOK AGAIN
700E   C3A043   00170         JP 17312       ;ELSE JUMP TO T-BUG
7000            00180         END     FLTST1
00000  TOTAL ERRORS
```

Now FILL2 and T-BUG are both resident in the system. Load the object code in Program 11-2, using the "M" function of T-BUG. Next, try out the default parameters with FILL2 by doing a J 7000 from T-BUG. Referring to Program 11-2, this will clear the screen, execute the FILL2 routine, and then hold the graphic on the screen until you strike the ENTER key (see lines 140 through 160). On striking the ENTER key, line 170 does a jump back to T-BUG. From there, you can make any corrections in FILL2; and if FILL2 did, indeed, draw a white rectangle in the upper-left corner of the screen, you are in a position to use T-BUG for setting some of FILL2's parameters to suit your own specifications.

While running from T-BUG, you can alter the parameter table according to the description in Chart 11-1. And when you've set up some of your own parameters, do another J 7000 to bring up the FLTST1 routine. It, again, will do the FILL operation you specified, and it will hold the figure on the screen until you strike the ENTER key to get back to T-BUG.

This notion of using FILL2, T-BUG, and the FLTST1 testing routine together leads to a powerful programming aid. It lets you tinker with the parameters to come up with any sort of graphic you want. The present scheme allows only one graphic to be displayed at any given time, but you can keep track of the parameters for any number of graphics. As demonstrated in the next section, they can be all worked together into a single program.

The testing routine, incidentally, can also be written under EDTASM. Saving its object code as FLTST1 makes it available for future use. Assuming, then, that you have FLTST1 available on tape, you can set up the test scheme as follows:

1. Load FILL2 under SYSTEM.
2. Respond to *? at the end of loading by operating the RESET push button.
3. Load FLST1 under SYSTEM.
4. Respond to *? at the end of its loading by operating the RESET push button.

5. Load T-BUG under SYSTEM.
6. Respond to *? at the end of its loading by entering a slash (/).

Now you can run the tests and determine FILL2 parameters as described earlier.

APPLYING AND REFINING FILL2

Table 11-1 shows the FILL parameters for drawing the four segments of a rectangular border figure. They were each generated by means of the technique just described—using Program 11-2 in conjunction with FILL2 and T-BUG. Now the trick is to work out yet another program that loads these parameters into the FILL2 parameter table and to draw them onto the screen. The idea is to run FILL2 four times in succession, loading the parameters for each of the rectangle elements.

Table 11-1. Memory Map for the FILL Parameter Table

Graphic	Parameter Addresses				
	4A00	4A01	4A02	4A03	4A04
Top line	83	00	3C	01	40
Bottom line	B0	C0	3F	01	40
Left line	BF	00	3C	10	01
Right line	BF	3F	3C	10	01

At this point the most straightforward way to build a rectangle-drawing program is under T-BUG. The program could, of course, be assembled under EDTASM, but T-BUG is already resident and the program is rather short. So why not try it with the tools already at hand? If it works, then it can be documented and assembled under EDTASM, prehaps with some refinements to FILL2.

A hand-assembled version of the rectangle-drawing program is shown as Program 11-3. With FILL2 loaded into the system, enter this program under T-BUG.

The program is divided into three basic sections: SET UP FILL ROUTINE, FIGURE TABLE, and DRAWING ROUTINE. FIGURE TABLE contains the four sets of parameters for the rectangle figure. Those parameters are to be loaded into FILL2's parameter table.

Referring to the DRAWING ROUTINE, it begins by clearing the screen, then pointing to the address of the first byte of data to be transferred from the FIGURE TABLE to FILL2's parameter table. The third line in the DRAWING ROUTINE then calls SET UP FILL ROUTINE.

Program 11-3. Assembled listing for a rectangle-drawing routine.

```
KB      7006
FLTST1  7000
;SET UP FILL ROUTINE
4A60  11 00 4A      LD DE,4A00H     ;BEGINNING OF DESTINATION
4A63  01 05 00      LD BC,5H        ;NO. OF BYTES TO LOAD
4A66  ED B0         LDIR            ;LOAD FILL PARAMETERS
4A68  CD 10 4A      CALL FILL2      ;DO FILL
4A6B  C9            RET             ;RETURN TO CALLING PROGRAM



;FIGURE TABLE
4A70  83 00 3C 01 40
4A75  B0 C0 3F 01 40
4A7A  BF 00 3C 10 01
4A7F  BF 3F 3C 10 01



;DRAWING ROUTINE
7100  CD C9 01              CALL 01C9H      ;CLEAR THE SCREEN
7103  21 70 4A              LD HL,4A70H     ;BEGINNING OF SOURCE
7106  CD 60 4A              CALL 4A60H      ;DRAW TOP LINE
7109  21 75 4A              LD HL,4A75H     ;SET UP BOTTOM LINES
710C  CD 60 4A              CALL 4A60H      ;DRAW BOTTOM LINE
710F  21 7A 4A              LD HL,4A7AH     ;SET UP LEFT LINE
7112  CD 60 4A              CALL 4A60H      ;DRAW LEFT LINE
7115  21 7F 4A              LD HL,4A7FH     ;SET UP RIGHT LINE
7118  CD 60 4A              CALL 4A60H      ;DRAW RIGHT LINE
711B  18 FE         LOOP    JR LOOP         ;LOOP TO SELF
```

SET UP FILL ROUTINE first points to the beginning of FILL2's parameter table, loads the number of bytes to be transferred, and then uses an LDIR instruction to make the transfer. By the time the program reaches the CALL FILL2 instruction, the parameters for the top line of the rectangle reside in FILL2's parameter table. Doing the CALL FILL2 then causes the system to draw that top line.

On returning to the DRAWING ROUTINE the system picks up the starting address for the second sequence of parameters—those required for drawing the bottom portion of the rectangle. And then it does the SET UP FILL ROUTINE again.

The scheme continues cycling in this fashion until the drawing is done. The final instruction in the DRAWING ROUTINE brings things to a halt by looping to itself. It is thus necessary to operate the RESET push button to get out of the loop; and returning to T-BUG is a matter of entering /17312 under the SYSTEM command.

So enter the instructions listed as Program 11-3. With both T-BUG and FILL2 also resident in the system, execute the program from T-BUG by doing a J 7100.

It should be apparent that any program using FILL2 to draw moderately complex figures should use the SET UP FILL ROUTINE and a FIGURE TABLE. The DRAWING ROUTINE will be different for every drawing program you devise, as will the FIGURE TABLE. But the SET UP FILL ROUTINE will remain the same, no matter what sort of figure you want to draw.

This leads to the notion that the SET UP FILL ROUTINE ought to be fit right into the FILL routine. It would also be nice if the FIGURE TABLE could be permanently defined at the end of that revised FILL routine. Things are tightened up this way in Program 11-4.

FILL3 is a revised version of the original FILL program. It has the T-BUG-tested SET UP FILL edited into the opening phase (lines 180 through 200) and a set of default FILL parameters defining the beginning of the FIGURE TABLE at the end (lines 640 through 680).

Using FILL3 is thus a matter of building an appropriate FIGURE TABLE, beginning at address 4A70H, and writing a calling program at some higher address location. Chart 11-2 documents the entry point and memory map for FILL3.

Chart 11-2. Overall Documentation for the FILL3 Routine

Memory Location:	4A00H–4A64H (101 bytes)
Entry Point:	4A10H
Figure Table:	4A70H–4AFFH (160 bytes)

NOTE: Prior to calling FILL3, the HL register pair must point to the first of 5 bytes of the FILL parameters.

The notion of writing one program, using it and testing it for a while, and then revising the original program is the usual procedure for building up truly useful machine-language programs. The various sections can be written under either EDTASM or T-BUG, depending on how extensive they are; more complex routines are better written under EDTASM. But they are tested and coordinated under T-BUG in order to provide instant feedback between tests and small modifications.

With the various sections thus written and debugged, they can be merged into a single program under EDTASM. In the previous example, FILL3 was generated by first loading FILL2 under EDTASM and then using EDTASM's editing features to add in the new sections. The result is a single program and an object code tape that loads the entire FILL3 routine.

Program 11-5 is an example of a program that calls the FILL3 routine to draw a rectangle on the screen. It begins by filling the FIGURE TABLE with the parameters for the rectangular figure (the same ones used in Program 11-3). The DEFS pseudo-op in

Program 11-4. Assembled listing for FILL3.

```
                00100   ;FILL ROUTINE -- VER 3: FILENAME FILL3
4A00            00110           ORG     4A00H
4A00    BF      00120           DEFB    191             ;CHARACTER TYPE
4A01    003C    00130           DEFW    3C00H           ;START ADDRESS
4A03    02      00140           DEFB    2               ;NO. OF LINES
4A04    04      00150           DEFB    4               ;CHAR PER LINE
4A05    46      00160           DEFM    'FILL OFLOW'    ;OFLOW MESSAGE
4A06    49
4A07    4C
4A08    4C
4A09    20
4A0A    4F
4A0B    46
4A0C    4C
4A0D    4F
4A0E    57
4A0F    00      00170           DEFB    0               ;ALWAYS '0'
4A10    11004A  00180   SETUP   LD      DE,4A00H        ;POINT TO PARAM TABLE
4A13    010500  00190           LD      BC,5H           ;SET NO. BYTES TO LOAD
4A16    EDB0    00200           LDIR                    ;XFER FROM FIG. TO PAR. TABLE
                00210   ;DO THE FILL ROUTINE
4A18    2A014A  00220   FILL    LD      HL,(4A01H)      ;FETCH START ADDR
4A1B    CD434A  00230           CALL    OFLO            ;VALID POINTER?
4A1E    3A034A  00240           LD      A,(4A03H)       ;FETCH NO. OF LINES
4A21    47      00250           LD      B,A             ;NO. OF LINES TO B
4A22    3A044A  00260   LINE    LD      A,(4A04H)       ;FETCH CHAR/LINE
4A25    4F      00270           LD      C,A             ;CHAR/LINE TO C
4A26    3A004A  00280           LD      A,(4A00H)       ;FETCH CHAR TYPE
4A29    54      00290           LD      D,H             ;SET LINE START
4A2A    5D      00300           LD      E,L
4A2B    77      00310   PLOT    LD      (HL),A          ;PLOT CHARACTER
4A2C    0D      00320           DEC     C               ;DECREMENT CHAR COUNT
4A2D    CA374A  00330           JP      Z,NLINE         ;IF DONE, DO NEXT LINE
4A30    23      00340           INC     HL              ;ELSE INCREMENT POINTER
4A31    CD434A  00350           CALL    OFLO            ;CHECK FOR OVERFLOW
4A34    18F5    00360           JR      PLOT            ;AND PLOT AGAIN
0001            00370           DEFS    1
4A37    05      00380   NLINE   DEC     B               ;DECREMENT LINE COUNT
4A38    C8      00390           RET     Z               ;RETURN IF DONE
4A39    214000  00400           LD      HL,64           ;SET LINEFEED
4A3C    19      00410           ADD     HL,DE           ;START OF NEW LINE
4A3D    CD434A  00420           CALL    OFLO            ;CHECK FOR OVERFLOW
4A40    18E0    00430           JR      LINE            ;PLOT NEW LINE
0001            00440           DEFS    1
4A43    3E3F    00450   OFLO    LD      A,3FH           ;SET MAX MSB OF VIDEO
4A45    BC      00460           CP      H               ;LESS THAN MSB OF VIDEO?
4A46    380B    00470           JR      C,FLOMES        ;IF SO,PRINT MESSAGE
4A48    7C      00480           LD      A,H             ;GET MSB OF VIDEO
4A49    FE3C    00490           CP      3CH             ;UNDERFLOW?
4A4B    3806    00500           JR      C,FLOMES        ;IF SO, PRINT OFLO
4A4D    3A004A  00510           LD      A,(4A00H)       ;ELSE RESTORE CHAR TYPE
4A50    C9      00520           RET                     ;AND RETURN
0002            00530           DEFS    2
4A53    21003C  00540   FLOMES  LD      HL,3C00H        ;ELSE SET VIDEO POINTER
4A56    11054A  00550           LD      DE,4A05H        ;POINT TO MESSAGE
4A59    1A      00560   MESCJ   LD      A,(DE)          ;GET MESSAGE CHAR
4A5A    FE00    00570           CP      0               ;DONE?
4A5C    2805    00580           JR      Z,LOOP          ;IF SO,LOOP
4A5E    77      00590           LD      (HL),A          ;PRINT CHAR
4A5F    23      00600           INC     HL              ;ELSE NEXT MESS CHAR
4A60    13      00610           INC     DE
4A61    18F6    00620           JR      MESCHR
4A63    18FE    00630   LOOP    JR      LOOP            ;LOOP TO SELF
000B            00640           DEFS    4A70H-4A64H-1   ;START OF FIG. TABLE
```

```
4A70   BF       00650         DEFB    191
4A71   003C     00660         DEFW    3C00H
4A73   02       00670         DEFB    2
4A74   04       00680         DEFB    4
4A18            00690         END     FILL
00000 TOTAL ERRORS

LOOP      4A63
MESCHR    4A59
FLOMES    4A53
NLINE     4A37
PLOT      4A2B
LINE      4A22
OFLO      4A43
FILL      4A18
SETUP     4A10
```

line 330 then skips over a lot of unused FIGURE TABLE memory, thus beginning the actual program at address 7000H. With this REC1 and FILL3 resident in the system, executing from address 7000H causes the rectangle figure to appear on the screen.

The object codes for FILL3 and REC1 can be saved separately on cassette tape. Getting the program running is then a matter of going through the following procedure:

1. Load FILL3 under the SYSTEM command.
2. Answer the *? at the end of the loading operation by operating the RESET push button.
3. Load REC1 under the SYSTEM command.
4. Answer the *? at the end of the loading operation by ENTERing a slash or doing /28672.

BUILDING A GENERAL-PURPOSE MOVE ROUTINE

Most animated graphics programs can be built around general-purpose FILL and MOVE routines. The FILL routine has just been described, and this section takes up the matter of a MOVE routine. In this case the idea is to move simple figures in any desired fashion on the screen. See the MOV1 routine in Program 11-6.

MOV1 has the same basic elements as the general-purpose FILL routines—a parameter table (4B00H through 4B04H) and a routine that uses those parameters (4B10 through 4B3E).

The parameter table consists of an address indicating the current video point on the screen, another address indicating the next video address, and a 1-byte motion code that indicates the direction of motion. Generally speaking, the program fetches the current video address (CPNT) and the motion code (MCODE) from the param-

Program 11-5. Assembled listing for REC1.

```
                00100 ;RECTANGLE-DRAWING SUBROUTINE -- VER 1:FILENAME REC1
4A70            00110        ORG      4A70H
                00120 ;LOAD FIGURE TABLE
4A70   83       00130        DEFB     83H
4A71   00       00140        DEFB     00
4A72   3C       00150        DEFB     3CH
4A73   01       00160        DEFB     1
4A74   40       00170        DEFB     40H
4A75   B0       00180        DEFB     0B0H
4A76   C0       00190        DEFB     0C0H
4A77   3F       00200        DEFB     3FH
4A78   01       00210        DEFB     1
4A79   40       00220        DEFB     40H
4A7A   BF       00230        DEFB     0BFH
4A7B   00       00240        DEFB     0
4A7C   3C       00250        DEFB     3CH
4A7D   10       00260        DEFB     10H
4A7E   01       00270        DEFB     1
4A7F   BF       00280        DEFB     0BFH
4A80   3F       00290        DEFB     3FH
4A81   3C       00300        DEFB     3CH
4A82   10       00310        DEFB     10H
4A83   01       00320        DEFB     1
257C            00330        DEFS     7000H-4A83H-1
4A10            00340 SETUP  EQU      4A10H
4A70            00350 TOP    EQU      4A70H
4A75            00360 BOT    EQU      4A75H
4A7A            00370 LEFT   EQU      4A7AH
4A7F            00380 RIGHT  EQU      4A7FH
7000   CDC901   00390 REC1   CALL     01C9H      ;CLEAR THE SCREEN
7003   21704A   00400        LD       HL,TOP     ;SET UP TOP
7006   CD104A   00410        CALL     SETUP      ;DRAW IT
7009   21754A   00420        LD       HL,BOT     ;SET UP BOTTOM
700C   CD104A   00430        CALL     SETUP      ;DRAW IT
700F   217A4A   00440        LD       HL,LEFT    ;SET UP LEFT
7012   CD104A   00450        CALL     SETUP      ;DRAW IT
7015   217F4A   00460        LD       HL,RIGHT   ;SET UP RIGHT
7018   CD104A   00470        CALL     SETUP      ;DRAW IT
701B   18FE     00480 LOOP   JR       LOOP       ;LOOP TO SELF
7000            00490        END      REC1
00000 TOTAL ERRORS

LOOP    701B
REC1    7000
RIGHT   4A7F
LEFT    4A7A
BOT     4A75
TOP     4A70
SETUP   4A10
```

eter table. Then it generates a new video point (NPNT) based on the values of CPNT and MCODE. The NPNT thus developed is loaded to the parameter table before the program returns to the calling, or controlling, routine.

Chart 11-3 documents MOV1. Note the motion-code parameters for stepping the video address from a current to a new point. Each time MOV1 is called and MCODE is not a STOP code, NPNT takes on a value representing a single step in the indicated direction. Using

209

Program 11-6. Assembled listing for MOV1.

```
               00100 ;MOTION ROUTINE -- VER 1:FILENAME MOV1
4B00           00110        ORG    4B00H
               00120 ;MOTION TABLE
4B00  003C     00130        DEFW   3C00H      ;CURRENT VIDEO POINT
4B02  003C     00140        DEFW   3C00H      ;NEW VIDEO POINT
4B04  00       00150        DEFB   0          ;MOTION CODE
000B           00160        DEFS   4B10H-4B04H-1
4B00           00170 CPNT   EQU    4B00H
4B02           00180 NPNT   EQU    4B02H
4B04           00190 MCODE  EQU    4B04H
4B10  2A004B   00200 MOV1   LD HL,(CPNT)      ;FETCH CURRENT VIDEO
4B13  3A044B   00210        LD A,(MCODE)      ;FETCH MOTION CODE
4B16  E603     00220        AND 3             ;ISOLATE HOR BITS
4B18  FE01     00230        CP 1              ;IS IT RIGHT?
4B1A  2807     00240        JR Z,RT           ;IF SO,MOVE RIGHT
4B1C  FE02     00250        CP 2              ;IS IT LEFT?
4B1E  2004     00260        JR NZ,UD          ;IF NOT, CHECK U/D
4B20  2B       00270        DEC HL            ;ELSE MOVE LEFT
4B21  1801     00280        JR UD             ;AND CHECK U/D
4B23  23       00290 RT     INC HL            ;MOVE RIGHT
4B24  114000   00300 UD     LD DE,64          ;SET UP VERT MOVE
4B27  3A044B   00310        LD A,(MCODE)      ;FETCH MOTION CODE
4B2A  E6C0     00320        AND 0C0H          ;ISOLATE U/D BITS
4B2C  FE04     00330        CP 4              ;IS IT UP?
4B2E  2807     00340        JR Z,UP           ;IF SO,SET UP
4B30  FE08     00350        CP 8              ;IS IT DOWN?
4B32  2006     00360        JR NZ,OUT         ;IF NOT, GET OUT
4B34  19       00370        ADD HL,DE         ;ELSE MOVE DOWN
4B35  1803     00380        JR OUT            ;AND GET OUT
4B37  AF       00390 UP     XOR A             ;ZERO CY FLAG
4B38  ED52     00400        SBC HL,DE         ;MOVE UP
4B3A  22024B   00410 OUT    LD (NPNT),HL      ;SAVE NEW VIDEO POINT
4B3D  C9       00420        RET               ;RETURN
4B10           00430        END    MOV1
00000 TOTAL ERRORS

OUT    4B3A
UP     4B37
UD     4B24
RT     4B23
MOV1   4B10
MCODE  4B04
NPNT   4B02
CPNT   4B00
```

this routine to create the effect of motion on the screen is thus a matter of calling it a number of times in succession.

Like most other kinds of general-purpose routines, MOV1 cannot be executed alone. It must be used in conjunction with a calling program that sets the CPNT and MCODE parameters and uses the NPNT parameter to draw the moving figure into its new place on the screen. See one such program, BNCE1, in Program 11-7.

BNCE1 calls MOV1 to create the impression of a white rectangle of light bouncing back and forth across the screen. It begins by initializing the CPNT parameter at 3D00H—a point at the left side of the screen, just a bit above center. The instruction in line 200

Chart 11-3. Overall Documentation for the MOV1 Routine

Memory Location:	4B00H–4B3E (63 bytes)
Entry Point:	4B10H
Parameter Table:	
4B00H	CURRENT VIDEO POINT (CPNT), 2 bytes
4B02H	NEW VIDEO POINT (NPNT), 2 bytes
4B04H	MOTION CODE (MCODE), 1 byte

Motion Codes (MCODE Values):

00H	STOP	08H	DOWN
01H	RIGHT	09H	DOWN/RIGHT
02H	LEFT	0AH	DOWN/LEFT
03H	STOP	0BH	DOWN
04H	UP	0CH	STOP
05H	UP/RIGHT	0DH	RIGHT
06H	UP/LEFT	0EH	LEFT
07H	UP	0FH	STOP

sets NPNT one character space to the right of CPNT. Then line 210 sets the initial MCODE for right motion. Those first steps, lines 160 through 220, initialize the parameter table for MOV1.

Label TRY marks the beginning of the actual animation sequence. The first set of steps determines whether or not the figure's NPNT value will carry it beyond the left or right extremes of the screen. Note that the decision is based on the value of NPNT that is fetched from the MOV1 parameter table at line 230.

If NPNT is going to put the figure beyond the right side of the screen, as determined by instructions in lines 270 through 280, the routine calls SETL to load the MCODE byte for left motion—to a value of 2. But if the instructions in lines 240 and 250 determine that NPNT is about to carry the figure beyond the left extreme edge of the screen, the scheme calls SETR to adjust the MCODE for right motion. Of course, no adjustments in MCODE are made if the figure is not reaching either extreme.

In any case, the routine finds its way to MOVIT at line 380, and that set of instructions calls MOV1 to set up the next NPNT value.

The figure is first erased from its current position and drawn in its new one by the instructions under label PLOT (lines 410 through 460). In those instructions the current video point (CPNT) is loaded from the parameter table of MOV1 to the BC register pair (line 410). A hexadecimal 20—ASCII code for a space—is then loaded to that point to clear the image from the screen. Line 440 fetches the new video point (NPNT) from MOV1's parameter table, and the remaining lines in PLOT print the TRS-80 graphic BFH (a solid rectangle) at that new point. The figure that appears to be moving on the screen is thus determined by the data byte that

Program 11-7. Assembled listing for BNCE1.

```
                00100  ;BOUNCE ROUTINE -- VER 1: FILENAME BNCE1
7000            00110           ORG     7000H
4B10            00120  MOV1     EQU     4B10H
4B00            00130  CPNT     EQU     4B00H
4B02            00140  NPNT     EQU     4B02H
4B04            00150  MCODE    EQU     4B04H
7000 CDC901     00160  BNCE1    CALL 01C9H        ;CLEAR THE SCREEN
7003 21003D     00170           LD HL,3D00H       ;SET INITIAL CURRENT POINT
7006 22004B     00180           LD (CPNT),HL      ;LOAD TO MOV1 PARAMETER TABLE
7009 23         00190           INC HL            ;SET INITIAL NEW POINT
700A 22024B     00200           LD (NPNT),HL      ;LOAD TO MOV1 MOTION TABLE
700D 3E01       00210           LD A,1            ;SET UP INITIAL MOTION CODE
700F 32044B     00220           LD (MCODE),A      ;LOAD IT TO PARAMETER TABLE
7012 2A024B     00230  TRY      LD HL,(NPNT)      ;GET NEW POINT FOR TESTING
7015 7C         00240           LD A,H            ;LOOK AT LEFT POSITION
7016 FE3D       00250           CP 3DH            ;IS IT AT LEFT EXTREME?
7018 3814       00260           JR C,SETR         ;IF SO,SET UP RIGHT MOTION
701A 3E3F       00270           LD A,3FH          ;SET UP RIGHT EXTREME
701C BD         00280           CP L              ;IS IT THERE?
701D 3808       00290           JR C,SETL         ;IF SO, SET UP LEFT MOTION
701F CD4070     00300           CALL PLOT         ;ELSE PLOT THE NEW POINT
7022 22004B     00310           LD (CPNT),HL      ;AND SET AS CURRENT
7025 180C       00320           JR MOVIT          ;AND DO THE NEXT STEP
7027 3E02       00330  SETL     LD A,2            ;SET UP LEFT MOTION
7029 32044B     00340           LD (MCODE),A      ;AND LOAD TO PARAMETER TABLE
702C 1805       00350           JR MOVIT          ;AND MOVE
702E 3E01       00360  SETR     LD A,1            ;SET UP RIGHT MOTION
7030 32044B     00370           LD (MCODE),A      ;AND LOAD IT TO PARAMETER TABLE
7033 CD104B     00380  MOVIT    CALL MOV1         ;DO THE MOVE
7036 18DA       00390           JR TRY            ;AND CHECK IT OUT
0008            00400           DEFS 8            ;LEAVE SOME MEMORY
7040 ED4B004B   00410  PLOT     LD BC,(CPNT)      ;FETCH CURRENT POINT
7044 3E20       00420           LD A,20H          ;SET UP ERASE
7046 02         00430           LD (BC),A         ;ERASE CURRENT POINT
7047 ED4B004B   00440           LD BC,(NPNT)      ;FETCH NEW POINT
704B 3EBF       00450           LD A,0BFH         ;SET UP CHARACTER
704D 02         00460           LD (BC),A         ;PLOT NEW POINT
                00470  ;DO A TIME DELAY
704E 060C       00480           LD B,0CH          ;SET MSB OF DELAY
7050 0EFF       00490  SETC     LD C,0FFH         ;SET LSB OF DELAY
7052 0D         00500  DECC     DEC C             ;COUNTDOWN LSB
7053 20FD       00510           JR NZ,DECC        ;IF NOT DONE, COUNT MORE
7055 05         00520           DEC B             ;COUNTDOWN MSB
7056 20F8       00530           JR NZ,SETC        ;IF NOT DONE, COUNT MORE
7058 C9         00540           RET
7000            00550           END    BNCE1
00000 TOTAL ERRORS

DECC     7052
SETC     7050
MOVIT    7033
PLOT     7040
SETL     7027
SETR     702E
TRY      7012
BNCE1    7000
MCODE    4B04
NPNT     4B02
CPNT     4B00
MOV1     4B10
```

is loaded to the A register in line 450. Change that byte, and the moving character will change its appearance.

The PLOT sequence is called from line 300. Looking over that portion of the routine, you can see that PLOT is called only if the next position on the screen is a valid one—not beyond either extreme edge.

Since machine-language routines execute so rapidly, it is usually necessary to insert a time delay between successive PLOTtings. A time-delay routine thus follows the PLOT routine. Using the values loaded to registers B and C, the rectangle of light requires roughly two seconds to cross the screen in either direction.

BNCE1 sets up an endless looping action. The animation thus cycles endlessly, and the only way out of it is by operating the RESET push button.

Thus far in this section we have generated two programs: MOV1 and BNCE1. MOV1 is a general-purpose, motion-generating routine, and BNCE1 uses MOV1 to achieve one particular sort of animation. A number of other routines can be written—all calling MOV1—to create complex sets of animated figures.

To run the suggested program, generate the MOV1 and BNCE1 object codes separately and under EDTASM. Then use the following procedure to get it going:

1. Load the MOV1 object code under SYSTEM.
2. Answer the *? at the end of the loading by operating the RESET push button.
3. Load BNCE1 under the SYSTEM command.
4. Start the program by answering the *? with a slash or a /28672.

APPENDIX A

Number System Base Conversions

Just about any computer (certainly the TRS-80) is essentially a binary machine; the Z-80 microprocessor does all its control, arithmetic, and logic operations in the base-2, or binary, number system. And it so happens that the Z-80 works with 8-bit binary numbers—a full byte of 8 bits.

People do not think and work with binary numbers very well, however. Such numbers, being made up of 1s and 0s, are very cumbersome. One alternative to purely binary representations of numbers is hexadecimal numbers. The hexadecimal (base-16) number system looks at binary numbers in groups of four; every group of four binary figures (sometimes called a *nibble*) can be represented by a single hexadecimal character. So, instead of having to work with strings of eight 1s and 0s in binary, it is possible to work with just two hexadecimal characters.

While, indeed, many machine-language programmers can learn to work with hexadecimal numbers with great proficiency, the general population still prefers the usual decimal number system. TRS-80 engineers were aware of that fact, and TRS-80 BASIC is built around the decimal number system exclusively.

As long as one works with TRS-80 BASIC in its most elementary fashion—doing no special addressing or machine-language work—there is no need to be aware of hexadecimal or binary numbers. But hexadecimal numbers become helpful when POKEing and PEEKing in memory, and they become quite necessary when doing extensive machine-language programming.

Then, too, binary numbering becomes important when attempting to write machine-language program for controlling custom circuitry connected to the TRS-80's output connector.

Thus, programmers working deeper and deeper into the TRS-80 system will find themselves having to make conversions between decimal and hexadecimal numbers and, eventually, between binary and hexadecimal numbers. The purpose of this appendix is to make such conversion tasks as simple as possible.

There are many ways to approach the conversions between these three different number systems; but, in this writer's opinion, the following are the most straightforward.

HEXADECIMAL-TO-DECIMAL CONVERSIONS

In the TRS-80/Z-80 system, data is carried as a 1-byte (two-hexadecimal-character) code, and addresses are carried as a 2-byte (four-hexadecimal-character) code. Table A-1 can be very helpful for translating hexadecimal numbers into their decimal counterparts. This sort of situation often arises when one is writing programs in both BASIC and machine language.

Table A-1. Hexadecimal to Decimal Conversion

4 Hex	Decimal	3 Hex	Decimal	2 Hex	Decimal	1 Hex	Decimal
0	0	0	0	0	0	0	0
1	4096	1	256	1	16	1	1
2	8192	2	512	2	32	2	2
3	12288	3	768	3	48	3	3
4	16384	4	1024	4	64	4	4
5	20480	5	1280	5	80	5	5
6	24576	6	1536	6	96	6	6
7	28672	7	1792	7	112	7	7
8	32768	8	2048	8	128	8	8
9	36864	9	2304	9	144	9	9
A	40960	A	2560	A	160	A	10
B	45056	B	2816	B	176	B	11
C	49152	C	3072	C	192	C	12
D	53248	D	3328	D	208	D	13
E	57344	E	3584	E	224	E	14
F	61440	F	3840	F	240	F	15

The table can be used for converting up to four hexadecimal places to their decimal counterpart. Note that there are four major columns, labeled 1 through 4. These column numbers represent the relative positions of the hexadecimal characters as they are usually written, with the lsb on the left and the msb on the right.

To see how the table works, suppose that you want to convert the hexadecimal number 1A3F into decimal. The first character on the left takes a decimal equivalent shown in column 4—4096. The second character from the left takes the value from column 3—2560. The last two figures get their decimal equivalents from columns 2 and 1—48 and 15, respectively. Then, to get the true decimal value, add those decimal equivalents: 4096+2560+48+15. That comes out to 6719. In other words, 1A3F (hexadecimal) is equal to 6719 (decimal).

If you are converting a two-place hexadecimal number, just use columns 2 and 1. Hexadecimal C3, for instance, is equal to 192+3, or decimal 195.

Table A-1 is adequate for hexadecimal-to-decimal conversions for all the usual sort of work on the TRS-80/Z-80 system.

DECIMAL-TO-HEXADECIMAL CONVERSIONS

When working back and forth between BASIC and machine language, it is often necessary to convert decimal data and addresses into hexadecimal notation. Table A-1 comes to the rescue here. The procedure is a rather straightforward one, but it involves several steps.

Suppose, for example, you want to convert decimal 65 into its hexadecimal counterpart. First, find the decimal number (in a decimal column) that is equal to, or less than, the desired decimal number—65 is the decimal number, and its closest, and less, value is 64. The 64 is equivalent to a hexadecimal 4 in column 2. Thus the most significant character in the hexadecimal representation is a 4.

Next, subtract that 64 from the number you are working with: 65−64=1. Now look up the hexadecimal value of the 1 in the next-lower column—the 1 column in this case. The hexadecimal version of that number is 1.

Putting together those two hexadecimal characters, you get a 41. Indeed, decimal 65 translates into hexadecimal 41.

By way of a somewhat more involved example, suppose you have to convert decimal 19314 into hexadecimal notation.

Looking through the columns of DEC numbers, you find that 16384 is the next-lower value; it translates into hexadecimal 4 in column 4. So you are going to end up with a four-character hexadecimal number, with the digit on the left being a 4.

To get the next place value, subtract 16384 from 19314: 19314−16384=2930. The next-lower decimal value in this case is 2816 from column 3; and that turns up a B as the next hexadecimal character. So far, the number is 4B.

Now do this: 2930−2816=114. The next-lower decimal value from column 2 is 112, and its hexadecimal counterpart is 7. And to this point, the hexadecimal number is 4B7.

Finally, do this: 114−112=2. From column 1, decimal 2 is the same as hexadecimal 2; so the final hexadecimal character is 2.

Putting this all together, it turns out that decimal 19314 is the same as hexadecimal 4B72. Fig. A-1 summarizes the operation.

DECIMAL ADDRESS TO 2-BYTE DECIMAL FORMAT

When POKEing addresses as 2-byte numbers into memory, it is necessary to convert the address to be loaded into a 2-byte format. In decimal, this isn't easy, but it is all a part of setting up address locations in decimal-oriented BASIC.

By way of an example, suppose you are to load a 2-byte version of decimal address 1234 into memory addresses 16787 and 16788. That number to be stored, 1234, has to be broken up into two parts: one for each of the places it is to be stored.

Before a decimal number can be divided into a 2-byte version, it must be converted into a hexadecimal form. Using the decimal to hexadecimal conversion described in the previous section, it turns out that 1234 decimal is equal to 04D2 in hexadecimal.

```
                        HEXADECIMAL
      DECIMAL           EQUIVALENT
      NUMBER            4  B  7  2
      19314
     -16384  — COLUMN 4 ——┘  ↑  ↑  ↑
       2930
      -2816  — COLUMN 3 ————————┘  │  │
        114
       -112  — COLUMN 2 ———————————┘  │
          2  — COLUMN 1 ——————————————┘

      19314 (DECIMAL) = 4B72 (HEXADECMAL)
```

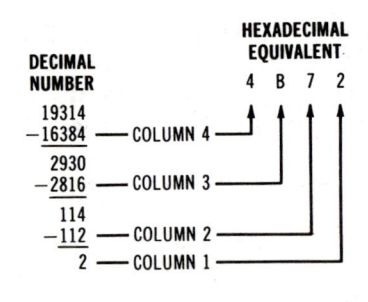

Fig. A-1. Converting 19314 decimal to 4B72 hexadecimal.

Next, divide that hexadecimal version into two bytes: the most significant byte (msb) is 04, and the least significant byte is D2. Divided this way, you get the combinations 04 D2.

Finally, convert those two sets of hexadecimal numbers into their decimal equivalents, treating them as two separate hexadecimal numbers. Thus 04 hexadecimal is 4 decimal, and D2 hexadecimal is 210.

The 2-byte version of decimal 1234 is thus 4 and 210, with 4 being the msb and 210 being the lsb.

That takes care of the conversion of an ordinary decimal number into a 2-byte version—also in decimal. This is the main point of the discussion at hand. But the example calls for POKEing these numbers into locations 16787 and 16788—both in decimal.

Now, almost without exception, you will find that the lsb of the 2-byte number must go into the lower-numbered address; so the BASIC operation for satisfying the requirements for the example looks like this:

```
POKE 16787,210:POKE 16788,4
```

No, it isn't a simple operation, but it's the price that must be paid for working with a binary/hexadecimal-oriented computer system in a decimal, BASIC-oriented language.

2-BYTE DECIMAL TO CONVENTIONAL DECIMAL

Suppose you are disassembling a machine-language program from BASIC. Under that condition, a 2-byte address will appear as a set of two decimal numbers; and if you want to get that pair of numbers into a conventional decimal format, you have to play with the numbers a bit.

Consider a case where 223 turns up as the lsb in decimal, and 104 is the msb. First, convert both sets of numbers into their hexadecimal counterparts: 223 decimal = DF hexadecimal, and 104 decimal = 68 hexadecimal.

That means DF is the lsb and 68 is the msb. Putting them together in the conventional order (msb first), the hexadecimal equivalent of the number under consideration is 68DF.

All that remains to be done is to convert that into a full decimal number: 68DF=24567+2048+208+15=26849 decimal. That's it—the conventional decimal version of the 2-byte decimal combination 104 223 is 26849. For one reason or another, the disassembled program is saving address 26849.

BINARY-TO-DECIMAL CONVERSION

In practice, most binary-to-decimal conversions are carried out with 1-byte (or 8-bit) binary numbers, although there are occasions when it is necessary to do the conversion from 2-byte (16-bit) numbers.

Fig. A-2A shows the breakdown of an 8-bit binary number. The positions are labeled 0 through 7, with zero indicating the least significant bit (lsb) position. Each of those eight bit locations will contain either a 1 or a 0.

To appreciate the relevance of this whole thing, suppose you want to POKE a decimal number into some address location, and select a number such that it looks like this in binary form: 01101011.

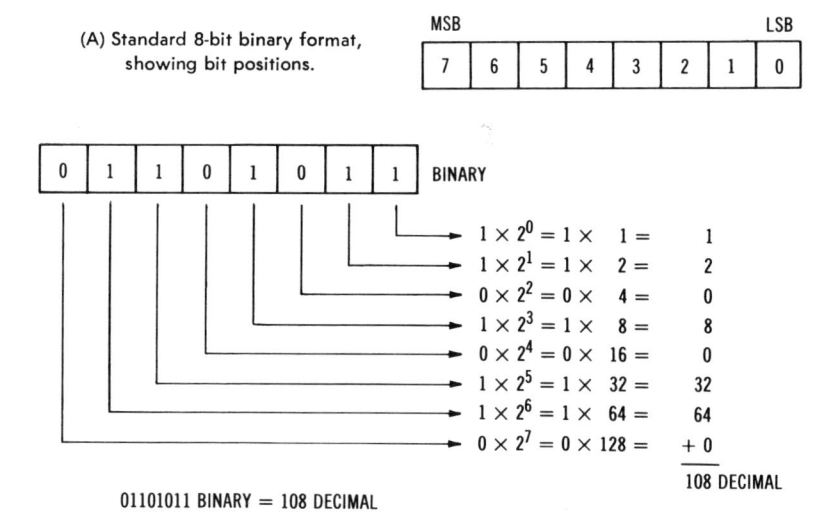

(A) Standard 8-bit binary format, showing bit positions.

MSB							LSB
7	6	5	4	3	2	1	0

| 0 | 1 | 1 | 0 | 1 | 0 | 1 | 1 | BINARY |

$1 \times 2^0 = 1 \times 1 = 1$
$1 \times 2^1 = 1 \times 2 = 2$
$0 \times 2^2 = 0 \times 4 = 0$
$1 \times 2^3 = 1 \times 8 = 8$
$0 \times 2^4 = 0 \times 16 = 0$
$1 \times 2^5 = 1 \times 32 = 32$
$1 \times 2^6 = 1 \times 64 = 64$
$0 \times 2^7 = 0 \times 128 = +0$

108 DECIMAL

01101011 BINARY = 108 DECIMAL

(B) Converting binary word 01101011 to decimal.

Fig. A-2. Power-of-2 place values of an 8-bit binary word.

So you want bit positions 0, 1, 3, 5, and 6 to be a 1, and the rest 0. But you have to POKE a decimal version from BASIC. Here's how to go about determining that decimal version.

First, multiply the 1 or 0 in each bit location times 2^n, where n is the bit's position value in each case. Then simply add the results. See the example in Fig. A-2B. That particular number in binary is equal to 108 decimal.

The same idea applies to converting 16-bit binary to a decimal equivalent. The place values run from 0 to 15 in that case, and Table A-2 can help you determine those larger powers of 2.

Table A-2. Powers of 2

n	2^n
0	1
1	2
2	4
3	8
4	16
5	32
6	64
7	128
8	256
9	512
10	1 024
11	2 048
12	4 096
13	8 192
14	16 384
15	32 768

BINARY-TO-HEXADECIMAL CONVERSION

Converting a binary number into a hexadecimal format is perhaps the simplest of all the conversion operations. All you have to do is group the binary number into sets of 4 bits each, beginning with the lsb, and then find the hexadecimal value for each group. Table A-3 helps with the latter operation.

Suppose the binary number is 10011101. Grouping this number into sets of 4 bits (or nibbles), it looks like this: 1001 1101. The hexadecimal equivalents for each group can be found in Table A-3: 9 D. The hexadecimal version of that 8-bit binary number is thus 9D.

The same procedure works equally well for 16-bit numbers, the only difference being that you end up with four hexadecimal characters instead of just two of them.

Incidentally, there is an algorithm for converting directly from binary to hexadecimal (without using the table), but its complexity far exceeds that of doing the job with Table A-3.

Table A-3. Binary to Hexadecimal Conversion

Binary	Hexadecimal
0000	0
0001	1
0010	2
0011	3
0100	4
0101	5
0110	6
0111	7
1000	8
1001	9
1010	A
1011	B
1100	C
1101	D
1110	E
1111	F

HEXADECIMAL-TO-BINARY CONVERSION

Converting a hexadecimal number to binary is a simple matter of applying Table A-3 to convert each hexadecimal character into the appropriate groups of 4 binary bits.

Example: Convert address 403D into binary. According to Table A-3, that hexadecimal number can be represented as

0100 0000 0011 1101

Nothing more, nothing less. That's all there is to it.

DECIMAL-TO-BINARY CONVERSION

There is a nice algorithm (several of them, in fact) for mathematically converting any decimal number into its binary format. But it is simpler in the long run, and probably more accurate as well, to use a two-step procedure.

The general idea is to convert the decimal number into its hexadecimal counterpart as described earlier in this appendix. Then convert the hexadecimal characters into their binary versions as described in the previous section. Besides, it is often handy to have the hexadecimal version available for later use.

Example: Convert 1234 decimal into binary. First, as described earlier, calculate the hexadecimal version of decimal 1234—that comes out to be 04D2. And that hexadecimal number, expressed in binary (from Table A-3) is 0000 0100 1101 0010. Thus 1234 in decimal is equal to 10011010010 in binary. You may retain the leading zeros if you wish.

APPENDIX B

Z-80 Instruction Set: Object and Source Codes

ADD WITH CARRY INSTRUCTIONS

8E	ADC A,(HL)
DD 8E byte	ADC A,(IX+indx)
FD 8E byte	ADC A,(IY+indx)
8F	ADC A,A
88	ADC A,B
89	ADC A,C
8A	ADC A,D
8B	ADC A,E
8C	ADC A,H
8D	ADC A,L
CE byte	ADC A,data
ED 4A	ADC HL,BC
ED 5A	ADC HL,DE
ED 6A	ADC HL,HL
ED 7A	ADC HL,SP

ADD INSTRUCTIONS

86	ADD A,(HL)
DD 86 byte	ADD A,(IX+indx)
FD 86 byte	ADD A,(IY+indx)
87	ADD A,A
80	ADD A,B
81	ADD A,C
82	ADD A,D
83	ADD A,E
84	ADD A,H
85	ADD A,L
C6 byte	ADD A,data
09	ADD HL,BC
19	ADD HL,DE
29	ADD HL,HL
39	ADD HL,SP
DD 09	ADD IX,BC
DD 19	ADD IX,DE
DD 29	ADD IX,IX
DD 39	ADD IX,SP
FD 09	ADD IY,BC
FD 19	ADD IY,DE
FD 29	ADD IY,IY
FD 39	ADD IY,SP

LOGIC-AND INSTRUCTIONS

A6	AND (HL)
DD A6 byte	AND (IX+indx)
FD A6 byte	AND (IY+indx)
A7	AND A
A0	AND B
A1	AND C
A2	AND D
A3	AND E
A4	AND H
A5	AND L
E6 byte	AND data

BIT-TEST INSTRUCTIONS

CB 46	BIT 0,(HL)
DD CB byte 46	BIT 0,(IX+indx)
FD CB byte 46	BIT 0,(IY+indx)
CB 47	BIT 0,A
CB 40	BIT 0,B
CB 41	BIT 0,C
CB 42	BIT 0,D
CB 43	BIT 0,E
CB 44	BIT 0,H
CB 45	BIT 0,L
CB 4E	BIT 1,(HL)
DD CB byte 4E	BIT 1,(IX+indx)
FD CB byte 4E	BIT 1,(IY+indx)
CB 4F	BIT 1,A
CB 48	BIT 1,B
CB 49	BIT 1,C
CB 4A	BIT 1,D
CB 4B	BIT 1,E
CB 4C	BIT 1,H
CB 4D	BIT 1,L
CB 56	BIT 2,(HL)
DD CB byte 56	BIT 2,(IX+indx)
FD CB byte 56	BIT 2,(IY+indx)
CB 57	BIT 2,A
CB 50	BIT 2,B
CB 51	BIT 2,C
CB 52	BIT 2,D
CB 53	BIT 2,E
CB 54	BIT 2,H
CB 55	BIT 2,L
CB 5E	BIT 3,(HL)
DD CB byte 5E	BIT 3,(IX+indx)
FD CB byte 5E	BIT 3,(IY+indx)
CB 5F	BIT 3,A
CB 58	BIT 3,B
CB 59	BIT 3,C
CB 5A	BIT 3,D
CB 5B	BIT 3,E
CB 5C	BIT 3,H
CB 5D	BIT 3,L

CB 66	BIT 4,(HL)		
DD CB byte 66	BIT 4,(IX+indx)		
FD CB byte 66	BIT 4,(IX+indx)		

COMPARE ACCUMULATOR INSTRUCTIONS

```
BE              CP  (HL)
DD BE byte      CP  (IX+indx)
FD BE byte      CP  (IY+indx)

CB 67           BIT 4,A
CB 60           BIT 4,B         BF      CP A
CB 61           BIT 4,C         B8      CP B
CB 62           BIT 4,D         B9      CP C
CB 63           BIT 4,E         BA      CP D
CB 64           BIT 4,H         BB      CP E
CB 65           BIT 4,L         BC      CP H
                                BD      CP L
CB 6E           BIT 5,(HL)
DD CB byte 6E   BIT 5,(IX+indx)
FD CB byte 6E   BIT 5,(IY+indx)

CB 6F           BIT 5,A
CB 68           BIT 5,B
CB 69           BIT 5,C
```

COMPARE AND INCREMENT/DECREMENT

```
CB 6A           BIT 5,D
CB 6B           BIT 5,E
CB 6C           BIT 5,H         ED A9    CPD
CB 6D           BIT 5,L         ED B9    CPDR
                                ED A1    CPI
CB 76           BIT 6,(HL)      ED B1    CPIR
DD CB byte 76   BIT 6,(IX+indx)
FD CB byte 76   BIT 6,(IY+indx)

CB 77           BIT 6,A
CB 70           BIT 6,B
CB 71           BIT 6,C
```

COMPLEMENT ACCUMULATOR

```
CB 72           BIT 6,D
CB 73           BIT 6,E
CB 74           BIT 6,H         2F       CPL
CB 75           BIT 6,L

CB 7E           BIT 7,(HL)
DD CB byte 7E   BIT 7,(IX+indx)
FD CB byte 7E   BIT 7,(IY+indx)

CB 7F           BIT 7,A
```

DECIMAL ADJUST THE ACCUMULATOR

```
CB 78           BIT 7,B
CB 79           BIT 7,C
CB 7A           BIT 7,D         27       DAA
CB 7B           BIT 7,E
CB 7C           BIT 7,H
CB 7D           BIT 7,L
```

DECREMENT INSTRUCTIONS

CALL INSTRUCTIONS

```
                                35              DEC (HL)
DC byte byte    CALL C,addr     DD 35 byte      DEC (IX+indx)
FC byte byte    CALL M,addr     FD 35 byte      DEC (IY+indx)
D4 byte byte    CALL NC,addr
C4 byte byte    CALL NZ,addr    3D              DEC A
F4 byte byte    CALL P,addr     05              DEC B
EC byte byte    CALL PE,addr    0D              DEC C
E4 byte byte    CALL PO,addr    15              DEC D
CC byte byte    CALL Z,addr     1D              DEC E
                                25              DEC H
CD byte byte    CALL addr       2D              DEC L

                                0B              DEC BC
                                1B              DEC DE
```

COMPLEMENT CARRY FLAG

```
                                2B              DEC HL
                                DD 2B           DEC IX
                                FD 2B           DEC IY
3F              CCF             3B              DEC SP
```

224

```
DISABLE INTERRUPT                             INCREMENT INSTRUCTIONS
-------------------------------------         ----------------------------------------

F3              DI                            34                     INC (HL)
                                              DD 34 byte             INC (IX+indx)
                                              FD 34 byte             INC (IY+indx)

                                              3C                     INC A
                                              04                     INC B
DECREMENT AND JUMP RELATIVE                   0C                     INC C
-------------------------------------         14                     INC D
                                              1C                     INC E
10 byte         DJNZ disp                     24                     INC H
                                              2C                     INC L

                                              03                     INC BC
ENABLE INTERRUPT                              13                     INC DE
-------------------------------------         23                     INC HL
                                              DD 23                  INC IX
FB              EI                            FD 23                  INC IY
                                              33                     INC SP


                                              JUMP INSTRUCTIONS
EXCHANGE INSTRUCTIONS                         ----------------------------------------
-------------------------------------
                                              C3 byte byte           JP addr
E3              EX (SP),HL                    E9                     JP (HL)
DD E3           EX (SP),IX                    DD E9                  JP (IX)
FD E3           EX (SP),IY                    FD E9                  JP (IY)
08              EX AF,AF'
EB              EX DE,HL                      DA byte byte           JP C,addr
D9              EXX                           FA byte byte           JP M,addr
                                              D2 byte byte           JP NC,addr
                                              C2 byte byte           JP NZ,addr
                                              F2 byte byte           JP P,addr
                                              EA byte byte           JP PE,addr
HALT INSTRUCTION                              E2 byte byte           JP PO,addr
-------------------------------------         CA byte byte           JP Z,addr
                                              38 byte                JR C,disp
76              HALT                          30 byte                JR NC,disp
                                              20 byte                JR NZ,disp
                                              28 byte                JR Z,disp
SET INTERRUPT MODES                           18 byte                JR disp
-------------------------------------

ED 46           IM 0
ED 56           IM 1                          LOAD INSTRUCTIONS
ED 5E           IM 2                          ----------------------------------------

                                              02                     LD (BC),A
                                              12                     LD (DE),A
INPUT FROM PORT INSTRUCTIONS                  77                     LD (HL),A
-------------------------------------         70                     LD (HL),B
                                              1                      LD (HL),C
ED 78           IN A,(C)                      72                     LD (HL),D
ED 40           IN B,(C)                      73                     LD (HL),E
ED 48           IN C,(C)                      74                     LD (HL),H
ED 50           IN D,(C)                      75                     LD (HL),L
ED 58           IN E,(C)                      36 byte                LD (HL),data
ED 60           IN H,(C)                      DD 77 byte             LD (IX+indx),A
ED 68           IN L,(C)                      DD 70 byte             LD (IX+indx),B
DB byte         IN A,(port)                   DD 71 byte             LD (IX+indx),C
                                              DD 72 byte             LD (IX+indx),D
ED AA           IND                           DD 73 byte             LD (IX+indx),E
ED BA           INDR                          DD 74 byte             LD (IX+indx),H
ED A2           INI                           DD 75 byte             LD (IX+indx),L
ED B2           INIR                          DD 36 byte byte        LD (IX+indx),data
```

FD 77 byte	LD (IY+indx),A	57	LD D,A
FD 70 byte	LD (IY+indx),B	50	LD D,B
FD 71 byte	LD (IY+indx),C	51	LD D,C
FD 72 byte	LD (IY+indx),D	52	LD D,D
FD 73 byte	LD (IY+indx),E	53	LD D,E
FD 74 byte	LD (IY+indx),H	54	LD D,H
FD 75 byte	LD (IY+indx),L	55	LD D,L
FD 36 byte byte	LD (IY+indx),data	16 byte	LD D,data
32 byte byte	LD (addr),A	ED 5B byte byte	LD DE,(addr)
ED 43 byte byte	LD (addr),BC	11 byte byte	LD DE,data data
ED 53 byte byte	LD (addr),DE		
22 byte byte	LD (addr),HL	5E	LD E,(HL)
DD 22 byte byte	LD (addr),IX	DD 5E byte	LD E,(IX+indx)
FD 22 byte byte	LD (addr),IY	FD 5E byte	LD E,(IY+indx)
ED 73 byte byte	LD (addr),SP		
		5F	LD E,A
0A	LD A,(BC)	58	LD E,B
1A	LD A,(DE)	59	LD E,c
7E	LD A,(HL)	5A	LD E,D
DD 7E byte	LD A,(IX+indx)	5B	LD E,E
FD 7E byte	LD A,(IY+indx)	5C	LD E,H
3A byte byte	LD A,(addr)	5D	LD E,L
		1E byte	LD E,data
7F	LD A,A		
78	LD A,B	66	LD H,(HL)
79	LD A,C	DD 66 byte	LD H,(IX+indx)
7A	LD A,D	FD 66 byte	LD H,(IY+indx)
7B	LD A,E		
7C	LD A,H	67	LD H,A
7D	LD A,L	60	LD H,B
ED 57	LD A,I	61	LD H,C
ED 5F	LD A,R	63	LD H,D
3E byte	LD A,data	64	LD H,E
		65	LD H,L
46	LD B,(HL)	26 byte	LD H,data
DD 46 byte	LD B,(IX+indx)		
FD 46 byte	LD B,(IY+indx)	2A byte byte	LD HL,(addr)
47	LD B,A	21 byte byte	LD HL,data data
40	LD B,B		
41	LD B,C	6E	LD L,(HL)
42	LD B,D	DD 6E byte	LD L,(IX+indx)
43	LD B,E	FD 6E byte	LD L,(IY+indx)
44	LD B,H		
45	LD B,L	6F	LD L,A
06 byte	LD B,data	68	LD L,B
		69	LD L,C
ED 4B byte byte	LD BC,(addr)	6A	LD L,D
01 byte byte	LD BC,data data	6B	LD L,E
		6C	LD L,H
4E	LD C,(HL)	6D	LD L,L
DD 4E byte	LD C,(IX+indx)	2E byte	LD L,data
FD 4E byte	LD C,(IY+indx)		
		ED 47	LD I,A
4F	LD C,A	ED 4F	LD R,A
48	LD C,B	DD 2A byte byte	LD IX,(addr)
49	LD C,C	FD 2A byte byte	LD IY,(addr)
4A	LD C,D	DD 21 byte byte	LD IX,data data
4B	LD C,E	FD 21 byte byte	LD IY,data data
4C	LD C,H	ED 7B byte byte	LD SP,(addr)
4D	LD C,L	F9	LD SP,HL
0E byte	LD C,data	DD F9	LD SP,IX
		FD F9	LD SP,IY
56	LD D,(HL)	31 byte byte	LD SP,data data
DD 56 byte	LD D,(IX+indx)		
FD 56 byte	LD D,(IY+indx)		

LOAD WITH INCREMENT/DECREMENT
```
ED A8        LDD
ED B8        LDDR
ED A0        LDI
ED B0        LDIR
```

NO OPERATION
```
00           NOP
```

NEGATE ACC. (2'S COMPLEMENT)
```
ED 44        NEG
```

LOGIC-OR INSTRUCTIONS
```
B6           OR (HL)
DD B6 byte   OR (IX+indx)
FD B6 byte   OR (IY+indx)

B7           OR A
B0           OR B
B1           OR C
B2           OR D
B3           OR E
B4           OR H
B5           OR L
F6 byte      OR data
```

EXCLUSIVE-OR INSTRUCTIONS
```
AE           XOR (HL)
DD AE byte   XOR (IX+indx)
FD AE byte   XOR (IY+indx)

AF           XOR A
A8           XOR B
A9           XOR C
AA           XOR D
AB           XOR E
AC           XOR H
AD           XOR L
EE byte      XOR dataa
```

OUTPUT TO PORT INSTRUCTIONS
```
ED 79        OUT (C),A
ED 41        OUT (C),B
ED 49        OUT (C),C
ED 51        OUT (C),D
ED 59        OUT (C),E
ED 61        OUT (C),H
ED 69        OUT (C),L
D3 byte      OUT (port),A
```

```
ED BB        OTDR
ED B3        OTIR
ED AB        OUTD
ED A3        OUTI
```

PUSH AND POP INSTRUCTIONS
```
F1           POP AF
C1           POP BC
D1           POP DE
E1           POP HL
DD E1        POP IX
FD E1        POP IY

F5           PUSH AF
C5           PUSH BC
D5           PUSH DE
E5           PUSH HL
DD E5        PUSH IX
FD E5        PUSH IY
```

RESET BIT INSTRUCTIONS
```
CB 86        RES (HL)
DD CB byte 86   RES (IX+indx)
FD CB byte 86   RES (IY+indx)

CB 87        RES 0,A
CB 80        RES 0,B
CB 81        RES 0,C
CB 82        RES 0,D
CB 83        RES 0,E
CB 84        RES 0,H
CB 85        RES 0,L

CB 8E        RES 1,(HL)
DD CB byte 8E   RES 1,(IX+indx)
FD CB byte 8E   RES 1,(IY+indx)

CB 8F        RES 1,A
CB 88        RES 1,B
CB 89        RES 1,C
CB 8A        RES 1,D
CB 8B        RES 1,E
CB 8C        RES 1,H
CB 8D        RES 1,L

CB 96        RES 2,(HL)
DD CB byte 96   RES 2,(IX+indx)
FD CB byte 96   RES 2,(IY+indx)

CB 97        RES 2,A
CB 90        RES 2,B
CB 91        RES 2,C
CB 92        RES 2,D
CB 93        RES 2,E
CB 94        RES 2,H
CB 95        RES 2,L

CB 9E        RES 3,(HL)
DD CB byte 9E   RES 3,(IX+indx)
FD CB byte 9E   RES 3,(IY+indx)
```

227

```
CB 9F              RES 3,A           ED 4D              RETI
CB 98              RES 3,B           ED 45              RETN
CB 99              RES 3,C
CB 9A              RES 3,D
CB 9B              RES 3,E
CB 9C              RES 3,H
CB 9D              RES 3,L

CB A6              RES 4,(HL)
DD CB byte A6      RES 4,(IX+indx)   ROTATE THROUGH CARRY INSTRUCTIONS
FD CB byte A6      RES 4,(IY+indx)   -----------------------------------

CB A7              RES 4,A           17                 RLA
CB A0              RES 4,B           CB 16              RL (HL)
CB A1              RES 4,C           DD CB byte 16      RL (IX+indx)
CB A2              RES 4,D           FD CB byte 16      RL (IY+indx)
CB A3              RES 4,E
CB A4              RES 4,H           CB 17              RL A
CB A5              RES 4,L           CB 10              RL B
                                     CB 11              RL C
CB AE              RES 5,(HL)        CB 12              RL D
DD CB byte AF      RES 5,(IX+indx)   CB 13              RL E
FD CB byte AF      RES 5,(IY+indx)   CB 14              RL H
                                     CB 15              RL L

CB AF              RES 5,A
CB A8              RES 5,B           1F                 RRA
CB A9              RES 5,C           CB 1E              RR (HL)
CB AA              RES 5,D           DD CB byte 1E      RR (IX+indx)
CB AB              RES 5,E           FD CB byte 1E      RR (IY+indx)
CB AC              RES 5,H
CB AD              RES 5,L           CB 1F              RR A
                                     CB 18              RR B
CB B6              RES 6,(HL)        CB 19              RR C
DD CB byte B6      RES 6,(IX+indx)   CB 1A              RR D
FD CB byte B6      RES 6,(IY+indx)   CB 1B              RR E
                                     CB 1C              RR H
CB B7              RES 6,A           CB 1D              RR L
CB B0              RES 6,B
CB B1              RES 6,C
CB B2              RES 6,D
CB B3              RES 6,E
CB B4              RES 6,H
CB B5              RES 6,L           ROTATE CIRCULAR INSTRUCTIONS
                                     -----------------------------------
CB BE              RES 7,(HL)
DD CB byte BE      RES 7,(IX+indx)   07                 RLCA
FD CB byte BE      RES 7,(IY+indx)   CB 06              RLC (HL)
                                     DD CB byte 06      RLC (IX+indx)
CB BF              RES 7,A           FD CB byte 06      RLC (IY+indx)
CB B8              RES 7,B
CB B9              RES 7,C           CB 07              RLC A
CB BA              RES 7,D           CB 00              RLC B
CB BB              RES 7,E           CB 01              RLC C
CB BC              RES 7,H           CB 02              RLC D
CB BD              RES 7,L           CB 03              RLC E
                                     CB 04              RLC H
                                     CB 05              RLC L

RETURN INSTRUCTIONS                  0F                 RRCA
-----------------------------------  CB 0E              RRC (HL)
                                     DD CB byte 0E      RRC (IX+indx)
C9                 RET               FD CB byte 0E      RRC (IY+indx)
D8                 RET C
F8                 RET M             CB 0F              RRC A
D0                 RET NC            CB 08              RRC B
C0                 RET NZ            CB 09              RRC C
F0                 RET P             CB 0A              RRC D
E8                 RET PE            CB 0B              RRC E
E0                 RET PO            CB 0C              RRC H
C8                 RET Z             CB 0D              RRC L
```

```
ROTATE ACC. AND (HL) INSTRUCTIONS           CB  C1              SET 0,C
-----------------------------------          CB  C2              SET 0,D
                                             CB  C3              SET 0,E
ED 6F                    RLD                 CB  C4              SET 0,H
ED 67                    RRD                 CB  C5              SET 0,L

                                             CB  CE              SET 1,(HL)
                                             DD  CB byte CE      SET 1,(IX+indx)
                                             FD  CB byte CE      SET 1,(IY+indx)
RESTART INSTRUCTIONS                         CB  CF              SET 1,A
-----------------------------------          CB  C8              SET 1,B
                                             CB  C9              SET 1,C
C7                       RST 00H             CB  CA              SET 1,D
CF                       RST 08H             CB  CB              SET 1,E
D7                       RST 10H             CB  CC              SET 1,H
DF                       RST 18H             CB  CD              SET 1,L
E7                       RST 20H
EF                       RST 28H             CB  D6              SET 2,(HL)
F7                       RST 30H             DD  CB byte D6      SET 2,(IX+indx)
FF                       RST 38H             FD  CB byte D6      SET 2,(IY+indx)

                                             CB  D7              SET 2,A
                                             CB  D0              SET 2,B
                                             CB  D1              SET 2,C
                                             CB  D2              SET 2,D
SUBTRACT WITH CARRY INSTRUCTIONS             CB  D3              SET 2,E
-----------------------------------          CB  D4              SET 2,H
                                             CB  D5              SET 2,L
9E                       SBC A,(HL)
DD 9E byte               SBC A,(IX+indx)     CB  DE              SET 3,(HL)
FD 9E byte               SBC A,(IY+indx)     DD  CB byte DE      SET 3,(IX+indx)
                                             FD  CB byte DE      SET 3,(IY+indx)
9F                       SBC A,A
98                       SBC A,B             CB  DF              SET 3,A
99                       SBC A,C             CB  D8              SET 3,B
9A                       SBC A,D             CB  D9              SET 3,C
9B                       SBC A,E             CB  DA              SET 3,D
9C                       SBC A,H             CB  DB              SET 3,E
9D                       SBC A,L             CB  DC              SET 3,H
DE byte                  SBC A,data          CB  DD              SET 3,L

ED 42                    SBC HL,BC           CB  E6              SET 4,(HL)
ED 52                    SBC HL,DE           DD  CB byte E6      SET 4,(IX+indx)
ED 62                    SBC HL,HL           FD  CB byte E6      SET 4,(IY+indx)
ED 72                    SBC HL,SP
                                             CB  E7              SET 4,A
                                             CB  E0              SET 4,B
                                             CB  E1              SET 4,C
                                             CB  E2              SET 4,D
SET CARRY FLAG                               CB  E3              SET 4,E
-----------------------------------          CB  E4              SET 4,H
                                             CB  E5              SET 4,L
37                       SCF
                                             CB  EE              SET 5,(HL)
                                             DD  CB byte EE      SET 5,(IX+indx)
                                             FD  CB byte EE      SET 5,(IY+indx)

                                             CB  EF              SET 5,A
                                             CB  E8              SET 5,B
SET BIT INSTRUCTIONS                         CB  E9              SET 5,C
-----------------------------------          CB  EA              SET 5,D
                                             CB  EB              SET 5,E
CB C6                    SET 0,(HL)          CB  EC              SET 5,H
DD CB byte C6            SET 0,(IX+indx)     CB  ED              SET 5,L
FD CB byte C6            SET 0,(IY+indx)
                                             CB  F6              SET 6,(HL)
CB C7                    SET 0,A             DD  CB byte F6      SET 6,(IX+indx)
CB C0                    SET 0,B             FD  CB byte F6      SET 6,(IY+indx)
```

```
CB F7                    SET 6,A              CB 2F                    SRA A
CB F0                    SET 6,B              CB 28                    SRA B
CB F1                    SET 6,C              CB 29                    SRA C
CB F2                    SET 6,D              CB 2A                    SRA D
CB F3                    SET 6,E              CB 2B                    SRA E
CB F4                    SET 6,H              CB 2C                    SRA H
CB F5                    SET 6,L              CB 2D                    SRA L

CB FE                    SET 7,(HL)           SHIFT LOGICAL INSTRUCTIONS
DD CB byte FE            SET 7,(IX+indx)      ----------------------------------------
FD CB byte FE            SET 7,(IY+indx)
                                              CB 3E                    SRL (HL)
CB FF                    SET 7,A              DD CB byte 3E            SRL (IX+indx)
CB F8                    SET 7,B              FD CB byte 3E            SRL (IY+indx)
CB F9                    SET 7,C
CB FA                    SET 7,D              CB 3F                    SRL A
                                              CB 38                    SRL B
                                              CB 39                    SRL C
                                              CB 3A                    SRL D
                                              CB 3B                    SRL E
SHIFT ARITHMETIC INSTRUCTIONS                 CB 3C                    SRL H
----------------------------------------      CB 3D                    SRL L

CB 26                    SLA (HL)             SUBTRACT INSTRUCTIONS
DD CB byte 26            SLA (IX+indx)        ----------------------------------------
FD CB byte 26            SLA (IY+indx)
                                              96                       SUB (HL)
CB 27                    SLA A                DD 96 byte               SUB (IX+indx)
CB 28                    SLA B                FD 96 byte               SUB (IY+indx)
CB 29                    SLA C
CB 2A                    SLA D                97                       SUB A
CB 2B                    SLA E                90                       SUB B
CB 2C                    SLA H                91                       SUB C
CB 2D                    SLA L                92                       SUB D
                                              93                       SUB E
CB 2E                    SRA (HL)             94                       SUB H
DD CB byte 2E            SRA (IX+indx)        95                       SUB L
FD CB byte 2E            SRA (IY+indx)        D6 byte                  SUB data
```

APPENDIX C

TRS-80 ASCII Character Set: Decimal and Hexadecimal Codes

Decimal	Hexadecimal	Character	Decimal	Hexadecimal	Character
32	20	space	80	50	P
33	21	!	81	51	Q
34	22	"	82	52	R
35	23	#	83	53	S
36	24	$	84	54	T
37	25	%	85	55	U
38	26	&	86	56	V
39	27	'	87	57	W
40	28	(	88	58	X
41	29	)	89	59	Y
42	2A	*	90	5A	Z
43	2B	+	91	5B	↑
44	2C	,	92	5C	↓
45	2D	-	93	5D	←
46	2E	.	94	5E	→
47	2F	/	95	5F	_
48	30	0	96	60	@
49	31	1	97	61	a
50	32	2	98	62	b
51	33	3	99	63	c
52	34	4	100	64	d
53	35	5	101	65	e
54	36	6	102	66	f
55	37	7	103	67	g
56	38	8	104	68	h
57	39	9	105	69	i
58	3A	:	106	6A	j
59	3B	;	107	6B	k
60	3C	<	108	6C	l
61	3D	=	109	6D	m
62	3E	>	110	6E	n
63	3F	?	111	6F	o
64	40	@	112	70	p
65	41	A	113	71	q
66	42	B	114	72	r
67	43	C	115	73	s
68	44	D	116	74	t
69	45	E	117	75	u
70	46	F	118	76	v
71	47	G	119	77	w
72	48	H	120	78	x
73	49	I	121	79	y
74	4A	J	122	7A	z
75	4B	K	123	7B	↑
76	4C	L	124	7C	↓
77	4D	M	125	7D	←
78	4E	N	126	7E	→
79	4F	O	127	7F	_

APPENDIX D

TRS-80 Graphics Character Set: Decimal and Hexadecimal Codes

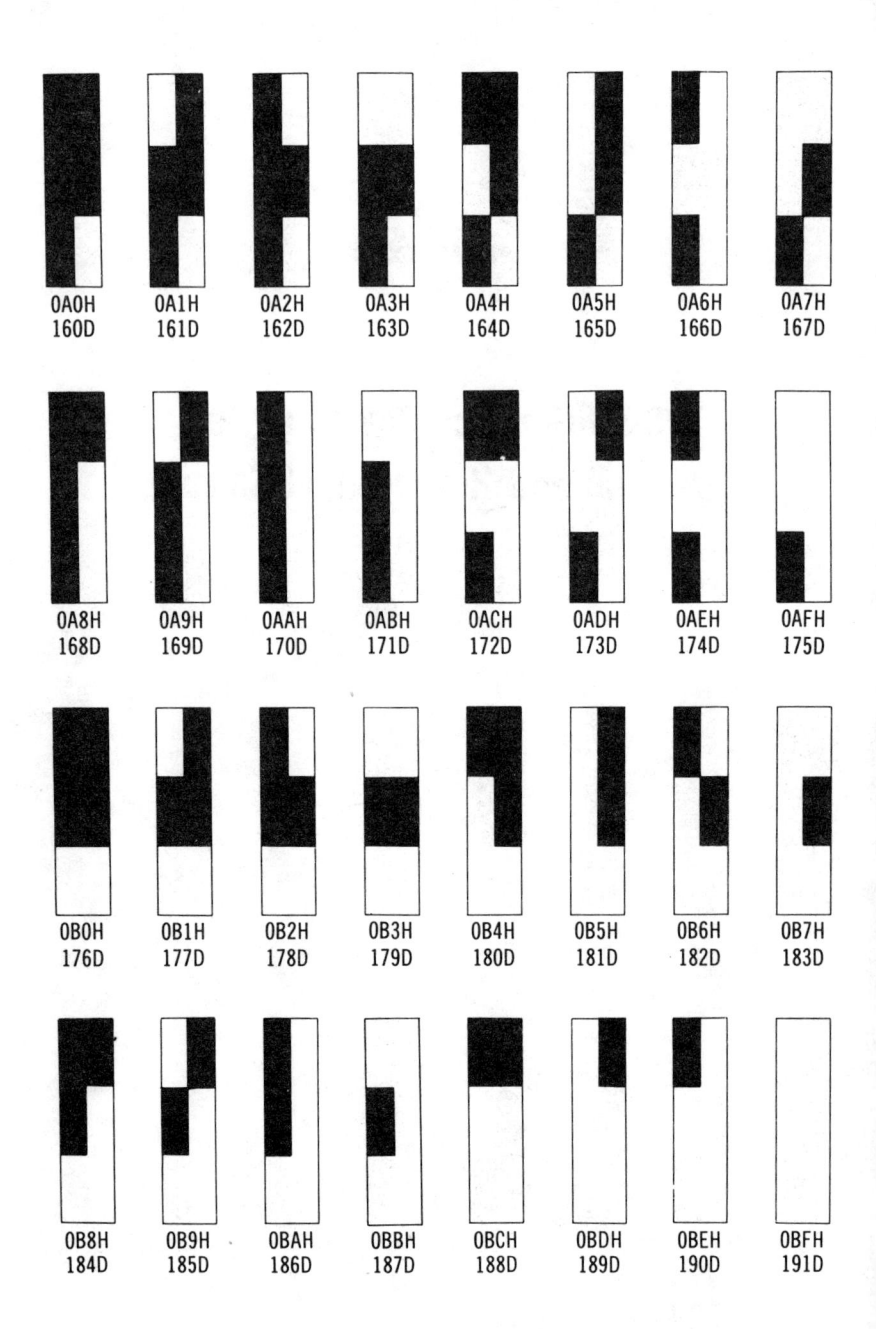

0A0H 160D	0A1H 161D	0A2H 162D	0A3H 163D	0A4H 164D	0A5H 165D	0A6H 166D	0A7H 167D
0A8H 168D	0A9H 169D	0AAH 170D	0ABH 171D	0ACH 172D	0ADH 173D	0AEH 174D	0AFH 175D
0B0H 176D	0B1H 177D	0B2H 178D	0B3H 179D	0B4H 180D	0B5H 181D	0B6H 182D	0B7H 183D
0B8H 184D	0B9H 185D	0BAH 186D	0BBH 187D	0BCH 188D	0BDH 189D	0BEH 190D	0BFH 191D

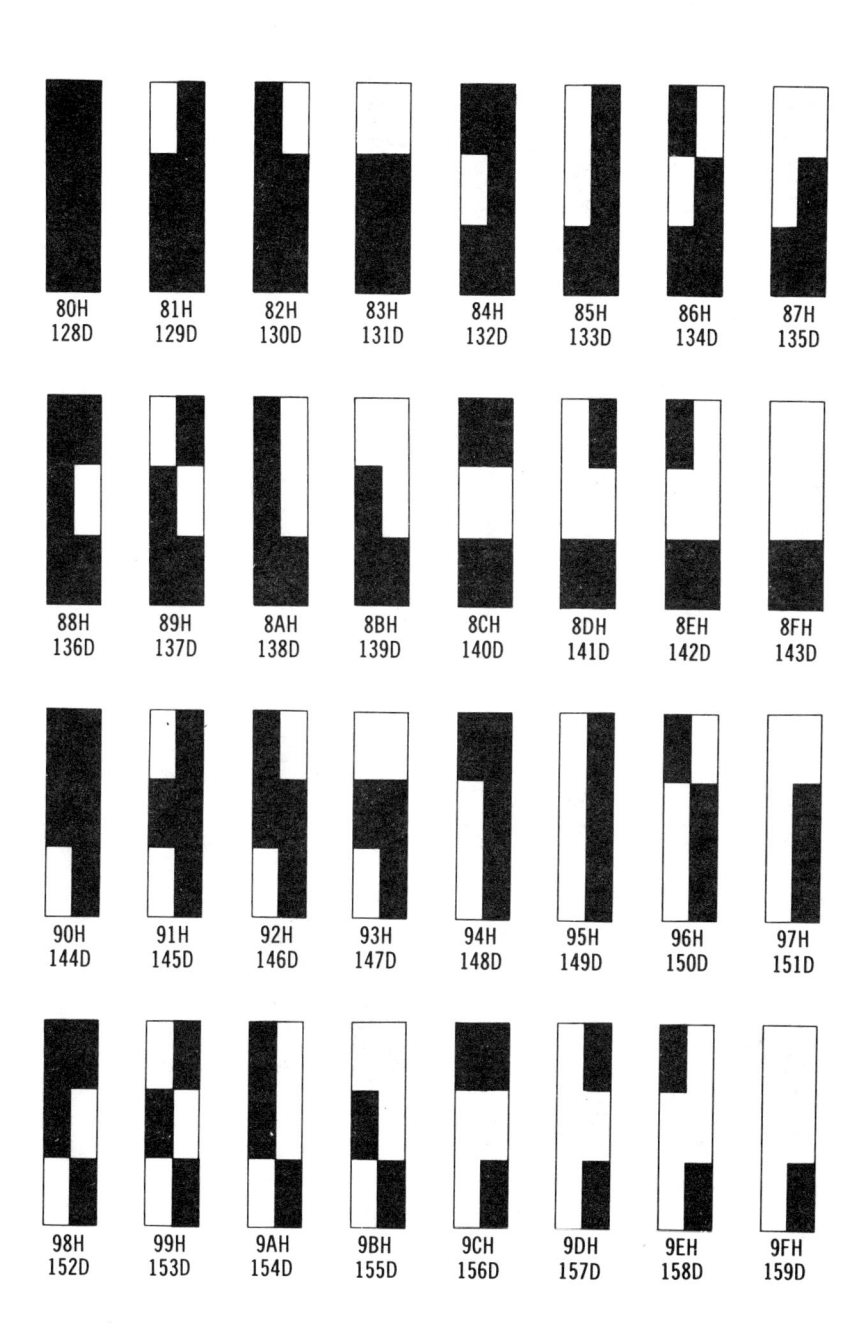

80H 128D	81H 129D	82H 130D	83H 131D	84H 132D	85H 133D	86H 134D	87H 135D
88H 136D	89H 137D	8AH 138D	8BH 139D	8CH 140D	8DH 141D	8EH 142D	8FH 143D
90H 144D	91H 145D	92H 146D	93H 147D	94H 148D	95H 149D	96H 150D	97H 151D
98H 152D	99H 153D	9AH 154D	9BH 155D	9CH 156D	9DH 157D	9EH 158D	9FH 159D

Index

A

Addressing, video, 23-26
  horizontal addressing with PRINT TAB, 30-32
  PRINT @ access to video memory, 25-28
  relative
    character-space, with TAB control codes, 32-34
    with primitive prints, 28-30
  SET/RESET memory, 36
  working directly with cursor counter, 34-36
Alphanumeric character codes, video data, 16-18
ASCII character set, 17, 232

B

BASIC-loaded, USR-linked programs, manipulating, 103-120
Binary
  to decimal conversion, 219-220
  to hexadecimal conversion, 220-221

C

Codes, video control. *See* Control codes, video
Character codes, alphanumeric, 16-18
Control codes
  and functions, summary, 38
  video, 36-43
Compression codes, 69-70
Cursor counter, working directly with, 34-36

D

Data, video, 15-23
  alphanumeric character codes, 16-18
  TRS-80 graphic codes, 19-23
Decimal
  address to 2-byte decimal format conversion, 217-218
  to binary conversion, 221
  to hexadecimal conversion, 216-217
DEFB and DEFW, defining memory contents with, 189-191

DEFL, redefining a label with, 186-187
DEFM, building necessary tables with, 191-196
DEFS, leaving memory space with, 187-189
Disassembling a BASIC program, 71-74

E

Editor/assembler, TRS-80, introducing, 163-180
EDTASM. *See* Editor/assembler, TRS-80
EQU
 operations with math expressions, 184-185
 pseudo-ops, simple, 181-184

F

FILL routine, building general-purpose, 197-204
FILL 2, applying and refining, 204-208
Free memory, 66

G

Graphic codes, TRS-80, 19-23
Graphics character set, TRS-80, 233-235

H

Hexadecimal
 programming with T-BUG, 121-140
 to binary conversion, 221
 to decimal conversion, 215-216
Horizontal addressing with PRINT TAB, 30-32

I

INKEY$ statement, standard, 49-57
INPUT statement, standard, 44-49
Instruction set, Z-80, 222-230
I/O buffer, user's memory environment, 68-70

K

Keyboard environment, 44-63
 sensing key depression with PEEK(14463), 57-60

Keyboard environment—cont
 standard
  INKEY$ statement, 49-57
  INPUT statement, 44-49
 working with the keyboard matrix, 60-63

L

Linking BASIC and machine language with USR, 81-102

M

Manipulating BASIC-loaded, USR-linked programs, 103-120
Matrix, keyboard, working with, 60-63
Memory environment, user's, 64-80
 disassembling a BASIC program, 71-74
 i/o buffer, 68-70
 organization of User's memory space, 65-68
 protecting memory space, 74-75
 special memory operations, 75-80
MOVE routine, building general-purpose, 208-213

N

Nibble, 215
Number system base conversions, 214-221
 binary
  to decimal, 219-220
  to hexadecimal, 220-221
 decimal
  address to 2-byte decimal format, 217-218
  to binary, 221
  to hexadecimal, 216-217
 hexadecimal
  to binary, 221
  to decimal, 215-216
 2-byte decimal to conventional decimal, 218-219

P

PEEK(14463), sensing key depression with, 57-60
POKE technique, 24
PRINT @ access to video memory, 25-28
PRINT statement summary, 28
PRINT TAB, horizontal addressing with, 30-32

Protecting user's memory space, 74-75
Pseudo-ops, real assembly power with,
    181-196
  building message tables with
    DEFM, 191-196
  defining memory contents with
    DEFB and DEFW, 189-191
  EQU operations with math
    expressions, 184-185
  leaving memory space with DEFS,
    187-189
  redefining a label with DEFL,
    186-187
  simple EQU pseudo-ops, 181-184

R

RAM space, user's available, 64
Real assembly power with pseudo-ops,
  181-196
Relative addressing, video, 28-36

S

Sensing key depression with
  PEEK(14463), 57-60
SET/RESET video memory
  addressing, 36
Split-screen formatting, 42
Standard
  INKEY$ statement, 49-57
  INPUT statement, 44-49

T

T-BUG
  exploring TRS-80 with, 141-162
  hexadecimal programming with,
    121-140
TRS-80
  ASCII character set, 17, 231
  graphics character set, 233-235
  2-byte decimal to conventional
    decimal conversion, 218-219

U

User's memory environment, 64-80
USR
  -linked, BASIC-loaded programs,
    manipulating. See Manipulating
    BASIC-loaded, USR-linked
    programs
  linking BASIC and machine language
    with, 81-102

V

Video environment, 15-43
  video addressing, 23-26
  video control codes, 36-43
  video data, 15-23

Z

Z-80 instruction set, 222-230

TO THE READER

Sams Computer books cover Fundamentals — Programming — Interfacing — Technology written to meet the needs of computer engineers, professionals, scientists, technicians, students, educators, business owners, personal computerists and home hobbyists.

Our Tradition is to meet your needs and in so doing we invite you to tell us what your needs and interests are by completing the following:

1. I need books on the following topics:

_____
_____
_____
_____
_____
_____

2. I have the following Sams titles:

_____
_____
_____
_____
_____
_____

3. My occupation is:

_____ Scientist, Engineer	_____ D P Professional
_____ Personal computerist	_____ Business owner
_____ Technician, Serviceman	_____ Computer store owner
_____ Educator	_____ Home hobbyist
_____ Student	Other _____

Name (print) _____
Address _____
City _____ State _____ Zip _____

Mail to: **Howard W. Sams & Co., Inc.**
　　　　Marketing Dept. #CBS1/80
　　　　4300 W. 62nd St., P.O. Box 7092
　　　　Indianapolis, Indiana 46206

21809